Ambivalent Europeans

Ambivalent Europeans [illegible] the implications of living on the fringe of Europe, [illegible] is dominated by the question [illegible] both at [illegible]—whether or not to join the EU—and at the level of national identity—whether or not Maltese are 'European'.

Jon Mitchell identifies a profound ambivalence towards Europe, and also more broadly to the key processes of 'modernisation'. He traces this tendency through [illegible] key areas of social life—gender, the family, community, politics, religion and ritual.

This book examines the potency of ritual with special reference to the island's *festi* (feasts), in particular that of the national patron St Paul, showing how they are used as a means for mediating and expressing anxieties about 'tradition' and 'modernity'. It also looks at the pervasive nostalgia that characterises contemporary Malta, a country where Roman Catholicism has historically been dominant, and where 'modernisation' and 'Europeanisation' are seen to threaten values, even as they promise greater affluence and economic stability. In addition, it demonstrates how the particular dynamics of Maltese political life have shaped debates concerning national identity.

The book contributes to contemporary theoretical debates, and highlights processes that may be observed outside of Malta as well. In so doing, it enriches our understanding of European integration, not least how Europe is viewed from its margins.

Jon P. Mitchell is Lecturer in Social Anthropology at the School of Cultural and Community Studies, University of Sussex, Brighton, UK

Jon P. Mitchell
University of Sussex, Brighton, UK

Ambivalent Europeans

Ritual, Memory and the Public Sphere in Malta

London and New York

First published 2002
by Routledge
11 New Fetter Lane, London EC4P 4EE

Simultaneously published in the USA and Canada
by Routledge
29 West 35th Street, New York, NY 10001

Routledge is an imprint of the Taylor & Francis Group

Typeset by Expo, Malaysia
Printed and bound in Great Britain by TJ International Ltd,
Padstow, Cornwall

British Library Cataloguing in Publication Data
A catalogue record for this book is available from the
British Library

Library of Congress Cataloging in Publication Data
A catalogue record has been requested

ISBN 0–415–27152–5 (hbk)
ISBN 0–415–27153–3 (pbk)

For my parents, Phyl and Peter

Contents

Figures

Preface

It is astonishing that a project that has taken as long to come to fruition as this one looks anything like the one I imagined at the outset. In 1992 I set out to research issues of Maltese national identity at a time when European integration was being discussed across the continent – the Maastricht summit giving impetus to pro- and anti-European agendas in both the countries that were already EU members and those that were on the fringes. These are the results.

In many ways, the theme of this book – ambivalence – was prefigured in the work of Thomas Pynchon. *V* was the first book I read during fieldwork. Its narratives follow the pursuit of the elusive V. from New York to Cairo to Alexandria to Malta by spies, sailors, priests and others. The search is as protracted as my own was for an understanding of my informants' orientation to the world. Like 'identity' itself, V. turned out to be everything and nothing:

> Truthfully, he didn't know what sex V. might be, nor even what genus and species ... If she was a historical fact then she continued active today and at the moment, because the ultimate Plot Which Has No Name was as yet unrealized, though V. might be no more a she than a sailing vessel or a nation. (Pynchon 1956: 226)

The chapter epigrams are taken from the Maltese sections of *V*, much of which take place during and immediately after the second world war – a time of crisis, when many of the institutions discussed in this book were questioned. It appeared to me that a similar questioning was taking place during the time of my fieldwork, and it is for this reason that I use these epigrams. They stand as a literary device to signal the relationship between outsiders' representation of Maltese ambivalence—both Pynchon's and my own—and those I examined as those of my informants. In many ways, the passages of *V* present an Orientalist—or Mediterraneanist (see Herzfeld 1987, chapter six below)—commentary on Maltese culture and society. But such Mediterraneanism is not the the preserve of the outsider. It is an image that is also prominent in indigenous representations of Malta—one which shapes an ambivalent self-identity that is simultaneously self-aggrandising and self-deprecatory. Indeed, as the Maltese philosopher Peter Serracino-Inglott has argued, *V* sums up this self-seduction and self-loathing, personifying its ambivalence in the character of V.—a transvestite, and part machine, with one eye replaced by a watch-face. Serracino-Inglott argues it is an appropriate image for Malta:

> The Maltese have shown a preference for, and excellence in, work as catalysts, brokers, middlemen, entrepôt traders, interpreters, translators, even as what one might call cultural transvestites ... (Serracino-Inglott 1988: 370)

In writing this book, I have tried to explore the implications of this ambivalence, tracing core anxieties about the process of European accession, of 'modernisation' and progress. I have tried to represent these anxieties as fully as possible, as they emerged during almost two years of fieldwork. Each chapter explores them in relation to a particular area of Maltese social life, and the chapters therefore deal with different ethnographic and theoretical material. They are intended to be semi-autonomous pieces—articulated parts of an ethnographic whole. The book combines ethnographic vignettes—some of which are explicitly reflexive—with more distanced analytical and theoretical analysis. As with the use of the Pynchon epigrams, this is intended to draw attention to the peculiar position of an ethnographer as both participant and observer—insider and outsider. Although I employ indigenous voices throughout the book, any misrepresentations are entirely my fault. All names contained herein, except those of prominent public figures, have been changed to preserve anonymity. Place names and street names remain accurate.

Most of my fieldwork was conducted in the Maltese language—*Malti*—and quotes from my interviews appear here as my translations. Similarly, quotes from Maltese language sources. All indigenous terms are italicised, including loan words from the English, for example *hobby, training* and *bastard,* which are indigenised versions of their English counterparts.

Inevitably in a project of this duration, I have many people to thank. The initial research was funded by ESRC. I am grateful to them and to the University of Edinburgh, University College London and the University of Sussex for providing resources to bring the project to fruition. In Malta, Jeremy and Inga Boissevain, Isabelle Borg, Paul Clough, Paul Sant Cassia, James and Pia Sapienza, Joe Vella, Raphael Vella and Ruth Azzopardi all helped to keep me sane. Lawrence and Miriam Carabott, Guzi and Polly Cremona, Simon Cumbo, Vince Farrugia, Charlie Grima, Guzi, Salvina, Paul Mario and John Sciberras, Freddie Sciberras, Joe and Carmen Verzin were patient in the extreme. The Chapter of St Paul's Shipwreck Church, *L-Ghaqda tal-Pawlini*, Institute of Tourism Studies, National Library of Malta, University of Malta Library, Valletta Rehabilitation Project all provided vital information. In the UK I am indebted to Anja-Maaike Green and to my two supervisors at Edinburgh, Tony Cohen and Judith Okely. Malcolm Anderson, Jeremy Boissevain, Isabelle Borg, Paul Clough, Robert Jones, Joao de Pina-Cabral, Jonathan Spencer, and an anonymous reviewer for Harwood Academic Publishers all provided valuable comments on various drafts at various times. Colleagues at University of Edinburgh, University College London and University of Sussex have helped probably more than they might imagine to enable this book's completion. Thanks to them. Chapter five is a revised version of a paper that appeared in *Ethnos,* 'The Nostalgic Construction of Community: memory and social identity in urban Malta' (**63,1:** 81–101). I am grateful to them for permission to publish this chapter. Finally, thanks to Hildi Mitchell, whose patience holds no bounds.

Italy
Sicily
Tunisia
MALTA
Mellieha
San
Pawl
il-Bahar
Mgarr
Naxxar
Mosta
San
Giljan
Paceville
SLIEMA
MSIDA
VALLETTA
BALZAN
BIRKIRKARA
HAMRUN
IL FURJANA
MDINA
RABAT
MARSA
Zabbar
Zebbug
QORMI
PAOLA
Dingli
Luqa
Zejtun
Siggiewi
Marsaxlokk
Qrendi
Zurrieq
Birzebuggia
0 kms 3
0 mls 3

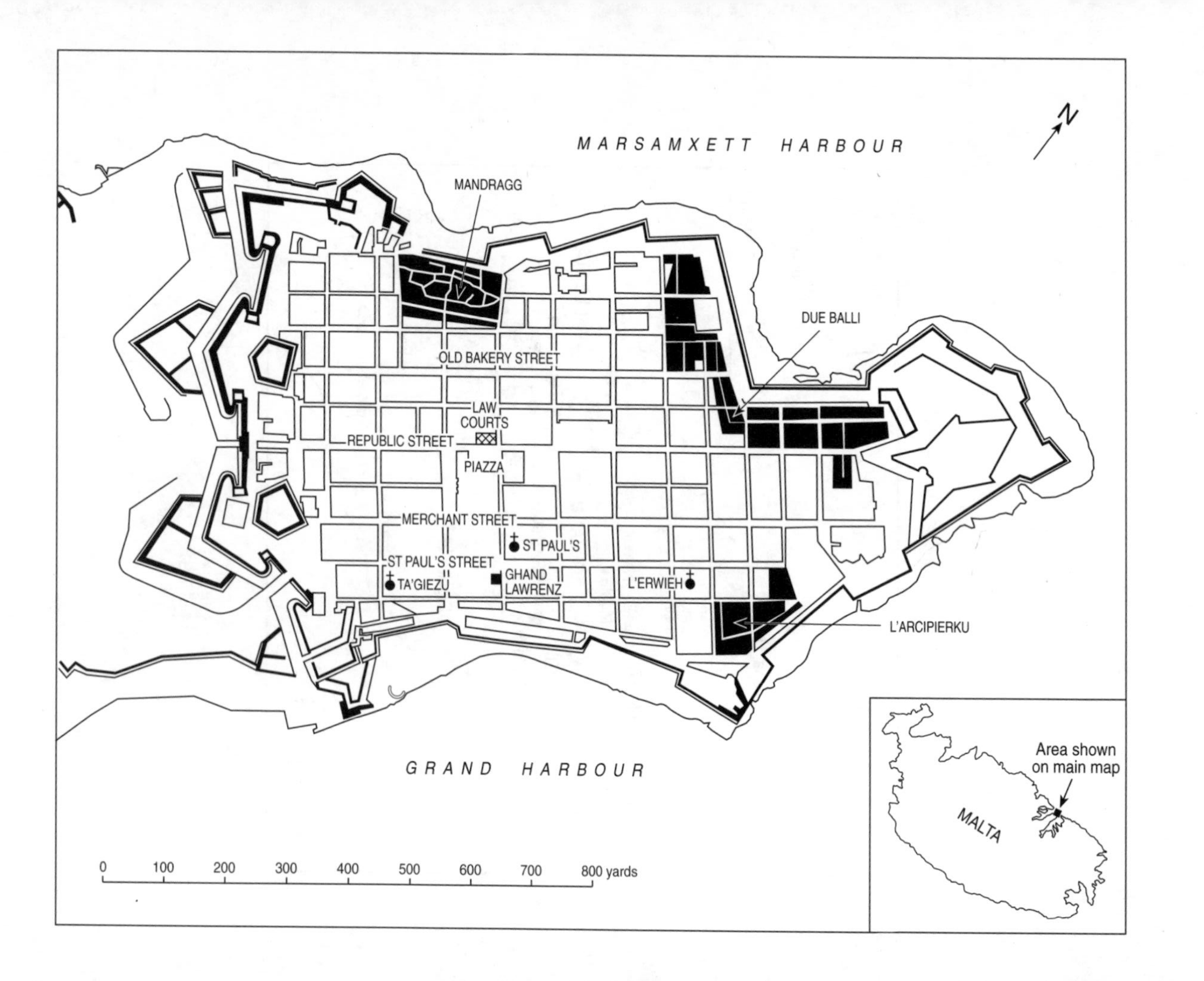
N
MARSAMXETT HARBOUR
MANDRAGG
DUE BALLI
OLD BAKERY STREET
LAW COURTS
REPUBLIC STREET
PIAZZA
MERCHANT STREET
ST PAUL'S
ST PAUL'S STREET
TA'GIEZU
GHAND LAWRENZ
L'ERWIEH
L'ARCIPIERKU
GRAND HARBOUR
0
100
200
300
400
500
600
700
800 yards
Area shown on main map
MALTA

CHAPTER ONE

Malta on the Margins of Europe—A History of Ambivalence

> Malta, and her inhabitants, stood like an immovable rock in the river Fortune ... The same motives which cause us to populate a dream-street also cause us to apply to a rock human qualities like "invincibility," "tenacity," "perseverance," etc. More than metaphor, it is delusion. But on the strength of this delusion Malta survived. (Thomas Pynchon, *V*: 325)

Contrary to what one might have expected, the last decades of the twentieth century saw a marked expansion throughout Europe of ritual celebrations (Boissevain 1992a). Both religious and secular, these rituals increased in scale and intensity. This revitalisation appears to have been particularly marked in places that are marginal, both politically and economically, to the centres of European power. Boissevain links the increase to a widespread critique of post-war industrialisation, and a consequent valorisation of 'tradition' (Ibid: 8–10). A crisis over the supposed homogenising effects of globalisation[1] and 'modernity' fuelled appeals to the 'authenticity' of 'traditional' ritual forms, which emerged as a means of identifying, strengthening and asserting the uniqueness of particular social—usually local—groups (11). Rituals, then, are seen as a form of resistance to wider social forces—a reassertion of localism in the face of the supralocal.

Although not primarily about ritual, this book has as its leitmotif a ritual that, like others, expanded exponentially in the late twentieth century. St Paul's feast, or *San Pawl* as I shall refer to it, takes place on February 10th each year in the parish of St Paul's Shipwreck, Valletta, Malta. It commemorates the patron saint of Malta, a country in which Roman Catholicism is not only the state religion, but also regularly practised by the majority of the population.[2] Like all Maltese feasts—*festi* sing. *festa*—it is organised by the people of the parish, and to this extent can be seen as a local celebration. As commemoration of the national patron it is also a national celebration. As such it could be seen as a means by which the integrity of Maltese 'tradition' is

introduction or chapter 1

reinforced against what is seen in many circles as an encroaching Europeanisation, that in turn is a source of dangerous and morally corrupting 'modernity'. However, it is far more than simply a form of resistance to supralocal forces. As Comaroff and Comaroff (1993) and Piot (1999) have argued for African contexts, ritual mediates the relationship between the local and the supralocal, serving as a means of expressing and therefore accommodating the dilemmas and ambiguities of this relationship. These ambiguities, as I argue below, are inherent in modernity itself, which can be identified, above all, by a tendency to divide the world into 'modern' and 'traditional'. By this reckoning, the invocation of ritual-as-tradition can be seen in itself as a 'modern' act—one which attempts to resolve or mediate the dilemmas and ambiguities of 'modernity'.

In 1990s Malta, these dilemmas were couched above all in terms of the country's ambivalent relationship to Europe. Thus *San Pawl,* which although in one sense can be seen as a conservative practice that communicates opposition to European 'modernity', is nevertheless also a celebration of Maltese European-ness—Maltese modernity. It commemorates the moment when St Paul the apostle was shipwrecked on Maltese shores, thereby ensuring that the country was part of Christendom—part of Europe.

This book suggests that such local festivities as *San Pawl,* on the margins of Europe, must be understood in the context of this all-pervasive ambivalence towards Europe. Although most Maltese would argue that their country falls into a wider European cultural region—notwithstanding arguments outlined below concerning Medieval Malta—and therefore that they are 'European', the category 'Europe' has since the mid-1980s increasingly come to stand for the European Union. On the one hand, this Europe is seen as positive—a source of wealth, education, democracy, 'modernity'—on the other hand it is seen as negative—a threat to local integrity, 'tradition' and morality. This ambivalence is signalled in *San Pawl* itself, which celebrates both Malta's inclusion within Europe and its separateness from it. Rather than unequivocally resisting these supralocal forces, then, the ritual can be seen as a means by which people manage, or accommodate, this ambivalence.[3]

To that extent, this book contributes to the argument set out by Boissevain, explaining the expansion or revitalisation of ritual across

Europe. Although focusing on the specific example of *San Pawl*, and the configuration of socio-cultural and historical factors that go towards making it a particularly poignant—or even semantically pregnant—ritual for those who participate in it, the book also has wider comparative applicability. Many of the processes described here are also prevalent in other parts of Europe—and other parts of the world—where geo-political marginality combines with a pervasive sense of nostalgia to produce an escalation of 'traditional' ritual practices. However, the book's central concern is with the lives of Maltese people, and particularly those of St Paul's parish, Valletta—to explore the various contexts in which ambivalence towards Europe, and particularly European integration, takes form and impacts upon their lives.

10th FEBRUARY 1994—ST PAUL'S FEAST, VALLETTA, MALTA

San Pawl ends with a climactic procession during which the massive monumental statue of St Paul is paraded through the parish, accompanied by a raucous brass band playing tunes to which the crowds sing along. Fireworks and petards are released intermittently, and streams of ticker-tape and confetti are released from overhanging balconies onto the statue below. As the 1994 procession drew to a close, I left my friends—a local Maltese artist and an American anthropology lecturer who worked at the University of Malta—to join the crowd of young men around the huge statue, in the hope of being able to take a turn at carrying it. I'd been eighteen months in Valletta, and spent much of my time with these people. I'd helped them with preparing the *festa*, attended meetings of the organising committee, and visited their houses, spending time sitting and chatting, over coffee or beer. In the few days prior to the procession, I'd attended *festa* with them—followed the noisy brass band marches around the city streets, attended the lengthy sermons that repeated the story of St Paul's shipwreck, and enjoyed the fireworks that punctuated the proceedings. Now as the young men struggled to 'take a piece'—*jieħu biċċa*—I too wanted to have a go at carrying St Paul.

Jostling to the front, I eventually found a place and lifted, the saint's weight bearing down on my shoulder as I tried to sway in time to the music, in approved fashion. Around the statue were crowds of people that I recognised from my fieldwork, shouting out—*Viva San Pawl!*—with arms aloft in supplication to the saint. It was a euphoric moment—a kind of epiphany at which the long hours of fieldwork research appeared to come together. In my physical engagement with the saint's statue—with the saint himself—I felt I understood the intensity of emotion behind people's commitment to the *festa,* to St Paul, and to Malta.

A little later, after I'd rejoined my friends, I tried to explain this moment—the first small steps in the writing of this book. They had been to the *festa* before, but as spectators—outsiders who didn't understand the full implications of the occasion. Yes, they knew it was a celebration of the national patron, and an important occasion for local political dignitaries—particularly the hierarchy of the Nationalist Party, which was in government during the years of my fieldwork. This much was clear from the presence of television cameras, of the Prime Minister, and of the Nationalist Mayor of Valletta. They also knew it was important to the local people of Valletta—that for them it was a time of emotion, jubilation and celebration. But they didn't really know why this was the case.

This book aims to explain the full implications of *San Pawl* for the people who organise it and participate in it. It argues that a full understanding of the texture of this *festa* can only come from an holistic ethnography, that takes account of the intersections and interconnections of different areas of social and cultural life—gender, family, community, stratification, politics, religion, ritual. Moreover, it can only be understood in relation to the pervasive nostalgia characteristic of 1990s Malta, and the particular features of Maltese public life. As a ritual that serves to alleviate the anxieties of geo-political marginality, it must be seen in these contexts.

ETHNOGRAPHIC HOLISM

Despite its increasing popularity as a subject of study, contemporary sociocultural anthropology often presents itself as being in crisis.[4] The current *bête noire* of the anthropological world is cultural studies, which is often seen as a threat to both the theory and practice of the social or cultural anthropologist. In a number of contexts, both formal and informal, anthropologists have been moved to explore the implications and effects of cultural studies for anthropology (Lave, Duguid and Fernandez 1992, Nugent and Shore 1997, Wade 1997). Of particular concern has been the tendency—in cultural studies—to move away from holistic ethnography, and focus on particular sociocultural phenomena, reading them as 'texts' that are separate—or separable—from the broader context in which they exist, and particularly from the people who practise them (Howell 1997: 108). For example, Howell (1997) laments the absence of people in Bennet's (1991) analysis of Expo '88:

> Bennet analyses the semiotics of the lay-out, architecture, posters and design as if they in themselves have some intentionality. I miss some reference to his interaction with local politicians, designers and exhibitors in order to elicit their intentions and hopes for the Expo, as well as with the various categories of the public who attended. (Howell 1997: 108)

In examining more mundane or everyday cultural phenomena, analysts do a similar injustice to the people involved in the production, and particularly consumption, of cultural 'texts'. For example, Ang's (1992) analysis of *Dallas* viewers was based on letters elicited by the researcher, assuming that their lives as *Dallas* viewers can be separated out from the rest of their lives, and analysed as separate.

Of course, this fragmentation of the subject has a certain currency in contemporary social theory (Giddens 1990, 1991). Indeed, contemporary socio-cultural anthropology often itself sees fragmentation where an earlier anthropology would have seen harmony. Building on the critiques of ethnographic representation that emerged in the 1980s (Clifford 1988, Clifford and Marcus 1986, Marcus and Fischer 1986), a number of scholars have proposed a movement away from holistic ethnography, which they associate with the essentialising and totalising tendencies of earlier anthropologists (Abu-Lughod 1991, Gupta and Ferguson 1997, Marcus 1989, Thornton 1988). They propose a more discursive theory of 'culture' that focuses on discontent, contest and negotiation rather than consensus and harmony. Such an approach is welcome, and—broadly speaking—is adopted here. Thus, where earlier ethnographers might have focused on 'Maltese culture' as a deterministic system, I examine Maltese peoples' debates and arguments *about* culture.

However, there seems no reason why paying attention to contest and negotiation should not also allow anthropological research to see people 'in the round'—holistically. Indeed, it is often not until we see people in their full contexts that we understand why they take particular stands on an issue—why they are prepared to enter into debate and contest. Thus, for example, a particular orientation to *Dallas* might be better explained when seen in the context of a particular subject's family life, their work life or even their party political allegiances. Naturally, eliciting this data requires much more long-term, in-depth fieldwork than some practitioners of cultural studies engage in, but it is my contention that the benefits of such long-term fieldwork outweigh the costs (see also Englund and Leach 2000: 238). It enables the holistic attention to interconnections that has been characteristic of anthropological ethnographies, in comparison to the 'ethnographies' of other cognate disciplines, which artificially fragment the subjects of enquiry—people's lives.

This book is intended to champion the value of such holistic orientation. It argues that in order to understand *festa,* we must first understand the lives of the people who participate in it 'in the round', with attention to the inter-connections between different areas of their lives. It is the result of nearly two years' fieldwork in Valletta, during which I lived among and with *Pawlini*—'Paulites', or followers of St Paul. This term broadly describes inhabitants or former inhabitants of the parish of St Paul, where the fieldwork was conducted. More specifically it describes the enthusiasts of St Paul's feast, *San Pawl,* and more specifically still, it describes members of the organisation that oversees the organisation of the *festa–L-Għaqda tal-Pawlini,* The Association of *Pawlini.* I use the term in each of these three ways throughout the book, allowing context to clarify exactly what is meant by *Pawlini* at any point. I saw the *Pawlini* in all areas of their lives, from work, leisure, family and in the ritual context of *festa.* I learned their language, Maltese,[5] and participated in their activities. Only with such immersion can full understanding be gained.

Three major themes emerged from the research, which are central to the understanding of Malta in the early 1990s. The first is the profound ambivalence towards not only Europe, but the processes of 'modernisation' more broadly. This has an historical provenance, and derives from Malta's historical and on-going situation on the margins of Europe. It provides an impetus for vigorous public debate about national identity and national foreign policy—should Malta be seen as part of Europe, and join the European Union, or not? Second is the particular dynamics of Maltese public life. Shaped by social stratification and political process, the Maltese public, in which debates about national identity take place, is characterised by an articulation of face-to-face communication and more attenuated communication in the broadcast media. This ensures that public figures—politicians, media personalities, intellectuals and civil servants—are also personally familiar. They can be, and frequently are, engaged with on a daily basis, despite also being 'distant' public figures. Third is the pervasive nostalgia, or sensitivity to the historical, that characterised early nineties Malta. I shall deal with each in turn, before moving on to discuss early nineties debates about St Paul, which bring the three themes together.

AMBIVALENCE, TRADITION AND MODERNITY

The first main theme relates to an overall sense of ambivalence towards processes of social change in general, and the influence of Europe in particular. Malta has always been on the fringes of Europe. The Maltese islands lie more or less in the centre of the Mediterranean, with Sicily—the nearest point of mainland Europe—93km to the north and Tunisia 288km south-west. Gibraltar lies 1,826km to the west and Alexandria 1,510km to the east. It is not surprising, then, that Malta has been called 'the crossroads of the Mediterranean'. As at any crossroads, a great deal of traffic has passed through Malta over the centuries, much of it in the form of colonising authorities. This history of external influence has polarised thinking on Maltese national identity, fuelling the kinds of anxieties and ambivalences towards Europe that preoccupied early nineties Maltese.

Archaeology shows that Malta was settled as early as 5,200BCE. Successive waves of peoples occupied the islands until the Romans established a colony in 218BCE (see Blouet 1993, Trump 1990). Malta seems to have been a rather affluent corner of the Roman empire (Laferla 1939: 33), and it was during this period that Malta is believed to have become Christian. St Paul's shipwreck on the islands is recounted in the Acts of the Apostles, and treated by most Maltese as evidence of a continuous Christian tradition since 60CE. Suggestions in the late 1980s that St Paul wasn't shipwrecked on Malta caused considerable controversy (see below, Mitchell 1998b). Similar controversy surrounds the so-called Arab period (870–1090/1270CE),[6] which some scholars argue led to widespread conversion of Maltese to Islam, thereby throwing into question the notion of a continuous Maltese Christian tradition.

By the fourteenth century, however, Christianity had certainly returned to Malta. From that time onwards, a number of monastic orders established convents on the islands, and began to acquire land (Bonnici 1967). Throughout the thirteenth, fourteenth and fifteenth centuries, the Maltese economy moved from one of subsistence agriculture to an increasing reliance on the cash crops of cumin and cotton (Blouet 1993: 412). This led in turn to the development of a small class of minor merchants who sat alongside the religious orders and the absentee Sicilian landowners as the islands' elite (Montalto 1979). This elite was subsequently displaced by another largely external authority—the Order of the Knights of St John. Set up as hospitallers in the eleventh century, the Knights of St John became a military order after their ejection from Jerusalem, and when their Rhodes headquarters fell to the Turks in 1511, they were given the islands of Malta by Charles V of Castille. Their arrival had a most profound effect on Maltese historical topography and economy (Blouet 1993), providing a veritable 'golden age' of secular and religious architecture, the implications of which are discussed in chapter two.

After the Order's rule came a brief but significant French occupation. The French Revolution had led to the seizing of the Order's land in France, creating an economic crisis in Malta. Despite their Roman Catholicism, the intellectual influence of the *philosophes* became popular among the Knights, and this led in the late eighteenth century to the development of a rudimentary language-based Maltese nationalism, particularly because of the intellectual achievements of Mikiel Anton Vassalli. Then regarded as a dangerous freemason, Vassalli is now seen as the 'father of the Maltese language' (Bonavia 1993). During this period, the self-conscious development of a distinctly Maltese language and culture first began. It was to re-emerge, with volatile consequences, in the party politics of the early twentieth century.

The revolutionary influence permitted a bloodless annexation of Malta by Napoleon's troops in 1798 (Montalto 1979: 340). Within two years, however, the French had been ousted, to be replaced by the British, who held the colony until 1964 and Independence. The reasons for Britain claiming dominion over Malta were, and remained, primarily strategic, and the characteristics of the colonial period reflect this realpolitik. The situation has been called 'fortress colonisation' (Frendo 1979), in which the British offered certain, limited, participation in decision-making to the Maltese, provided they did not interfere with their military and strategic aims. This had two consequences. First, it led to the emergence of an elite of doctors, lawyers and priests who were involved in the political process. Second, it meant that the colonial authorities were uninterested in providing social services or education for the local population. During my fieldwork it was commonly said that the British deliberately kept the Maltese poor and ignorant, because it served their interests.

The representative legislature offered the Maltese was seen in various forms from 1821 to 1964, and its presence allowed the development of the political polarisation characteristic of twentieth-century Malta. Party politics developed in the late nineteenth century, when the *Partit Nazzjonalist* (Nationalist Party) was set up. As discussed in chapter six, the Nationalist Party became strongly pro-Italian, drawn as it was from the ranks of the established bourgeoisie—lawyers, priests or wealthy merchants who had links with Italy. This was not least because of the powerful social control they could exert by maintaining Italian as the principal language of church, state and legislature (Frendo 1979: 208). This powerful Italianate group saw a danger in the British presence in Malta, who they believed threatened not only to Anglicise the state, but also to Protestantise the Church. Protestantism was associated with the linguistic proto-nationalism of Vassalli, so that promoting the Maltese language became itself connected to Anglicisation and freemasonry (Sant 1992). This framed the principal line of debate between the emerging political parties at the end of the nineteenth century. On the one hand, Nationalists supported the development of Italian culture and greater links with Italy. On the other hand, British authorities produced commissions suggesting the development of indigenous culture and language, and through that, the use of English. By the turn of the twentieth century, the Maltese trade union movement that developed around the country's dockyards took on this commitment to Anglicisation, as it took on the struggle to improve the lot of the Maltese worker (Zammit 1984: 15).

The debate crystallised in the 1920s and 30s around the issue of language and education. Whilst Nationalists wished to develop Italian, some even suggesting an integration of Malta into Mussolini's Italy, the Constitutional Party that emerged as champion of British interests argued for the development of Maltese and, *pari passu,* English (see Hull 1993). By the 1950s the Constitutional Party had been replaced by the Malta Labour Party as the Nationalists' main opponents, and continued the policy of developing Malta's cultural and linguistic discreteness whilst forging links with Britain. This came to a head in 1956, when the MLP government tabled a referendum proposing that Malta be integrated into the United Kingdom (see Austin 1971). The Nationalist Party, and particularly its Church allies, strongly objected, as it threatened the pre-eminence of the Catholic Church. The referendum was defeated, following unequivocal opposition by the Church. This began a period of Church-Labour hostilities that culminated in the severance of all relations after Labour Party members were interdicted in 1961 (see Hill 1986, Koster 1984). Following this defeat, the Labour Party dropped their pro-British stance, opting for a radical particularism that was in many ways more genuinely nationalist than the Nationalists. Meanwhile the Nationalists themselves, who had by this time abandoned hopes of integration with Italy, fought for Independence from Britain, which came in 1964.

Although the Nationalists claimed this was the final deliverance from colonial subjugation, the Labour Party disagreed, campaigning for Republic status and the ousting of British troops. Despite administrative withdrawal in 1964, Malta remained an important British naval and military base, with preferential leasing conditions that made the rents of Maltese territory very cheap. The Labour Party argued that, under these circumstances, the colonial era had not really ended, and when it came to power in 1971 immediately started planning a Maltese Republic (established in 1974) and attempted to negotiate more lucrative terms with the British. Protracted and hostile discussions went on throughout the 1970s between the Admiralty and the Maltese Prime Minister Dom Mintoff. The ensuing crisis provoked a rapprochement between Church and Labour Party, with Archbishop Gonzi being used in negotiations (see Attard 1988). However, after Mintoff had ejected NATO's Mediterranean headquarters and raised the rents, the British eventually withdrew, and in 1979 the last British ship left Grand Harbour bound for Portsmouth. Mintoff also began to introduce social welfare and housing reform, the implications of which are discussed in chapter five.

The 1980s saw the Labour government developing a notion of national identity based on a pan-Mediterraneanism. Opposed to Europe and the Nationalist *Italianità*, this account of Maltese identity focused on the African/Arabic/Semitic links evident in Maltese language and folklore, emphasising Malta's role as a bridge between north and south, east and west. Stronger links were developed with Gaddafi's Libya and Soviet Russia, and a protectionist economic policy was adopted, reducing European imports. The implications of this policy for Maltese consumption patterns is discussed in chapter four. For Nationalists, these policies represented a denial of European roots and a threat to two of their main constituents—the established bourgeoisie and the Church. In the early 1980s their opposition became increasingly violent—both vocally and physically.

Politics in the 1980s became an increasingly dangerous game, with riots and shootings common in the leads-up to general elections. There were also accusations of gross abuse of power by the Labour government (see chapter six), and by the time of the 1987 election even Labour supporters were prepared to vote tactically against what was turning out to be an increasingly tyrannical administration. The sense of injustice about this period is discussed in chapter five. The Nationalists won the 1987 election on a manifesto of democracy, justice and pro-Europeanism. Indeed European accession was seen as a strong support for democracy, which would simultaneously weaken the power of the state and encourage the development of civil society. They applied to join the European Union in 1990, and a second election victory in 1992 was seen by them as a mandate for accession to Europe. However, following a rather negative response by the European Commission in 1993 (see chapter six), and controversy over the introduction of VAT, they lost the 1996 election, only to return to power and the pursuit of their European goals in 1998.

Malta in the 1990s was dominated by the question of Europe, and indeed more fundamentally, by the question of identity. To its supporters, Europe was seen as a source of potential economic security and stability for a country that was vulnerable. Since the withdrawal of the British forces, Malta had become increasingly dependent on tourism—an inherently unstable economic sector.[7] Moreover, with economic security would come strategic protection for a country that had historically been threatened. To its detractors, however, Europe itself was a threat to national sovereignty and national identity. Its influence was evident in various areas of life, and stimulated vigorous argument about the erosion of Maltese 'tradition' in the face of European 'modernity'. These arguments are examined throughout this book, in a variety of contexts. Chapter three deals with debates about 'traditional' Maltese family and gender relations, chapter six examines 'traditional' and 'modern' political processes and chapter seven looks at arguments concerning the 'traditional' Maltese *festa*.

The social and historical sciences have been preoccupied with defining the nature and consequences of 'modernity' (Collier 1997: 9–16, Giddens 1990, 1991, Habermas 1987, Miller 1994, Spencer 1996). Indeed, a central feature of what Piot (1999) describes as the classic Euroamerican epistemology is the tendency to divide the world into the 'modern' and the 'traditional', which translates into 'Western' and 'non-Western' and therefore ultimately 'us' and 'them'. The proposition of such theories, then, is to describe and discuss the processes of capitalist expansion, development and globalisation as ones through which a non-Western 'them' becomes increasingly like 'us'. There are clearly dangers in such arguments, of becoming overly deterministic, assuming that the increased globalisation of world economy necessarily entails a homogenisation of socio-cultural forms. Modernity, in this reading, comes to define a way of life or mode of being, raising questions about whether the people who don't live that way are really modern or not. Such an approach represents difference as (temporal) distance, denying the coevalness—to use Fabian's useful phrase (1983: 31)—of 'moderns' and 'non-moderns'.

A counter-stream to the homogenisation theory focuses on the heterogeneity of global modernity (Robertson 1995: 25–28). A number of scholars have examined the ways in which particular societies respond to, accommodate or resist capitalist development and modernisation (see for example Comaroff 1985, Gudeman and Rivera 1990, Taussig 1980). This more subtle analysis treats modernity as the product of an encounter between capitalist and non-capitalist societies, that produces distinctive mutual understandings and misunderstandings not only about who is modern and who is not, but about what it means to be modern. Such work tends to pluralise modernity, focusing on multiple modernities, conceived as local understandings of global process (see for example Featherstone, Lash and Robertson 1995, Mills 1999, Rofel 1999).

This pluralising of 'modernity' appears to absolve analysts of the essentialising tendency inherent in a monolithic concept of modernity, yet it can risk reproducing it, in the same way that simplistic cultural relativism risks reifying difference whilst attempting to understand it (cf. Englund and Leach 2000: 237). Van der Veer (1998) is critical of the pluralising move, arguing that modernity should be seen as a singular phenomenon, but rather than use the term to classify an historical or social epoch, it should be seen first and foremost as a political project linked to the development of the nation-state (see also Piot 1999: 173). The multiplicity of modernity lies not in a plurality of modernities, but a plurality of histories of the singular modernity, in which the emergence of the nation-state has differed (Van der Veer 1998: 285).

The process of modernity nevertheless shares certain features, chief among them being the discursive division of the world into 'traditional' and 'modern'. This is achieved, according to Van der Veer, for two main reasons (292). First, so that 'tradition' can be discarded as backward. Second, so that new traditions can be invented through which the 'modern' can be promoted (see also Chatterjee 1993). To this extent, modernity itself can be described as a 'tradition'—which produces 'tradition' as its antithesis and purports to displace it (Collier 1997: 11). By this reading, what Piot describes as the classic Euroamerican epistemology, with its tendency to divide the world into 'modern' and 'traditional' is the epistemology of modernity itself, 'whose aim has always been to center the West and marginalize the rest' (1999: 173). To this extent, modernity can be seen as a mode of symbolic domination.

Using the example of Cyprus, Argyrou (1996) argues that in using the categories 'tradition' and 'modern'—particularly as they refer to 'non-Western' and 'Western'—Cypriots demonstrate the extent to which they have become subjects of Western hegemony; victims of symbolic domination. Even when they appear to resist Westernisation, he argues, they 'reproduce the conditions of their subjectification' (170) by presenting such resistance as (non-Western) tradition. Subtle though his analysis is, Argyrou risks romanticising Cypriot culture, in treating it as a *dominated* culture (see also Kahn 1997). For example, he presents the example of Eleni, an educated Cypriot feminist who berates the attachment of many of her compatriots to what she regards as an outmoded version of gender relations. Her case, he argues, demonstrates the plight of Cypriot culture:

> By embracing a *hegemonic* identity, Eleni may be able to achieve legitimation *as a woman*. At the same time, however, inadvertently but inevitably, she reproduces the conditions of being dominated *as a Cypriot*. (Argyrou 1996: 174, emphasis in original)

By this logic, the history of modernity is one in which cultures such as Cyprus are produced as subjects of Western hegemony:

> as the Cypriot case demonstrates, modernization or Westernization is not a means by which societies become Western, even though it is often presented as such. It is the mechanism by which they constitute themselves and are constituted as Western *subjects*. (183, emphasis in original)

In arguing thus, Argyrou, like Eleni, risks also reproducing the allochronic discourse of West–rest that modernity itself produces (see Fabian 1983). He separates West from rest, Europe from Cyprus, and in doing so implies that the subjectification of the latter is different from that of the former—the rest are different from the West because they have had the West foisted upon them; been subjected to it. To present modernity straightforwardly as symbolic domination, however, is to take modernity at face value—to assume its terms of reference and accept that the distinction traditional–modern can be achieved. This is not unproblematic. As a number of scholars have pointed out, modernity contains within it an inherent ambiguity or ambivalence (Bauman 1991, Wagner 1994). Latour (1993) argues that the characteristic feature of modernity is its tendency to divide and classify—what he calls the work of purification. However, he argues, this work is doomed to failure, because each division entails a prior assumption of unity—each proposition of difference must begin with an assumption of sameness. By this logic, each attempt to divide the world into 'traditional' and 'modern'—a 'Western' and a 'non-Western'—must begin with the assumption of a shared historical trajectory. This shared trajectory is identified by Friedman (1992) as inherent in a global economic system, which has enabled 'the rest' to not merely capitulate to the power of the 'the West' but to actively participate in its development. Similarly, Piot argues that rather than being opposed to modernity, African society must be seen as part of it:

> Africa has been an integral part of Europe over [a] 400-year period. Not only did African peoples like Kabre supply the plantation labor that helped create Europe's wealth in the Americas; they also contributed to cultural practices—music, cuisine, social sensibilities—that became central to the culture of modernity. By this line of reasoning, modernity's roots lie in Africa as much as in Europe. (1999: 21)

Comaroff and Comaroff (1992) elaborate this shared trajectory, in comparing the modern projects of missionisation in late nineteenth-/early twentieth-century London, Liverpool and South Africa. They argue persuasively that the 'civilising' missions to British inner cities were guided by the experiences of missionisation and colonisation in South Africa:

> in seeking to cultivate the "savage"—with, as we said, variable success—British imperialists were actively engaged in transforming their own society as well (293)

The modernity of South Africa and that of London is therefore a shared modernity—a singular modernity. If this is the case for Africa, then it is even more so for Mediterranean societies such as Cyprus or Malta, which have been incorporated into wider European economic trade networks for thousands of years (Frank and Gills 1996). Yet to proclaim such societies' participation in modernity is itself important mainly at a symbolic level. What is more important empirically is to explore both the specific histories of such participation—which is not the primary aim of this book—and the sense that people make of such participation at a daily level—which is. This book therefore treats modernity as a discursive field within which Maltese people in the early 1990s discussed their current predicament, their past and their future. Characteristically, this field was oriented around the polarity 'tradition' and 'modernity', which I treat as indigenous categories, and which embody or encompass an inherent ambiguity. On the one hand, 'tradition' was associated with Catholic morality, a way of—particularly family—life based on it, and practices such as *festa* that bolstered it. On the other hand, it was associated, particularly by younger Maltese, with a 'backward' and increasingly anachronistic orientation to the world, that bore the hallmarks of Church hegemony. Similarly, 'modernity' encompassed an inherent ambivalence. On the one hand, it was associated with education, material wealth and progress, but on the other hand with material excess and the erosion of 'traditional' morality (see also Mitchell 2000). Thus, at times 'modernity' was positively valued, at other times negatively. Similarly, 'tradition' was sometimes lauded, at other times criticised.

This tension permeated discussion about Maltese identity, and particularly those surrounding European accession. Being on the margins of Europe was seen as being on the margins of modernity. An early nineties attempt by a local sociologist to locate Maltese society on a gradient of 'tradition' and 'modernity' concluded that Malta was 'neo-traditional'—'traditional' because it maintained a Catholic morality, 'neo-' because it also incorporated a modernist orientation to economy and rationality (Abela 1991). In invoking the Catholic 'tradition', Malta placed itself both inside and outside European 'modernity'. Catholicism was used as a means of legitimising the calls for accession to Europe, but also a means of resisting it, or keeping it at arm's length.

Debates about Maltese identity, and its relationship to Europe, took place in various public fora—television, newspapers, public discussions, face-to-face conversations in public places. Indeed, since Anderson's (1983) exploration of the origins and spread of nationalism, it has been assumed if not wholly acknowledged that national identity is produced and disseminated in the public sphere. The 'imagined community' is dependent on media technologies for its effectiveness. However, for Anderson—and Habermas, who is perhaps the most influential theoretician of the public sphere—the public sphere is monolithic. The messages it carries are both unambiguous and determinate, unequivocally producing national identity. Clearly, such an approach is not appropriate in the Maltese context, where national identity was debated, contested and challenged. Neither is Habermas's determinate history of the public sphere's transformation. Like modernity, the public sphere has had different historical trajectories in different socio-cultural contexts. These contexts shape both the form and content of public debate, and are important when trying to understand such debate. Before describing the particular contours of the Maltese public, however, I will present Habermas's thesis and some recent critiques of his argument.

PUBLIC SPHERE—PUBLIC CULTURE

The 1989 publication of an English edition of Habermas's *Strukturwandel der Öffentlichkeit—The Structural Transformation of the Public Sphere*—coincided with a wave of research across a range of disciplines examining the media, the public sphere and public culture. Much of this work has concerned itself with the implications of Habermas's argument for the development of democracy (Dahlgren and Sparks 1991, Fraser 1987). For Habermas, the public sphere is above all the institution that guarantees democratic representation, providing it operates in the right kind of way. It should be a productive and open sphere in which public opinion is produced through the communicative deployment of reason (1989: 28). As such its position within civil society is to act as a prophylactic against the potential despotism of periodically-elected governments and establish the genuine influence of the citizen on the state:

> By 'the public sphere' we mean first of all a realm of our social life in which something approaching public opinion can be formed. Access is guaranteed to all citizens ... Only when the exercise of political control is effectively subordinated to the democratic demand that information be accessible to the public, does the political public sphere win an institutionalised influence over the government through the instrument of law-making bodies. (Habermas 1974: 49)

Historically, such a public sphere developed in the coffee-houses and salons of eighteenth century Britain and Germany. Such places were the loci of a bourgeois public sphere which was 'above all ... the sphere of private people come together as a public' (Habermas 1989: 27). Through reasoned debate about issues of common concern, the participants in this public sphere became the representative mouthpiece of a wider public (37)—generative of public opinion. Habermas contrasts this almost nostalgic image of the eighteenth century public sphere with its twentieth century counterpart (Dahlgren 1991: 5). Rather than bringing private people into the public to produce public opinion, the latter is characterised by the opposite movement. Changes in the organisation of capital, the nature of politics and in the technology of communication transformed the public sphere from being an arena of production into an object of consumption, in which the public is brought into and intrudes on private life (Habermas 1989: 162). This transformed public sphere is anti-democratic, in that it turns the table from the production of public opinion to its consumption and from participation to exclusion. Rather than listening to its citizens as purveyors of reason, 'the state has to "address" its citizens like consumers' (195). This process reaches its apogee in the news or current affairs programmes that promote style over content and are viewed primarily as entertainment.

Critics of this rather pessimistic view point towards the creative potential of the new media. They argue that although it is true that in the mainstream media public opinion has become an object of consumption, consumption in itself can be seen as a creative act, and the proliferation of new technologies opens up new possibilities for a genuinely productive public sphere:

> In effect, what we have here is the emergence of a plurality of dynamic alternative public spheres ... an inverse complement to the mainstream media's audience segmentation. (Dahlgren 1991: 14)

Other critics question the gendered and class-based assumptions behind Habermas's theory, arguing that he over-plays the significance of the male-dominated bourgeois public sphere to the exclusion of other publics (Eley 1992, Fraser 1990). The eighteenth century coffee-shops that he almost idealises were primarily male domains and domains of the bourgeoisie. His critics point towards the existence of other, feminine and proletarian, public spheres during the earlier phases of his analysis, and to the emergence of ethnic- or sexuality-based publics more recently (Calhoun 1992: 37). This argument, deriving broadly from the American agenda of a 'politics of recognition', posits the existence of multiple public spheres, geared towards the interests of different groups within society. As Calhoun has pointed out, this argument implies an atomisation of society's constituent groups and their respective publics:

> It seems to me a loss simply to say that there are many public spheres . . . for that will leave us groping for a new term to describe the communicative relationships among them. (Calhoun 1992: 37)

Taylor suggests that we employ a metaphor of 'nesting', with alternate public spheres 'nested' within and impacting upon the 'hegemonic' (1995: 22). However, Calhoun proposes another solution, which not only allows us to understand the relationship between different publics in any one society, but also permits an analysis that is sensitive to the differences in the public sphere between societies. Rather than using the fixed architectural metaphors of 'alternate' and 'nested' publics, he concludes that it might be more useful to think of the public sphere in terms of a 'field of discursive connections' (1992: 37), a phrase that coincides with Appadurai and Breckenridge's definition of 'public culture'.

Attuned to cross-cultural differences in the organisation of the public sphere, they defined 'public culture' as 'a *zone* of cultural debate' (1988: 6—emphasis in original). They are particularly concerned with how this zone has drawn such economically and politically marginal places as India 'into the cosmopolitanism of the rest of the world' (5), but argue that neither the process nor the media through which it occurs are uniform. Thus, 'every society appears to bring to [this] form . . . its own special history and traditions, its own cultural stamp, its own quirks and idiosyncracies' (Ibid).

This movement away from the public sphere as an entity towards public culture or public debate takes us away from the rather prescriptive analysis presented by Habermas towards a more descriptive, ethnographic approach. Rather than assuming the public sphere is an ideal to which societies should aspire, such an approach traces the dynamics of public debate in particular contexts. Such investigation reveals the 'quirks and idiosyncracies' of particular public cultures, and particular public spheres.

A SEMI-TRANSFORMED PUBLIC

If Habermas contrasts a 'non-transformed' face-to-face public with a 'transformed' public of the mass media, then Maltese public debate takes place in what one might describe as a 'semi-transformed' public. This public sees an articulation of face-to-face discussion in clubs, bars, churches and grocery shops with more attenuated discussions in public meetings or in the public media of television, radio and the press. The contours of this public reflect the relationship more broadly between 'public' figures and non-public.

As discussed in chapter four, Maltese society of the 1990s made a distinction between 'high' and 'low' society, which were respectively well- and less well-connected to the centres of power—government and bureaucracy. Most of the fieldwork on which this book is based was conducted among groups who regarded themselves as the wider populace, rather than élites. They referred to the latter as being *tal-klikka*—of the clique—the assumption being that at the centre of Maltese society is a self-interested clique who know each other and manage politics and bureaucracy in their own interests. This clique, however, are not entirely remote. In comparison with other societies, there are more intimate relationship between politicians and the electorate, and between prominent public figures and the wider public. This is partly because of the small size of Malta and partly because of the personalised nature of politics and political canvassing (see chapter six). Like politicians, the public figures who write for the newspapers or appear on radio and television are also personally familiar. They are people 'at a distance', because participating directly in the rarified zone of mass media, but they are also people 'close by', because they are people with whom one could have, or conceive of having, personal, face-to-face relationships. Through such relationships 'the public' are brought close to and engage with the well-connected elites. Despite the fact that those involved in both political and public culture are the relatively well-connected, they are nevertheless 'open', to be engaged with, rather than closed off from wider public attention.

The media are particularly well developed in Malta, considering the country's relatively small population. In the early nineties, the press included one English language and two Maltese dailies, four Sunday newspapers—two in each language—and a number of fortnightly and monthly publications.[8] The Maltese language publications were directly linked to the political parties—both Labour and the Nationalists had their own dailies and Sunday newspapers, and Alternattiva Demokratika, the small centrist party, published fortnightly. The Church also published two weeklies in Maltese. The English language newspapers were independent, although the oldest and most influential, *The Times of Malta*, was regarded as being pro-Nationalist and pro-clerical. All the newspapers, but particularly *The Times* and its Sunday counterpart *The Sunday Times (Malta),* had a long tradition of vitriolic letters to the editor. Radio, since its deregulation in 1992, provided another discursive medium, with phone-in and discussion programmes abounding on the ten national stations.[9] Television was dominated by Italian channels, but there was a single government channel that in the early nineties broadcast an increasing number of locally-oriented programmes between the British- and American-made dramas.[10] These were mostly discussion programmes in the form of public debates about the state of Maltese society.

The extent of this media output would suggest a fully 'transformed' public sphere, but in Malta the mass media operates in articulation with face-to-face communication. Indeed, the forms the media themselves take serve to emphasise the sense in which public figures can be approached on a personal basis. The preponderance of phone-in radio shows on national and local radio have meant that the broadcast radio operates as a node for private telephone calls, or a public version of interactions which could just as easily occur face-to-face. The media are used to personalise the space of public debate, and indeed to personalise the nation as a whole. The public media are not dislocated spaces of an abstract imagined national community that produces debate for passive consumption by the populace. Rather, both newspaper and radio lie somewhere between the categories of public and private communication, for although they are key elements in a national public culture, and key zones for national public debate, the persons involved in creating these debates are personally familiar. They may be friends, neighbours, acquaintances.

This articulation of face-to-face and mass media ensures that Maltese public culture includes moments of productive debate—in Habermas's terms—and moments of consumption. The consumption, however, feeds into new production in a cyclical, generative fashion that throws up new topics for debate. This serves to give a sense of inclusion or incorporation of the broader citizenry in national debate. However, to say that participation in such debate was equal and open, in the ideal expressed by Habermas, would be wrong. Given the significance of bars and clubs in such debate, women were often *de facto* excluded (see chapter three), although they often did participate in radio debates. Similarly, the inclusiveness was cross-cut by a sense of limits defined by respectability and connectedness such that 'the people' saw public culture dominated by people *tal-klikka*—a central, influential clique that governed public debate and public culture.

This central *klikka* consisted of the well-placed, the well-connected, the influential—bureaucrats, politicians, professionals, intellectuals and priests. In such a strongly Catholic country, priests are ever-present and involved in public culture, combining their roles of public orator—from the pulpit—and private counsellor—from the confessional—with those of writer or media personality. Priests were leaders and representatives of their congregation, but also intimate confidantes. They led debate, particularly when religious or moral issues were introduced into the on-going debates about national identity.

NOSTALGIA, NATIONAL IDENTITY AND THE LEGACY OF ST PAUL

The third major theme running through this book concerns a pervasive nostalgia, or concern with the past. This is partly a result of the ongoing anxieties about 'tradition' and the erosive effects of 'modernisation' and Europeanisation. As chapter five demonstrates, however, it also relates to party political allegiance, and claims against the state. Nostalgia for the part of St Paul's parish known as *L-Arċipierku*, large parts of which were demolished during the 1970s Labour modernisation programme, channelled claims that the state should intervene, and shaped the demonisation of Labour in general and Dom Mintoff in particular, by the predominantly Nationalist *Pawlini*. They argued that with the demolition of *L-Arċipierku*, a functional and unified community was destroyed, marking a significant phase in the erosion of 'traditional' Maltese life. This nostalgia for *L-Arċipierku* matched a more general nostalgia for the former glories of Valletta as a whole, that is discussed in chapter two.

This retrospective tendency related not only to Valletta, however, but to Malta as a whole. In a context dominated by vigorous public debate about national identity, national history became implicated, with competing narratives of the national past serving to justify competing accounts of national identity, and therefore competing arguments about Malta's future destiny. For *Pawlini* this identity was rooted in the legacy of St Paul's arrival on Maltese shores, which was seen as a point of national origin that not only confirmed Malta's Christian, Catholic heritage but also played the country into a distinctly European sphere of influence. However, a competing national narrative emphasised the years of Arabic rule, suggesting a Mediterranean provenance.

Debates that emerged in the late 1980s and early 1990s demonstrate the inter-relationship of this nostalgia with the prevailing ambivalence about national identity that characterised Malta at the time. These debates took place in Malta's semi-transformed public. The elaboration of these debates, then, unites the three main themes of this book—ambivalence, public culture and nostalgia.

At the centre of the controversy was the story of St Paul's shipwreck. The story is described in St Luke's *Acts of the Apostles* (28:1). Having been arrested in Caesarea for preaching Christianity, Paul was taken by boat to Rome, where he was to stand trial before Caesar. With him went several other prisoners, and Roman guards. While passing Crete, a storm brewed, which set them off course and floating for fourteen days, propelled by a strong wind. Finally, they struck land, but were shipwrecked. All the mariners were saved, and discovered that the land they hit was called Melite—a Roman colony governed by a man named Publius. Publius' father was sick, and Paul cured him, and converted him to Christianity. Since the nineteenth century it has been confirmed by the Vatican that the Melite referred to in Luke's account is Malta, and indeed even before this, the inhabitants of Malta have been convinced that Melite was Malta. Quintinius, whose *Insulae Melitae Descriptio*—A Description of the Island of Malta—was published in 1536, refers to well-established local oral traditions dedicated to St Paul (Luttrell 1977: 114).

In 1987, however, the German theologian Heinz Warnecke published his doctoral thesis, entitled 'The Real Journey to Rome of the Apostle Paul',[11] in which he argued that rather than being shipwrecked in Malta, the hapless apostle had in fact been washed up on the shores of the Aegean island of Cephallonia. The thesis was well-received in the German press, warranting favourable review in *Die Zeit* and other German newspapers. In Malta, however, it was received with consternation, sparking off a debate that was largely ignored by international scholars, but had immense local significance. Warnecke's argument was initially publicised in *The Sunday Times (Malta)*, where a lengthy article appeared in February 1989.

The Sunday Times (Malta) is a curious publication, occupying a space somewhere between a serious tabloid such as *The Daily Express* or *USA Today* and a scholarly journal. Each edition usually contains at least one learned article, usually by a local historian, that is well-researched, containing footnotes and a bibliography. It is therefore a medium for scholarly, as well as political, debate, which takes place not only in the articles but also in the lengthy 'Letters' section, where replies to the articles and debates make it something of a forum for discussion of topical issues. The practice of using pseudonyms when writing letters about particularly sensitive issues demonstrates the extent to which this sphere of debate, although in the public media, has immediate personal consequences. Letters are discussed in face-to-face contexts and replies can as easily come from these quarters as from other letter-writers. This articulation of public media and face-to-face communication is also demonstrated by the regular reporting, in *The Sunday Times (Malta)*, of the public debates and other fora that take place throughout Malta.

One such forum took place in May 1989, to debate the value of Warnecke's thesis. Warnecke himself had been invited to explain his thesis, in discussion with a number of prominent Maltese scholars, including one of the canons from St Paul's parish church. *Dun*

Ciarlò—*Dun* is the honorific term used for priests, as in the Italian *Don*—was popular and well-respected in the parish, as an authority on both historical and moral issues. In the events following the news of Warnecke's thesis, he emerged as a champion of the *Pawlini,* defending the integrity of the Pauline story in various public fora.

The forum appears to have begun with a friendly and jovial atmosphere, but become rather heated, as local priests defended the integrity of their belief in the *Acts* account. The debate continued periodically in the Maltese press over the next few years, and was still prominent when I began fieldwork. In 1992, *Dun* Ciarlò published, with local historian Michael Galea, an official refutation of the Warnecke hypothesis (Galea and Ciarlò 1992). It brought together contributions from theologians, historians, folklorists and even the Pope. The arguments were based on a re-examination of Warnecke's evidence, new analyses of the *Acts* accounts and evidence of a long folk tradition dedicated to St Paul. The Papal statement that opens the book, taken from an address to the Maltese during his 1991 visit, confirms from the highest religious authority that Malta and St Paul are inextricably linked:

> [Malta's] religious and spiritual history is closely *tied to the figure of the Apostle of the Nations, St Paul.* (Galea and Ciarlò 1992: 129—emphasis in original)

The volume was well-received in the Maltese press, confirming the popular opinion that Warnecke's thesis was at best misguided, and at worst a malicious attack on Maltese history and identity. Many commentators pointed to the fact that Warnecke had never been to Malta before writing his thesis, arguing that had he visited the island, it would be clear from the strength of local belief that St Paul had really been there. As *Dun* Ciarlò put it to me, 'You just have to be Maltese to know that St Paul was shipwrecked here'.

This line of argument raises issues concerning the legitimacy of non-Maltese arguments about Maltese history. In many ways it mirrors Herzfeld's conclusions about Greek folklorists, whose writings represent a defence of the integrity of national identity and national history against the incursions of Anglo-American ethnographers (1987: 66). In the Maltese context, the writings of local theologians represent a defence of the integrity of national historical memory against the threat of Warnecke, who came to represent foreign biblical scholarship more generally. A dominant strand of this defence was the suggestion that such scholars, because they were outsiders, were *ipso facto* unqualified to comment. They did not understand the weight of tradition behind the story of St Paul.

Paul Guillaumier, a regular correspondent in *The Sunday Times (Malta)*, conceded the absence of solid documentary or archaeological evidence for Christianity in Malta before the fourth century, but like *Dun* Ciarlò suggested that the sheer weight of tradition should be enough to prove that Luke's Melite was Malta:

> No ... histrionics or acrobatics are needed to substantiate the humble but venerable origins of Maltese Christianity. In the absence of more historical evidence, there need be no taboo either in admitting that, so far, the aetiology of Maltese Christianity does not yield a date earlier than the third-fourth century ... Nor, from the lack of mention of conversions in the Acts, should one necessarily prescind from the possibility that St Paul may have preached the Gospel and left a nucleus of faithful, first among whom Publius; a possibility, backed by a belief enshrined in the history, culture and identity of the local inhabitants as Maltese and Christians. (*The Sunday Times (Malta)* 8/11/92: 42)

This passage clearly demonstrates the central importance of the St Paul story in debates about Maltese identity. These debates took place within Maltese public culture, a zone of debate that included both face-to-face and more attenuated media communication. Most of this debate took place among priests and other biblical scholars, who were public figures but also personally familiar. They, above all, were characteristic of Malta's 'semi-transformed' public culture. They were also instrumental in defending the integrity of the Pauline story, as defenders of the faith, but also—consequently—of national history and a particular version of national identity. Inevitably, given the long association between the Church and the Nationalist Party, it was a Nationalist history that was emphasised, that linked Malta, via Christianity, to Europe. Indeed, it is significant that *Dun* Ciarlò's co-editor Galea was also a committed Nationalist who, among other things, had written an extensive biography of the former Nationalist prime minister, Gorg Borg Olivier (1989, see chapter six).

The Pauline story established the Maltese as not only European, but arguably *aboriginal* Europeans, converted to Christianity even before the establishment of Rome (Sant Cassia 1999: 248). This conversion was narrated as an inevitable moment in national development, making the pre-conversion Maltese proto-Christians and proto-Europeans. As one of the preachers during *San Pawl* 1993 put it:

> When Paul came to Malta, it wasn't just by chance. The storm was a providential storm. Paul was an Apostle. But he was meant to be the Apostle of Malta. Paul of Malta and Malta of Paul. This was what God—God who controls the whole history of humanity—this was what God intended. And when Paul came, the Maltese were ready. When they saw the ship coming towards the island, they saw their salvation.

The rather hyperbolic Maltese claims to European aboriginality are mirrored in other Southern European countries. A similar process has been observed by Herzfeld in Greece, where folklore and archaeology have served to assert Greece's claims to being the original European culture (1980, 1987). In Sicily, aboriginal identity is claimed via Greeks, Arabs, Normans and the direct intervention of the Virgin Mary (Fentress, pers. comm. 1997). These claims are directly related to a sense of marginality from the economic and political centres of Northern Europe, carrying with them the rhetorical message that rather than being marginal to Europe, they are central.

In the Maltese context, these claims to European aboriginality enabled particularly Nationalist supporters to maintain a commitment to European accession and 'modernity' whilst also emphasising the importance of local 'tradition'. European accession, although politically desirable, presented a threat to traditional morality, and particularly the position of the Church. If it could be established, however, that Malta's accession would reacquaint Europe with its religious origins, the tables would be turned. Rather than Europe threatening Maltese morality, Malta would launch its attack on European immorality. By this logic, rather than Malta being dependent on Europe, Europe is dependent on Malta.

It is not only Pauline story that emphasises Malta's Europeanness. Accounts of other events point to the significance of Malta to

Europe—as defenders of Christendom during the time of the Knights of St John and of the North African campaign during the Second World War. During the Independence celebrations of 1993 there was great jubilation at the apparent acknowledgement of this central historical role by Jacques Delors, then European Commissioner. The Maltese Prime Minister read out a statement made by Delors in Brussels that referred to 'a small country that has made a large contribution to European history—Malta'.

Clearly such linking of Maltese and European histories was beneficial to the Nationalist project of European accession. Indeed, more broadly, the establishment of Malta's Christian credentials through the defence of the Pauline story gave legitimacy to Nationalist claims to European-ness, particularly via the related notions of *Italianità* and *Latinità*—Latin-ness (Frendo 1992: 735, Hull 1993: 100–101). If it could be established that Maltese were the original Christians, then that made them the original heirs to the Latin church. Hence they were not only linked culturally to Italy, but in some senses the founders of a tradition that led to the establishment of Rome and—later—Italy itself. The linkage of European identity to *Latinità* and *Italianità* derived from the Nationalists' strongly pro-clerical orientation, and long-term commitment to the linkage of religion and the nation—*Religion e Patria* (see Frendo 1979).

Among Labour supporters, this association was less significant. Since its formation, the Labour Party has been more interested in developing the idea of Malta's distinctly Mediterranean identity—in contrast to Latin Italian—at times stressing the cultural links between Malta and Arab-Semitic culture (Frendo 1988). This emerged most notably during Mintoff's Labour administration of the 1970s and 80s, when the slogan *Malta L-Ewwel u Qabel Kollox*—Malta First and Before Everything—emerged as part of Labour's anti-colonial repertoire. The focus on Malta's cultural and political independence was combined, however, with a strengthening of political and cultural ties with Gaddafi's Libya, which proved particularly irksome to the religious authorities and the Nationalist opposition (Koster 1984: 219ff). The notion of *Malta Maltija*—'Maltese Malta'—however has an earlier provenance in which the British colonial powers were seen as cultural allies, or even long-lost cousins.[12]

The development of these contrasting accounts of Maltese cultural origins, related to contrasting political agendas, and contrasting traditions of national history (Sant Cassia 1993). On the one hand, there was religious or church history, that was broadly hegemonic and continues to be so.[13] It stresses the continuity of the Christian tradition, seen in the form of a direct genealogical line back to St Paul. On the other hand, there was a folkloric tradition that sought, through the investigation of Maltese language and folk customs, to identify cultural links between Malta and the Semitic-Arabic world. This tradition saw its origins in the late nineteenth century, but can be linked back to the work of early Maltese language pioneers, particularly Mikiel Anton Vassalli (1764–1829) who in 1993 was honoured with an exhibition that confirmed him 'Father of the Maltese Language'—*Missier l-Ilsien Malti*. Initially, folklore was not concerned explicitly with historical narrative, but with an exploration of cultural traits, locating them in a pan-Mediterranean context that incorporated and emphasised the Phoenician, Syrian and Semitic origins (Cassar Pullicino 1992). However, as it gained legitimacy it began to influence historical scholarship that criticised the hegemonic account of Malta's continuous Christian tradition.

In the late eighties and early nineties, a particular controversy emerged regarding the so-called 'Arab Years' of Maltese history (870–1090), during which Malta came under Islamic rule. According to 'hegemonic' Maltese history, this occupation failed to threaten the well-established Christian tradition in Malta. Rather, Christianity lived on until the reconquest of Malta by Count Roger the Norman, whose arrival in 1090 is narrated as a liberation.[14] However, in 1989 Maltese historian Godfrey Wettinger published an account of the 'Arab Years' which questioned this commitment to Malta's continuous Christian heritage (Wettinger 1989). In it, he described the assimilation of local people to the culture, language and religion of their conquerors. The Maltese, he argued, converted to Islam.

Published in *The Sunday Times (Malta)*, his article provoked substantial public debate. Chief among the defenders of Christian continuity was Mark Brincat, an obstetrician and gynaecologist who was nevertheless committed to defending religious history. As with the defenders of the Pauline story, Brincat based his argument on strength of belief, and commitment of the Maltese populace to a particular version of the past:

> There are those of us who unlike Professor Wettinger believe that Christianity continued as a significant element in the population of the Maltese Islands during the Arab period. (*The Sunday Times (Malta)* 11/02/90)

An exchange ensued in the pages of the press, on radio and television. The terms of this debate became increasingly political. In particular it was suggested that Wettinger must have a political motive in questioning the continuity of Maltese Christianity, that motive being to jeopardise the Nationalists' European ambitions and revitalise the country's ties with North Africa.

Brincat ended one article with an appeal to the Maltese to celebrate the 'victory of Western European Christian culture in Malta', and drew attention to the coincidence of the 900th anniversary of the 'Norman Conquest' with Malta's application to join the EEC/EU (Ibid). This explicitly drew attention to the links between the religious historiography that stressed a continuous Christian tradition and the politics of EU accession supported by the Nationalist Party.

It was into this highly politicised historical milieu that the news of Warnecke's St Paul thesis had arrived. However, there was a reluctance to explicitly draw politics into the debate. This was largely because the story of St Paul was intended to be inclusive—to mark a point of origin for the whole nation. Indeed, if its primary intention was to establish Malta as both European and Catholic, then the story would work well. Although non-Nationalists were more sceptical about Malta's EU ambitions they nevertheless by and large regarded themselves as both European and Catholic. However, to trace their Catholicism explicitly to St Paul would be to collaborate in perpetuating the national importance of what was broadly regarded as a Nationalist project—a Nationalist *festa* and a Nationalist history.

These Nationalist links were down-played by *Dun* Ciarlò, Guillaumier and Galea. Rather, they focused on the legitimacy of foreign scholars' intrusion into local historical debate, presenting the challenge to the Pauline story as an offence against the whole nation, not just the Nationalist half. Their argument was that denying Malta's Pauline origins threatened the integrity of all claims to European or Catholic identity. There are two possible reasons for this. First, that denying Maltese Catholic origins is denying their right to claim

Christianity. This denial coming from another Christian country—albeit a northern one—suggests a politics of legitimacy about who is able to discuss religious origins and who is not. Second, that it is tantamount to saying that the Maltese were Arabic. The alternative to European-ness, as suggested by folkloric historians, and indeed by Wettinger, placed Malta in an Arabo-Semitic, or even Islamic cultural sphere. Given that these were the two dominant streams in Maltese historiography, it can be seen how, when alienated from the very foundational moment of their European identity, Maltese were left to opt for the only other source of cultural identity—the Semitic Mediterranean. Coming from a Maltese scholar, such as Wettinger, this kind of argument was regarded as political. From Warnecke—an outsider—it was more problematic. As one *Pawlini* informant put it: 'It seems like an insult—almost a racist one'.

That such an argument should be interpreted as racist obviously contains its own racist assumption—that calling the Maltese Arabic is inevitably to insult them. But it also reveals the kind of awkward relationship Maltese have had with their history and identity. As shown in chapter six, there is a habitual self-essentialising tendency in Maltese public debate. This can lead to a kind of self-Orientalism or Mediterraneanism that presents their own difference as inferiority. Implicit in this process, however, is that the Maltese are assumed to have a monopoly over the articulation of such inferiority. Thus, whilst self-essentialisation as 'Southern' or even 'Arabic' is an acceptable strategy in the management of ambivalent identities, essentialisation from another, particularly a powerful other, is unacceptable. Hence, whilst Wettinger's challenges to the integrity of national identity are interpreted as 'political', for Warnecke the charge is more substantial—that of racism.

Both challenges to the integrity of Malta's claims to a continuous Christian tradition struck at the very core of the assumptions behind Nationalist accounts of the Maltese nation, and their ambitions for the future. For *Pawlini*, they marked a significant challenge to the very integrity of the practice for which they were constitutionally responsible—St Paul's *festa*. The importance of continuity, for them, was related to the status of the *festa* as a commemorative event that celebrated the foundation of the national religious tradition. In order to successfully discharge these commemorative duties, they needed to find a formula which was inclusive of the whole nation and which maintained its sense of 'tradition'. At the centre of this 'tradition'—or at its point of origin—is the story of St Paul, that was the object of public debate in the early 1990s.

NOTES

1 Although fears about the homogenising effects of global culture and capital appear unsubstantiated (see Hannerz 1996 and contributors to Featherstone 1990), they are nevertheless important in their effect. Even if we are not becoming 'all the same', if people think we are, they orient their lives and practices around this fear.

2 Ninety-eight per cent of the population are members of the Catholic Church and of these, eighty-five per cent practice their faith at least weekly.

3 A similar argument has been made by the Comaroffs (1993) about ritual in Africa, which they see as a means by which an encroaching market economy—conceived as 'modernity'—is accommodated by local ritual practices.

4 Indeed, it has been argued that anthropology sees itself in a perpetual crisis.

5 Maltese—*Malti*—is joint official language of Malta, with English. *Malti* is based on an Arabic-Semitic structure, with a large Romance vocabulary, derived mainly from Italian.

6 The 'emancipation' of the Maltese from 'Arabic Rule' is given different dates by different scholars.

7 In 1991, for example, the gross income from tourism was Lm (Maltese Liri) 175.3 million out of a total GNP of Lm 635.7 (Department of Information 1992: 18).

8 Since then, one of the English Sunday papers has gone daily, and another English-language weekly has been added.

9 By June 1994 there were ten national stations broadcasting on the radio, and plans to set up both more national stations and local stations. By summer 1995, a local station had been set up, serving the villages of Naxxar, Mosta and Għargħur. Since then, the number of national stations has expanded, and a number of other local stations have been set up.

10 In 1994, a second television station was set up by the Labour Party, which argued that the state station was simply a mouthpiece for the PN government. This was followed by the founding of stations by the Nationalists themselves and the Church. The advent of cable television in 1993 has expanded the range of overseas stations available to Maltese, giving them access to BBC and SKY broadcasts.

11 *Die tatsächliche Romfahrt des Apostels Paulus.*

12 Gerald Strickland, a leading figure in the so-called 'Language Question' of the early twentieth century, and leader of the pro-British Constitutional Party, was

Prime Minister from 1927 to 1932. He is well-known for his argument that Maltese racio-cultural origins—like those of many Britons—were Phoenician. According to Frendo (1988), 'He wanted to show, basically, that the Maltese were Aryans not Semites nor Latins.' (196)

[13] This is the version of history found in Maltese schools and in the influential doctrine classes attended by virtually all Maltese children. It constitutes the dominant narrative of national history.

[14] Local oral tradition sees the Count being welcomed into the then capital, Mdina, with huge and grateful crowds waving palm branches in scenes reminiscent of Christ's entry into Jerusalem (Cassar Pullicino 1992).

CHAPTER TWO

Valletta—Glory, Decline, Rehabilitation

A city uninhabited is different. Different from what a 'normal' observer, straggling in the dark—the occasional dark—would see. It is a universal sin among the false-animate or unimaginative to refuse to let well enough alone. (Thomas Pynchon, *V*: 323)

28TH MARCH, 1993—VALLETTA FOUNDATION DAY

On this day in 1566 Jean Parisot de La Valette, Grand Master of the Order of the Knights of St John of Jerusalem, laid the foundation stone of his new city. It was less than a year after the Knights' successful defence of Malta against a Turkish invasion force who occupied large parts of the island in what was to be known as the Great Siege. The foundation of Valletta acknowledged the Knights' long-term commitment to Malta—they were to stay until 1798—and their determination to defend the island against the Turks. It set in motion the building of one of the most impressive Baroque cities in the world—a purpose-built headquarters for the Knights, and the world's first planned 'new town'.

In the evening of the 1993 Foundation Day, a public meeting was held in the Old University building in Valletta. Entitled 'How can we *really* give life to the city of Valletta?'—*Kif nistgħu* verament *ngħatu ħajj lil-Belt Valletta*?—the forum brought together local politicians and other public figures, with members of the public, to discuss Valletta's problems. It was a public recognition of the city's decline from the glories of the Knights' era to the present situation of both infrastructural and social decay. The title of the forum was an acknowledgement that much of the discussion of Valletta's decline had hitherto focused on purely architectural issues. Valletta as a whole was designated a UNESCO World Heritage Site in 1980, which focused attention on its architectural riches. The European Community-funded *Malta Structure Plan* (1990), which outlined suggestions for an integrated environmental policy, proposed a 'Valletta Harbours Heritage Conservation and Improvement Area...[as Malta's]...jewel in the crown.' (93). The Valletta Rehabilitation Project (VRP), which had been set up in the late 1980s to deal with the city's decline, had focused most of its attention on the restoration of important buildings and churches associated with the Knights. *Really* giving life to Valletta, as the forum suggested, would involve going beyond these architectural, infrastructural or monumental issues, to address the quality of city life.

The forum was a further example of the kind of 'semi-transformed' public debate outlined in chapter one. It began with a series of speeches by the invited dignitaries. The University Rector, Father Peter Serracino-Inglott opened the proceedings, referred to Valletta as 'one of the finest elements of European heritage', but lamented the decline of daily life in the city. Valletta had been a lively city with a sizeable population—a vibrant hub of administration, trade and entertainment. With the decline of shipping in the post-Independence period, however, and particularly the withdrawal of the British fleet in 1979, the harbour economy had declined. At a national level, economic policy moved towards tourist development, which brought with it a movement of the country's entertainments centre away from Valletta to the coastal resort towns of Paceville and St Julians. Coterminously, Valletta ceased to be a fashionable place of residence, and the increasingly efficient communications coupled with increased availability of private cars led to a bourgeois exodus to the more fashionable suburbs. At the same time, a number of post-war slum clearance projects further reduced the city's population, leading to a staggering decline from 15,000 in the 1960s to 9,000 in the 1990s (Piano 1989, see chapter five).

Its remaining population was ageing and vulnerable to increased petty crime—frequently drug related. Empty buildings provided places for junkies to shoot up and crash out, but were as decrepit as some of the regular inhabitants. The problems of Valletta, argued politician John Bonaci, centred around its ageing population and ageing buildings. Another politician, John Spiteri, also emphasised the needs of Valletta as a residential area. While it was good to see churches and historical places being restored, it was also necessary to restore Valletta's housing, to encourage younger families to repopulate its empty streets. Although large numbers still flocked to the city during the day, after the last shops shut at 7 pm, the streets were dead. Valletta had the feel of a depopulated downtown area characteristic of many of the world's cities—the decaying downtown of an island city state. What was needed was a balance between the need for social rehabilitation and the need for structural and architectural restoration—a balance summed up by the architect Alex Torpiano, who argued that the only solution to the current problems was to work for *Belt Barokk, perot Belt Modern*: 'A Baroque City, but a Modern City.'

The contrast between Baroque and Modern was endemic in early nineties debates about Valletta, and indeed aesthetics more generally (see chapter seven). It would be tempting to see the contrast as a conflict of interests between outsiders to the city, and insiders. On the one hand we had the educated elites who perpetuate the image of Valletta as a Baroque city *par excellence*, for whom all interests appeared to be subsumed under a policy of preservation aimed partly at maintaining the national patrimony, and partly at encouraging tourist development. This position was summed up in the forum by a spokesman for the Maltese National Trust, *Din L-Art Helwa*—This Sweet Land—who argued that when discussing Valletta, we are always discussing the cultural, historical and patrimonial heritage of Malta. It was also the position associated with State-sponsored organisations such as the VRP. On the other hand we had the local people of Valletta, the interests of whom appeared to be constantly subsumed under this hegemony of heritage, and who struggled to come to terms with the implications of living on a monument. Such an argument echoes that of Herzfeld in discussing the Cretan town of Rethemnos (1991). Herzfeld characterises this conflict as one between two modes of temporality—monumental time and social time. In Rethemnos, large parts of the historical 'old town' were defined by the state as 'archaeological sites'; monuments to Cretan history. For the people who lived in Rethemnos, this monumentalisation of their surroundings contrasted and contradicted their normal mode of life—the monumental time of the state contradicted the social time of their lives. The problem was that by listing the buildings, many of them dwellings, as archaeological sites, the state were both forcing them to take on costly restoration works that did not square with their intentions and ambitions, and forbidding them from modifying their houses in ways that did. As a result, the Rethemniots resorted to a number of strategies aimed at resisting and subverting the state's policies.

In the Valletta situation, there is a similar antagonism. One of the more memorable events of the Foundation Day forum was when a man appeared at the door of the hall and began shouting abuse at the panel. Their actions and opinions were typical of the egotism and arrogance of their type, he argued. How could they possibly understand the problems of Valletta, as most of them lived outside the city, or were aloof politicians? They were only interested in monuments and politics—not in people's lives. It turned out his anger was directed at the person who had parked in front of his house on the street below the Old University. The car was so close to his door he could not get into his house. We might take this as an appropriate metaphor for the hegemony of particular elite outsider ideas about the rehabilitation of Valletta. Whilst care was taken to make sure that people could visit important monuments such as the Old University Building, nobody worried about whether this prevented people from living in Valletta. However, reducing the complexity of issues surrounding Valletta's rehabilitation to a simple model of dominant/subordinate or hegemonic/resistant is to over-simplify a much more complex picture.

First, although it is true that some Vallettans—*Beltin*—complained about the spending on monumental restoration, many others themselves subscribed to a monumentalist reading of Valletta's importance. They were aware and proud of the city's former glories and its rich architectural heritage. Living on a monument is not necessarily alienating, it can also be enriching, lending a certain civic pride to the narration of self. Second, many of the 'outsiders' who appeared to be determining or defining the terms for debate about the city's rehabilitation were not true outsiders. Given the city's rapid depopulation, and particularly the exodus of bourgeois families, the proportion of people in Maltese public life with Valletta connections is high. Many of these 'outsiders' are people whose families come from Valletta, and perhaps were even themselves brought up in the city. Moreover, they were people who had worked or studied in the city—at the law courts, government offices, or at the University, which was based in Valletta until 1968. Their investment in issues relating to the city, then, is more than those of a disinterested, aloof elite attempting to profit from an over-bearing monumentalism. Rather, theirs is also a personal investment anchored in genuine nostalgia and memory.

I shall return to this personal nostalgia of former Valletta residents at the end of this chapter. First, though, I shall examine the emergence of 'memory' as a key concept in late twentieth century social science, suggesting a need for clarification of the different types of memory, from personal through to historical. This serves as a prelude to a discussion of Valletta's history, and the kind of monumentalist nostalgia that surrounds the city—particularly for the City Gate and Opera House sites. This monumental nostalgia contrasts with what I identify as a quotidian nostalgia—for everyday life in Valletta—that makes the city more than merely a symbolic *tabula* upon which the elites can write their monumenalist fantasies.

MEMORY, NOSTALGIA AND THE PAST

Memory has become something of a buzz word in the social and cultural sciences in the last ten or fifteen years—largely prompted by the rediscovery or rehabilitation of Halbwachs' work of the 1930s (Coser 1992). Halbwachs, and others of his era, challenged the notion of memory as an information storage device, that holds data in pristine condition, ready for retrieval at a later date. Rather, memory should be seen as an active process that works on data from the past, transforming it and shaping it to the needs of the present (see also Bartlett 1932). In particular, memory is linked to the production of social identity, a feature of the work which can be traced back to the oral history movement, which sees narrating the past as simultaneously a process of producing the self (Tonkin 1992, Thompson and Samuel 1990).

This is clear in Passerini's examination of Turin working class memories of life under fascism (1988). She observed that the subjects of her research nearly always narrated events in such a way as to produce themselves as the protagonist. For example, the now elderly Maddalena Bertagna recounts her version of the events of 1st May, 1920—a day Passerini describes as a major historical turning-point, as it was the last May Day before the Communist Party split from the

Socialists. For Maddalena, however, it was memorable as a day on which she had transgressed the normal rules of feminine etiquette. She had attended a large public demonstration, run in a large group when the royal guards fired on the crowd, then fallen and let her hair fall loose. Finally, she returned home late to find her husband struggling to prepare soup for dinner (19–21). This demonstrates not only Maddalena's unwillingness to adopt the 'official' or hegemonic version of the day's events, but also the importance of her own version in the production of herself as a woman who 'breaks the rules'.

It would be wrong, though, to assume that the significance of such past narratives in the constitution of the self makes memory an essentially individual process. Halbwachs was sceptical of overly individualistic theories of memory, arguing that above all people remember as part of a social group (1992). It is clear that without the social category 'woman' and the notion of appropriate feminine roles, it would be impossible for Maddalena to construct her narrative in the way she does. A range of work on the self testifies to its social origins, and just as it is now received wisdom that the self is socially constructed (Carrithers, Collins and Lukes 1985, Cohen 1994, Morris 1994), so it is also firmly established that memory—a significant process in the constitution of the self—is a social process (Fentress and Wickham 1992).

The recognition that memory is both an active and a social process has fuelled a host of studies which examine the 'work of memory' required in the production of collective political movements—particularly regionalist or nationalist movements, which use the past to produce present and future (Chapman, McDonald and Tonkin 1989, Denich 1994, Hobsbawm and Ranger 1983). Memory is considered by definition a counter-hegemonic process, which again mirrors developments in oral history and 'history from below' that aimed at a critique of nationalist historiography (Appleby, Hunt and Jacob 1994, Burke 1991, 1997, Thompson 1978). The oral history movement has been concerned to acknowledge and write the history of social groups that were excluded from the grand historical narratives of political or military history. To replace the history of kings, queens, politicians and generals came working class history, women's history, black, gay, lesbian history. These different histories constituted alternative, or even subversive historiographies that would challenge the traditional form. They were explored through oral narrative, based on the personal recollection of individual subjects. Because of this, oral historians became interested in memory, as an avenue for emancipatory or counter-hegemonic historiography.

A similar interest in forms of resistance emerged in sociocultural anthropologists' readings of Foucault, Gramsci and Bourdieu (Comaroff and Comaroff 1992, Dirks, Eley and Ortner 1994). A concern to recognise or rehabilitate subaltern voices and trace the means by which the disenfranchised negotiate and oppose their own subordination has led to a similar pursuit of the authentic, counter-hegemonic narrative. This orientation has been maintained throughout the proliferation of 'memory' studies, and would be tempting to apply to the Valletta situation. One could envisage a rewriting of Valletta history that opposed or ignored its baroque glory, focusing instead on the everyday experience of a small urban populace. It would focus on the 'authenticity' of people's daily lives, and the generalisations made by official elite history. If I paint a caricatured picture, it is only in order to demonstrate the dilemmas of focusing too clearly on the 'forgotten voices' of memory. To do so is to eschew the complexity of attitudes towards the city's past.

The problem with much 'memory' research is that it fails to adequately outline the different forms taken by people's engagement with the past. Different authors have described as memory everything from the social history of bodily posture to the experiences of Holocaust survivors; from the development of nationalist mythologies to the cognitive operation of the human brain. In order to understand the full implications of past narratives in the Valletta context, it is important to make more rigorous distinctions between different forms of memory.

The problem is not so much with those who use memory to describe personal recollection of autobiographical events. This seems a perfectly sensible use of the term. The problems come when using 'memory' to describe social or collective processes. Psychologists distinguish between episodic memory and semantic. The former refers to autobiographic recollection and the latter to socially agreed scripts or narratives about the past that provide the general information necessary to function in a particular social milieu (Tulving and Donaldson 1972, Schachter 1996). As a form of social memory, semantic memory comes very close to an anthropological concept of culture. As with culture, there is a tendency to see such memory as composed of items, traits, practices or narratives which are handed down from one generation to the next in relatively pristine form.[15] The focus on content rather than process exacerbates the elision of differences between types of memory. By describing all types of scripted, semantic memory as social memory glosses the different processes involved in their scripting—their becoming social.

Where other authors have seemed happy with the single category social memory, I identify three processes contained within that category.The first lies at the cross-over of the personal and the social. I will call it collective memory. This is where autobiographical memories of personal experience are—more or less—shared by a number of people. For example, the collective experience of war or displacement which allows soldiers or refugees to script a collective memory of past events. This memory is collective inasmuch as it represents or incorporates the sum of its parts—the aggregation of multiple personal memories. Of course, such memories are often mediated by communicative media. For example, the collective memory of a particular battle would be shared not only by those who are present but also by those who receive letters or read contemporary press accounts of it. The feeling of involvement in distant events has recently been explored in the context of so-called 'flashbulb memories' of particularly shocking or surprising events, which resonate within a social group creating a vivid and detailed memory (Brown and Kulick 1982, Wright and Gaskell 1992, Whitehouse 1996, see chapter eight). The events surrounding the assassination of John F Kennedy are a celebrated example of such flashbulb memories, which encompass in collective memory not only those who were in Dallas at the time of the shooting, but also those who saw it on television or read about it later in the press.

The second process I would identify is social memory proper. This is where autiobiographical memory is carried across the generations even following the death of those who actually experienced the events referred to. The memory becomes socially significant either because of its former prevalence as collective memory, or its salience in evoking a collective pride or tragedy. Such social memory often refers to military triumphs or defeats, such as Gallipoli (Kapferer 1988) or in the Maltese case, the Great Siege (Bradford 1964). Ritter (1996) cites the example of the Japanese bombing of Pearl Harbour in 1941, to demonstrate the process of social memory. He was born in 1943, after the event, and yet has a detailed knowledge of what happened, why, and how significant it was. He links this to his being told as a child by his father that the day of the bombing was one of infamy. His father's memory of the bombing was derived from what I have called collective memory—the aggregation of actually recollected experience. Ritter's, on the other hand, comes from social memory. With the death of the generation that actually experienced the memory of Pearl Harbour, the collective memory will also die, leaving social memory. The significant difference is that the autobiographical component of 'I remember when...', still present in collective memory, disappears.

Social memory is reinforced by the third level of memory, which is history. Ritter argues that his 'memory' of Pearl Harbour was reinforced by reading accounts of, and looking at newsreels and photographs of it, which shaped his knowledge of the bombing. These accounts are even further scripted, written down and certified as official memory. The historical element is often state-sponsored, with a distinct mode of production and dissemination. It may contradict personal, collective of social memory, and indeed frequently does—such is the complaint from oral historians. It is nevertheless a powerful process, creating the same impression of accurate memory as those less formalised processes. As Ritter points out, the combination of collective, social and historical memory form a powerful picture of the past in people's lives:

> I may come to behave as if I have a direct personal memory of reports of the event, or even in some sense direct experience of the event itself. (1996: 17)

This vicarious memory can be powerfully invoked through people's engagement with the places where such events occurred. Recent academic work has firmly established the relationship between place and memory, suggesting in particular the extent to which place serves not only as the content of memory, but also its medium (Feld and Basso 1997, Boyarin 1994, Schama 1995). Thus, for the Ilongot headhunters of Rosaldo's ethno-historical monograph, for example, remembering the landscape is also remembering the events that took place in it (1980).

The work on memory and place can be analysed to reveal a similar set of distinctions between social, collective and historical memory. They are easily illustrated by a single example. Kugelmass (1995) describes an encounter in 1990s Poland between an aged Pole, a Jewish American scholar (himself) and a Jewish Pole. They travel to the concentration camp at Treblinka, a major site of Jewish, Polish and Jewish-Polish memory. He explains that in official Communist history, or historical memory, Jews had not existed in post-war Poland. Their regime was premised on non-ethnic, non-religious statehood within which the actually substantial Jewish population was seldom acknowledged, and even then only as a strategic scapegoat. This picture of a non-Jewish Poland was also propagated by official historical memory among Jewish Americans, for which the country was simply seen as a graveyard, and sites such as Treblinka and Auschwitz served as confirmation of this. Through their expansion into sites of pilgrimage tourism, Poland had been built up as 'a theater prop in a Jewish pageant about national catastrophe and redemption.' (281). Yet for many Jewish Americans they are also sites for social memory, as people who go there do so to experience the places they have been told about by parents or elderly relatives. For the latter group, including Kugelmass's companions, they are places of personal and collective memory. Kugelmass describes the way the aged Jewish Pole—himself a survivor of Treblinka—took over the day's proceedings, making himself the host. His familiarity with the camp's geography was testimony to his memory of having been there. His lighting of candles in commemoration of those who died was testimony to the experience's collective nature. But the trip was also collectively significant for the aged Pole. He too shared bloody memories of wartime and after, but only in order to separate himself from the Jewish memory. Kugelmass is pessimistic about the possibilities of Polish historical memory reincorporating the presence of the Jews, yet there is enduring tension between this official denial, and the vivid collective memory of those who cannot quite accept it.

Such tensions between the different levels of memory are endemic, and fully evident in the different accounts of the past which surround Valletta. We have already seen how the monumentalist historical memory of the city's glorious baroque past conflicts with the quotidian collective memory of everyday life. Such a process produces a rift between the local Valletta people and elite planners and historians such as those who spoke at the Foundation Day forum. Yet the distinction is not a simple one, between an officialising elite memory and a more organic collective version. The narratives of Valletta's past cross-cut and interpenetrate. Social and historical memory contribute to the experience and identity of those living in the city, and in important ways the elite themselves maintain a collective memory of life in Valletta.

Attitudes towards the past in Valletta are characterised by a profound nostalgia that sees the past as not only qualitatively different from the present, but demonstrably better. Etymologically, nostalgia derives from the Greek *nostos*, meaning 'return home', and describes a wistful or regretful longing for a particular place, normally associated with childhood (Lowenthal 1985: 10, Shaw and Chase 1989). Such homesickness is evident in Maltese attitudes towards Valletta, which as the capital city is the national 'home'.

Capital cities are always important foci for the nation, both as sites for national monuments and as contexts for important state occasions. Much of their importance is a consequence of public culture—the imagined geography of the nation, as centred on the capital, being reproduced in the media of the imagined community (Said 1978, Anderson 1983). Many nationals seldom—if ever—actually visit the capital, but they are nevertheless familiar with its street-names, its buildings and its sights. At least that is the case with the larger nations. In Malta, a smaller nation, the engagement with the capital is less imagined than known. Valletta, to Maltese, is not known as Valletta, but 'the city'—*Il-Belt*. It is a hub of activity. From the bus terminus outside the main city gate, one can catch a bus to any part of the island. It is an important national shopping centre, with retail outlets of all descriptions, and two major markets: the covered *Suq tal-Belt* which sells food and drink, and the open *Monti* which daily blocks off Merchant Street, one of the city's main roads, for stalls selling clothes, electrical goods, household items and video cassettes. Between them, the *Suq* and the *Monti* provide considerable employment to the city's inhabitants—*Il-Beltin*. As well as a centre for shopping, Valletta is also a major administrative centre. It is the seat of Maltese parliament, houses the country's law courts and most of the government ministries. Most shipping companies have their offices in

Valletta, and it has become an important centre for the country's burgeoning financial sector, providing office space for insurance companies and financial institutions. As a consequence, Valletta is well-used by Maltese from all over the country, despite its small residential population. In 1989 it was estimated that over 29,000 people passed through the city every day (Piano 1989). Because of this daily engagement, Valletta has adopted a specific position in the national imagination. Even for those whose families do not come from the city, it is still an important focus. On the centennial Foundation Day in 1966, Gorg Borg Olivier, the first post-Independence Prime Minister of Malta, acknowledged this symbolic centrality:

> For us Maltese, Valletta constitutes a fine showpiece, a perennial emblem of our fortitude and a symbol of national unity. Every inhabitant of these islands is at heart a citizen of Valletta. (*Times of Malta* 28/03/66)

Yet Valletta is also 'home' in a more substantive way. Borg Olivier was among a larger number of elite Maltese in prominent government positions who were originally from Valletta. The depopulation of the city from the 1960s to the 1990s was mainly at the expense of such elite families. In this sense, attitudes towards Valletta revealed a combination of monumentalist historical and collective nostalgia, born of a simultaneous acceptance of a glorious historical past, and an intimate lived past.

VALLETTA AS MONUMENT: THE HISTORICAL PAST

Most Maltese, and certainly the better educated, know the story of Valletta's foundation, at the height of hostilities between the Knights and the Turks. Its fortifications betray its origins as a military centre, and evoke the social memory of the Great Siege. Maltese schoolchildren are taught of the valliant, unified defence by Knights and Maltese during the Siege, and Valletta itself has become a monument to this important piece of history. Whilst I was engaged in a spell of temporary teaching at the University of Malta in early 1996, a student—not himself from Valletta—explained to me his feelings about Valletta:

> Whenever I see Valletta and its bastions—you can see them from here [the University]—it always reminds me of the Siege. It just brings to mind an image of the Turkish firing on the city. It's funny, because Valletta didn't exist then. I suppose it just shows how we understand the past.

In 1565, the Xiberras peninsula—on which the city was subsequently built—was uninhabited, and overlooked the old capital of Birgu. Under a commander called Dragut, the Ottomans set up artillery on its hill, from which they were able to bombard the tightly-packed Birgu with impunity. The siege was finally lifted following Dragut's death from flying shrapnel when one his of cannons exploded, and the new city was erected in the name of the architect of Birgu's defence. These events are important in the national consciousness and Cassar (1994) has argued that they marked an important moment in the development of Early Modern Maltese identity. As the events of the Siege became transformed, from collective to social memory, the image of Knights and Maltese standing side by side in defence of a common enemy became distilled in such a way as to enable a local claim to the glories and achievements of what was essentially a colonizing power. Through invoking its events, the Maltese were able to appropriate the Knights as their own. Valletta, originally the Knights' city, became the Maltese city—its glories reflecting the glories of the nation.

The design and building of Valletta took place in a context of widespread European preoccupation with the notion of an ideal city. The sixteenth century was a great time of city planning, partly because developments in military technology had made the older cities vulnerable, and partly because of philosophical changes sparked by the renaissance of classical philosophy (Mumford, 1970: 73–83). During the period, the themes of unity and integration came to the fore, influenced by Alberti (1404–1472) who described the city as no more than a great house. Like a great house it must be aesthetic and rational in its whole and in its parts.

Ideally, the city was round, with a defensive perimiter wall that often served to define the size of a city, rather than vice versa (Mumford, 1970: 85). In the case of Valletta, this ideal had to be abandoned due to the topology of the site, which favoured a more rectangular or elliptical design. Other elements of the idealised city were maintained, however, with important consequences. Valletta was designed by Francisco Laparelli, a student of Michelangelo, with Alberti's vision in mind (DeGiorgio 1985). His design was completed quickly—in just six days—because of the immediate threat of an Ottoman re-invasion. This speed suggests he was working to a pre-existing plan, or formula. Mumford has observed a tension in what he calls the Baroque city plan, between order and emotion, geometry and sensuousness (1961: 351). This is fully apparent in Laparelli's design, which specified a central, straight avenue running from the city gate at the land-side end of the peninsula, to the small Fort St Elmo at it's tip. On either side of this ordered bisection, the other streets would be 'serpentine', in keeping with Alberti's vision of streets that were both easily defended and elegant (Hughes, 1969: 68–69).

Throughout Europe, the sixteenth century saw a movement away from the evolved disorder of the Medieval city. Planning, and particularly military planning, was considered paramount to the Order's architects. Indeed, military considerations appear to have shaped religious ones. Unlike previous capitals of the Order, Valletta was to have no *collachio*, or concealed retreat area for the Knights to withdraw into reflective isolation. Rather, the whole of Valletta would be the Knights' *collachio*, with access forbidden to all but members of the Order. This plan had to be scrapped as increasing building costs necessitated the sale of plots within Valletta, to merchants and traders who were free to live there, provided they developed their land according to the central plan.

In 1569, Laparelli was replaced as chief architect by Girolamo Cassar, whose plans dictated that—among other things—all street corners in Valletta should be properly decorated. Consequently, Valletta became a city of statues, with religious imagery spilling out of the numerous churches and onto the streets. Having learnt his architecture in Rome, Cassar was preoccupied with the bluff, mannerist style of the Renaissance (Hughes 1969: 79). He designed a number of Valletta buildings for the Knights, including the conventual church of St John—now St John's Co-Cathedral—which in form is a representation of the Order's dual identity as religious and military. Recognisably a church, it is nevertheless clearly also defendable as a small fortress.

As a further concession to their military constitution, the Order abandoned Laparelli's plans for 'serpentine' side-streets, in favour of a strictly regimented grid pattern, with not one but two central avenues. At a symbolic level, this represented the militarisation of the city. Straight lines not only demonstrate the triumph of rationality and order, they also enable their representation:

> In the new city ... the building forms a setting for the avenue, and the avenue essentially a parade ground: a place where spectators may gather ... to review the evolutions and exercises of triumphal marches of the army ... (Mumford, 1970: 97)

Valletta's central straight avenues and open squares, then, provided a stage on which the Knights could demonstrate their power and glory. This practice is still maintained in the capital. On important state events such as the commemoration of Independence and Republic Days, military bands and guards of honour march through the streets, crowded with onlookers from the city and elsewhere. Similarly, on religious celebrations such as Good Friday and Our Lady of Sorrows, and the main Valletta saints' feasts of St Paul and St Dominic, processions and pilgrimages utilise this grid pattern.

By the seventeenth and eighteenth centuries, the immediate military threat of Turkish invasion subsided, and with it went the preoccupation with such functional architecture. The result was an expansion of the Baroque. Many of the plainer Valletta buildings were renovated in the excessively decorative style characteristic of that period. By the start of the nineteenth century, Valletta was referred to by the young Disraeli as 'equal in its noble architecture, even it does not excel any capital in Europe' (Bonnici 1989: 3).

Although many of Valletta's buildings were rebuilt or had facades replaced during the British colonial era under private, colonial or church patronage, the strict grid pattern was maintained to preserve the integrity of the city. New additions were embellishments, rather than replacements, of the original plan, and in early 1990's historical consciousness, Valletta was seen as largely intact until the rupture of the Second World War. During the war, many buildings were destroyed during the bombing, and thousands of people displaced as evacuees or refugees. The destruction of Valletta housing prompted widespread post-war rebuilding and redevelopment projects. These took on a particularly brisk momentum in the lead-up to Independence in 1964, as concern for Malta's post-Independence development came to the fore. Following Independence, the concern with housing in Valletta continued, but was joined—particularly under the Nationalist Government of 1987 to 1992—with a concern to restore the city to its former architectural, monumental glory.

MONUMENTALISM

Monumentalism combines social and historical memory to provide a powerful image of the past and suggest an agenda for preservation and restoration. In Herzfeld's Rethemnos context, it provided legitimacy to a centralised Greek state that sought to control development in the town. There, the Venetian Baroque buildings were perceived to be under threat from locals' attempts at modification and conversion. As a result, the planning authorities produced a set of coherent guidelines for preservation, which effectively sentenced the local people to living in a decaying ruin. As Herzfeld puts it, '[t]he national Archaeological Service has waged a principled battle against the heedless pursuit of comfortable modernity and the consequent destruction of the architectural heritage.' (1991: 34). The resulting tension between a monumental nostalgia and a more quotidian pursuit of modernity mirrors those that emerged at the 1993 Foundation Day forum. It is essentially a tension between cities as dwellings and cities as museum pieces.

The tension has been to the fore in post-war Valletta planning, which has taken two main forms. The first was primarily oriented to social policy, and comprised a variety of urban renewal and slum clearance projects. Harrison and Hubbard (1945), in a Government report prepared immediately following the second world war, identified various areas of the city which were either war damaged or considered 'obsolescent' because they were unfit for habitation. Subsequent governments set about replacing these problematic areas, and generally improving the city's living environment. As agents of the British colonial administration, Harrison and Hubbard inevitably preserved its political agenda—to maintain Malta and Valletta as a functioning fortress base for the Imperial fleet. Their recommendations, however, became the subject of political debate among local authorities, as successive pre- and post-Independence Governments sought to rebuild Valletta (see chapter five). The newly built housing blocks came in a variety of architectural styles. It was not until the late 1980s that serious concern was expressed about the sensitivity with which buildings should be replaced.

The second area of planning reflected monumental concerns. During the Nationalist government of 1958–62, the main gate of the city was replaced and an imposing new Neo-Classical law courts building erected in the city's central Great Siege Square. A grant was obtained from the British colonial authorities to restore the fortifications. The Nationalist Party in general became associated with the pursuit of monumental glory, whilst it opposed much of the slum clearance on the grounds that it was Labour policy. In 1981 Ray Bondin, who was later to become a Nationalist MP, wrote that the Labour Government (1971–1987) appeared to have forgotten that Valletta is not just a city, but the capital city (Bondin 1981: 11). As such, it should be a '[well] organised and modern city, without reducing the importance of its historical parts ... a city that is very much the centre of the country's culture, and that we admire' (17–18).

This policy was not only linked to a monumental nostalgia. It also reflected the political-economic agenda of the new government. The Nationalist Government of 1987 to 1996 were preoccupied with the issue of European accession, and Valletta became an important symbol of Malta's claims to being recognised as European. As the capital of the Knights of St John, an Order drawn from the highest ranks of Europe's aristocracy, Valletta was a quintessentially European city. Indeed Patrick Brydone, an eighteenth century British traveller to Malta referred to the city as 'an epitome of all Europe' (Luke 1960: 155). If it could be demonstrated that Malta was heir to an important part of the European *patrimoine*, then the claims to European accession would be given fresh vigour. Likewise the Maltese economy which, following the withdrawal of the British navy, was increasingly dependent on tourism. The Nationalists were wary of the mass sun-and-sand tourism associated with other parts of Southern Europe, opting instead to develop a heritage-cultural tourism that not only attracted a more discerning, higher-spending tourist, but also drew attention to the country's—and Valletta's—monumental splendour (see Mitchell 1996b).

Bondin proposed a central and permanent office dedicated to administering the rehabilitation or reconstruction of Valletta. He was eventually to become head of the Valletta Rehabilitation Committee—later Valletta Rehabilitation Project (VRP)—following the election of a Nationalist Government in 1987. The VRP set about the restoration of several historical buildings and churches in Valletta, including the Knights' former conventual church, the Grand Master's palace and the Manoel Theatre—a magnificent eighteenth century theatre tucked away in one of the narrower side-streets. In 1989 it commissioned a plan for the rehabilitation of the city from the workshop of Italian architect Renzo Piano, most famous for his design of the Centre Georges Pompidou in Paris (Piano 1989). The plan included solutions for the city's parking problems and suggestions for new pedestrian zones, as well as the design for a new City Gate complex. By this time, near-consensus had been reached that the Nationalists' 1960s gate was an eye-sore, and needed to be replaced.

The original gate was the only landward breach in the massive Valletta fortifications. Flanked on either side by two vast cavalier defences, it was a small chink in the city's armour. Entering the city over a narrow drawbridge that spanned the deep ditch cut by the Knights, visitors passed through an ornate gate and into the streets beyond. John Galt, a traveller of the early nineteenth century, revived Alberti's notion of the city-as-house when he described the entrance as 'in some respects more like the vestibule of a great mansion, than the portal of a city.' (Galt 1812: 116). Nowadays, the entrance is less enchanting. The entrance is larger—more open. In front of the gate is the central bus terminus with a large Triton fountain beyond which a wide tarmacked walkway leads into the city. The gate itself is a massive marbled dolmen in an architectural style reminiscent of Mussolini's state-sponsored Neo-Classicism. Large and square, in beige concrete, it is topped with flag-poles and flanked with two large Imperial wreaths.

The style reflects the era of its building. Immediately post-war the Nationalist Party were keen to challenge Malta's colonial past, present and short-lived future, and establish their own hegemony over the national monumental iconography. The old city gate, which had been damaged during the war, was seen as stylistically anachronistic—a symbol of the old order. The choice of new style reflected the long-standing links between the Nationalists and the Italian nation, and particularly their involvement in Italian irredentism during the fascist era. The architect chosen for the gate was productive during that time, designing many prominent buildings for Mussolini. This fact has since been picked up by critics of the gate who argue that a fascist's work is not fitting for the gateway to a city that was beseiged by Hitler's fascist powers during the war.

Today the gate is home to a number of bread and lottery vendors. After passing through, visitors find themselves in an open square used as a car park, with the pedestal ruins of the old Opera House directly in front. The Piano plan outlined a refurbishment of the entire city threshold, incorporating the gate, square and Opera House ruins. They were all to be replaced by a modern, integrated entrance complex which according to the Organization of World Heritage Cities, 'makes no concessions to any form of historicism or attachment to the past' (OWHC 1996).

The Opera House was designed and built by the English architect E.M. Barry in the late nineteenth century, as a place of entertainment for Maltese high society and the British forces. It was renowned as the first port of call for touring opera companies, and thus the first place in Europe to hear new productions and new performances (Sant Cassia 1992). The Opera House was bombed by the Germans in 1942, and some argue that its targeting had been a deliberate attempt to reduce Maltese-British morale by ridding them of an important (high) cultural edifice—thus reproducing the 'Baedecker bombings' of Exeter. The building was badly damaged, but not destroyed. Later it was condemned as dangerous by the British authorities and completely demolished. This was seen as a double injustice by local Maltese. Not only had they suffered the hardships of war and the relentless German bombing raids, but also the British, with whom they had fought, were now finishing off the job rather than preserving this symbol of Maltese—and Vallettan—urbanity.

The Opera House became important in Valletta collective and social memory as a symbol of lost cultural glories. Its prominence reflects the extent to which monumentalism, far from being the preserve of the elites and state organisations such as the VRP or the Greek Archaeological Service, can enjoy a popular significance. Vallettans—or *Beltin*, and particularly older *Beltin*—would tell me about the glories of the building. It was perfectly proportioned and a fine sight for those entering the city. Its design was both practical and symbolic, with the classical pillars that flanked the main entrance representing the continents in which the British held colonies. The *Beltin* appreciated this ingenuity of design, despite its direct association with colonial rule. Several showed me photographs of the Opera House, to demonstrate its beauty. Its demolition was an important moment in the monumental decline of the city, and the remembrance of its quality a significant element in its monumental nostalgia. The elderly *Beltin* with whom I enjoyed many hours' conversation would also point out the significance of the Opera House as a social space. They would describe how as children they had congregated outside the building before performances to observe the elegantly dressed society figures as they met, talked and eventually climbed the stairs into the foyer. With the demolition of the Opera House, there was no longer such a focus for mass spectatorship of the elites. With it, an important part of popular culture disappeared. Likewise high culture. The Opera House was routinely praised by those who had never witnessed a performance there for its excellent acoustics. One man in particular explained to me that he had once been taken into the building by his father, who was a cleaner there:

> The sound was crystal clear. You could hear a pin drop on the stage from the back of the auditorium. It was the best opera theatre in the whole of Europe.

This image of quality contributes to the sense of pride and nostalgia for a lost glory of both monumental and cultural quality. Its disappearance is associated with a decline in the quality of not only Valletta's cultural life, but also that of Malta as a whole. The Opera House was never properly replaced, and its ruins stand as a monument to this decline.

The praise of the Opera House's value in the social and collective memory of ordinary *Beltin* contrasts with other evidence and demonstrates the extent to which such nostalgia might display a reconstitutive or even inventive edge. Such is the work of memory. Harrison and Hubbard summed up the glories of the Opera House as follows:

> The Opera House, which is not a historical monument, was marred by serious practical defects. It was very generally agreed

> that the acoustics were execrable; that the line of sight of a higher proportion of the seats was unsatisfactory; that the number of seats was, from the point of view of an impresario, insufficient, that the stage, with its wings and loft, were too small...(Harrison and Hubbard 1945: 71)

However, even at the time of their report, they found considerable support for the preservation of the building, based on local understanding of its practical and social value; support which appears to have increased with the passage of time as memory has developed through nostalgia. Since its demolition, it has come to be seen alongside City Gate as an eyesore, and an area fit for redevelopment.

The Piano plan was seen as basically too modern, and with its focus on shopping malls an inappropriate legacy to the cultural glories of the Opera House. As a consequence, the newly re-elected Nationalist Government in 1992 organised a competition in which Maltese architects were invited to submit plans for a new Arts Centre development on the site. The competition was overseen by the VRP, and attracted applicants from all the main architects in Malta. The submissions led to a lively public debate about the most appropriate style of building for the Arts Centre and revealed key tensions between traditionalists and those who thought the development should be modern.

On the traditionalist side, opinions were divided. On the one hand were those who favoured a Baroque building and on the other those who pressed for the rebuilding of Barry's original Opera House. Those who favoured the former emphasised the fact by rehabilitating Alberti's—and indeed Galt's—rhetoric of the city as a single grand building. Architect Leonard Mahoney, one of the entrants to the competition, compared Valletta to 'a big cathedral with the National Arts Centre as the façade' (*The Sunday Times (Malta)* 24/01/93: 18). He emphasised the need for harmony in the design, pointing out that as most of Valletta's existing buildings were Mannerist or Baroque so too should be the design for the new Opera House. Valletta should remain a monument to the Renaissance, in keeping with the social and historical memory invoked by its extant churches and Knights' palaces.

This monumental nostalgia, based on a social memory concerned to approximate style, rather than accurately rebuild, contrasts with the other form of traditionalism at play, which was based on a collective memory of how things used to be. Those who favoured the rebuilding of Barry's Opera House were by and large more elderly elites for whom the actual memory of the Opera House held sway. Their arguments were based upon the same criteria as those of the *Beltin* outlined above—that the original had been a temple of culture, sophistication and urbanity. Mahoney was critical, largely because Barry's design had been so clearly British in its Classicism, and therefore failed to fit his idea of the Valletta cathedral's façade:

> The storm troopers of the pro-Barry Brigade ... believe that there is a chance that the Royal Opera House will be rebuilt as it was before the war. These well-intentioned but misguided persons fail to appreciate that the Royal Opera House did not belong with the Valletta environment, that in the words of a visitor, "it was so obviously British that one might as well be in London, or Manchester, or Liverpool." (*The Sunday Times (Malta)* 13/12/92)

Defenders of rebuilding—and indeed those of the modernist plans—argued that Valletta had never been all that integrated, and had always comprised a hodge-podge of different architectural styles. The calls for integration represented a retrospective projection of stylistic integrity—a kind of architectural gestalt harking back to a mythical golden era of completeness. Another architect, Renato La Ferla, argued that the new design must be for a building 'for its time and of its time, and any masquerade of any of the dead styles is inadmissable.' (*The Sunday Times(Malta)* 31/01/93). Needless to say, La Ferla's design was decidedly modernist. Mahoney's represented a kind of pastiche of architecture from the period of the Knights.

Mahoney and La Ferla kept up a lively debate in the press throughout late 1992 and early 1993, following the decision of the competition jury to reject all 13 submissions and launch a new, international competition. This was a higly controversial decision, that raised serious questions about the Government's commitment to Valletta's rehabilitation, and the appropriateness of giving over the responsibility for such an important national site to a foreigner. Given the tensions between traditionalists and modernists, however, it was perhaps the only decision possible. It certainly represented the Maltese predicament at a time when 'tradition' and 'modernity' were central discursive co-ordinates in debates about the nation.

Paul Sant Cassia, in a piece prepared for *The Sunday Times (Malta)*, described the debates about the Opera House—and indeed City Gate—as being primarily to do with cultural identity. In particular, he argues that the debates signalled differential attitudes towards Malta's European-ness. While both traditionalists and modernists agreed that the significance of the City Gate and Opera House developments was that they should represent Maltese European identity, there was disagreement over whether this should be a Europe of the past or of the present:

> Both hark, or beckon, to a period when the City Gate expressed (or will express) Valetta's [sic], and Malta's identity as a 'European' society—either in the past or in the future. (Sant Cassia 1992: 1)

He ends on a slightly mischievous note, arguing that the replacement Opera House should incorporate the existing ruins, thus combining the new building with an 'archaeology of [the Opera House's] memories and of itself' (5) and that the City Gate should be left alone. After all, he argues, all Maltese agree that in its present incarnation it is horrendous and inappropriate, 'we *all* agree quite spontaneously that we hate it' (5). Given this consensus, what's the point in arguing about its replacement?

At a national level, the debates about City Gate and the Opera House took place in the national press and particularly, as observant readers will be aware, *The Sunday Times (Malta)*. Along with *The Malta Independent*—first published 1992—this publication provides an important forum for the discussion of significant national issues. As an English-language newspaper, it is both a symbol of and an important element in the public sphere of the nation's elites. Debates held in this forum can therefore be seen as elite debates, but they are not exclusively so. As argued above, the local inhabitants of Valletta are also enaged in debates about the city's architecture, just as they engage in debates about Maltese religious history (see chapter one). Such is the character of Malta's 'semi-transformed' public. However, there is another reason why the elite debates should not be seen as overly divorced from the everyday realities of life in Valletta. This is because many of the people engaged in the public monumentalist debates themselves have personal experiences and memories of Valletta. Thus, whilst there is a tendancy to over-emphasise a dichotomy between subordinate collective memory of everyday life and hegemonic social memory of historical glory or monumental spendour, in the Maltese situation such a dichotomy is inappropriate. Elites share with *Beltin* both a collective memory of experiencing Valletta and a social or historical memory of its past glories. This is partly a consequence of Valletta's position within the wider national sphere.

QUOTIDIAN MEMORIES: VALLETTA AND EVERYDAY LIFE

Since its foundation, Valletta has been a focal point of Maltese life. At its foundation it was ear-marked as the Order's capital and went on to perform that role for the Knights, the British and the Independent Maltese to the present. As well as an administrative capital, Valletta has also been an important focus for economic activity in a country that since the arrival of the Knights has been totally dependent on external trade. The Valletta harbours were a significant focus of trading activity, and in the later sixteenth and early seventeenth centuries, a large and vibrant mercantile class developed, based on trade and investment in shipping (Cassar 1994: 123–139). Cassar describes Valletta as a 'gateway community', as in it was managed the country's contact with the outside world (101). It was also a hub for domestic activity. It became a centre that attracted farmer-traders and workers from the more rural areas of Malta, who travelled to the city on a daily basis to engage in economic activity (Cassar 1988)—and indeed continued to do so until the early 1990s. Alongside the strictly mercantile activity there developed a vibrant entertainments sector in the city. By the later seventeenth century, Valletta had become something of a centre for prostitution. Cassar cites the presence of 165 *donne publiche*—public women—in the 1667 *Status Animarum* for the parish of Our Lady of Porto Salvo, out of a total population of nearly 3,000 (1994: 188).[16] This trade continued until the 1970s. Valletta became a 'sailor town' with numerous bars, brothels and night-clubs providing auxiliary services to the harbour economy. The withdrawal of the British fleet signalled a decline in the sailor town. As the coastal resorts became more fashionable, life in Valletta declined to the levels that provoked such anxieties in the early 1990s. Yet to be gentrified, this decaying downtown then attracted—and continues to do so—the nostalgia of those who remembered its more lively days.

The nostalgia is not only monumental, nor only related to the evocation of 'culture' and sophistication emerging from the debates about Valletta's Opera House. It is a nostalgia for the time when Valletta was a vibrant entertainments centre and, for large numbers of suburbans of both elite and non-elite families, a place of up-bringing—home. Among them the tutor I engaged to help me learn the Maltese language. Peter Schembri was a former Jesuit and gifted linguist who gave up his vows to become a secondary teacher, marry and have children. He was a prominent leader of opinion, particuarly in religious matters, and wrote frequently for the fortnightly religious newspaper *Il-Gens*—The People. During my Maltese lessons he would talk not only about the language, but also about his childhood in Valletta, of which he was clearly fond. He had lived in the low-lying area close to Fort St Elmo known as the *Due Balli*: a poor neighbourhood renowned for its supply of prostitutes to the bars and dance-halls of Strait Street—known as The Gut. During the second world war, his family had been evacuated to the wealthier and safer town of Sliema. There they found living conditions more comfortable and rather than move back to the city, decided to stay.

In Valletta, Peter's family had lived in a single room with only shared sanitation facilities. As in the cliché, they were poor but happy. Life was simple. Peter recalled playing football for hours on end on the open space outside the Fort, that at other times was used as a parade ground. The soldiers would move them on when it was parade time, and join in their games at other times. He also recalled directing visitors from Britain and elsewhere to the local 'chapel of bones'—a small but impressive ossuary that was destroyed during the war. It had been a prominent tourist attraction, and featured in a number of travel guides to Malta. Peter told me of his childhood on a walking tour of Valletta, during which he also alluded to the lively entertainments in The Gut. Like all children of respectable families, he had been forbidden from going into The Gut—a narrow alley-street then lined with bars and dance-halls of which only the frontages and sign-posts remain. He described how he had used to sneak into the street with his friends, to observe the drunken goings-on of the sailors and their paid escorts. As we walked up the gently-sloping street, he told me to write down the names of the various establishments—The Cotton Club, Cape Town, The Garden of Eden—all names he associated with his childhood, with home and with the erstwhile vibrancy of this now-defunct red light area of a declining city.

This nostalgia for the former liveliness of the now quiet city is shared by both elite outsiders such as Peter Schembri and the local people of Valletta. They come together on such occasions as *festa* and football matches, when large numbers of former *Beltin*—or indeed the offspring of former *Beltin*—return to their city to revitalise it, if only temporarily. On such occasions, the streets of the city are filled with locals and non-locals alike, all concerned to preserve Valletta tradition. According to many, if such tradition disappears, the battle to save Valletta would be lost. This anxiety about the future formed a constant back-drop to my research in the city. With it came the notion that a palatable future could only be guaranteed by ensuring continuity with the past—modernity was only possible through tradition. This continuity in turn was manifest, objectified, in traditions such as *festa*. The importance of maintaining these traditions was most eloquently summed up by an informant called Lawrence, who was the proprietor of a local Valletta bar that provided a locus for much of my research:

> Look at Valletta—Valletta is dying. All we've got left are traditions. If you take off traditions and the *festa*, we've got nothing. If you take it away there'll be nothing left for our kids.

The objectification of ritual traditions should be seen as an inherently modern act, encompassing the characteristic ambivalence of modernity. It complements the objectification of historical and social memory inherent in the monumentalisation of Valletta. In both cases, the appeals to preservation contrast or even contradict the collective memory of everyday life. While monumentalism focuses on perceived or actual glories that are evoked by the presence of a building, the tradition of *festa* focuses on the relatively extraordinary events associated with the commemoration of a patron saint. In each case, they become the focus of anxieties created by an apparent decline in everyday life—hence the trend in ritual revitalisation that went alongside calls for the city's rehabilitation.

Rehabilitation was a national concern, not simply one of local, parochial significance. This is partly because of the city's prominence in the life of the country as a whole, and partly because of its position in the individual biographies of people such as Peter Schembri—well-placed figures of Maltese society, who mix with the highest echelons, but who nevertheless maintain a nostalgia for the city grounded in the actual experience of collective memory. This collective memory feeds into the more social or historical memory that contributes to the monumental nostalgia for Valletta as a place of Baroque architecture, and stimulates debate about rehabilitation and refurbishment. To call all these things social memory would be to oversimplify a set of more complex processes, involving an interplay of personal, collective, social and historical memories. To rigidly distinguish between a hegemonic social and a subordinate collective memory would likewise elide the genuinely shared nostalgia and memory for a place of monumental significance that was also quite literally a home to much of the nation's population.

NOTES

[15] For a detailed discussion of concepts of culture and their implications see Abu-Lughod 1991, Barnard & Spencer 1996, Kahn 1989.

[16] *Status Animarum*, or 'State of Souls' is an annual census performed by parish priests since the Council of Trent. In it they record the age, sex and occupation of all parish inhabitants.

CHAPTER THREE

Gendered Lives—Women and Men in Valletta

> How many other families have cared for her? All our babies have had only one father, the war; one mother, Malta her women. But lookout for the Family, and for mother-rule. Clans and matriarchy are incompatible with this Communion war has brought to Malta. (Thomas Pynchon, *V*: 325)

FIELDWORK IN VALLETTA: FROM OUTSIDER TO INSIDER

In the early days of fieldwork, I found myself wandering the streets of Valletta, from the central, commercial zone close to City Gate, to the bustling Valletta markets: the *Suq tal-Belt* or food market, and the *Monti*—the daily open air market selling clothes, cosmetics and electrical goods. From these relatively anonymous zones which buzzed with people from all over Malta and beyond, I would descend to the quieter, more intimate residential areas, stopping occasionally in an attempt to start up provisional conversations in my rudimentary Maltese.

In my initial sojourns I was demonstrably an outsider—*barrani*—a foreigner, even a tourist. Tourists are ubiquitous in Malta, but particularly in Valletta, where they are quietly tolerated. They are regarded as good for business, but their presence is seen by many as morally problematic, as particularly the younger tourists introduce Maltese to 'modern' ways. *Barrani/ja*—pl. *barranin*—derives from the stem *barra*, meaning 'outside'. It literally translates as 'outsider', although it can also mean 'foreigner'. It is used in a variety of contexts, from nationality, to village, community, *festa* and household. As Dubisch has demonstrated in a modern Greek context, such categories of 'inside' and 'outside' are flexibly applied to different levels of inclusion and exclusion, providing a 'rhetoric of segmentation, merging or separating social units according to specific situations.' (1993: 273). Thus, people who in one context would be referred to as 'insiders' would in another be classed as 'outsiders', *barranin*.

The process of integrating into Valletta life became one of moving from 'outsider' to 'insider'. As I gradually developed an ear for the Maltese language, *Malti*, and began to speak it, people assumed that I was the son of an emigré, returning from Australia or Canada to start a new life. No longer an absolute *barrani*, the ability to speak even rudimentary Maltese made me—at least linguistically—an insider. *Malti* is perhaps the ultimate marker of inclusion and exclusion in Malta. Although most Maltese are multilingual, speaking both English and Italian, *Malti* is the main medium of everyday discourse, and a powerful symbol of national uniqueness. Like all identity markers in Malta, its true nature is contested, most notably during the so-called 'Language Question' of the early twentieth century (Hull 1993, see chapter one). Its Semitic structure suggests cultural links with the Arab world, but a vocabulary derived in large parts from Italian and French bears the hall-mark of Malta's Europe-oriented history (Aquilina 1989). The language is therefore grist to the mill of both pro- and anti-European elements in Maltese political discourse.

As well as being a symbolic marker of Maltese exclusiveness, *Malti* is also a practical tool for the exclusion of ever-present foreigners—*barranin*—from local discourse (Gullick 1975). In a situation where the country is over-run by tourists for much of the year, it achieves a kind of closure from the rest of the world, allowing the Maltese to speak among themselves without being heard. As my competence in the language developed, I was able to enter this world of Maltese-speakers, and become increasingly integrated. I clarified my status as a student of Maltese culture and society, and eventually, became known as *Ġanni L-Ingliż*—Jonny the English—acknowledged as an insider by dint of being nick-named, but forever branded an outsider by that nickname's reference to nationality. I was also *L-Ingliż li joqgħod Għand Dupont*—the Englishman who stays at the Dupont house'.[17]

The Duponts—Ray and Mary, and their adult daughter Gabriella—were my hosts for the first nine months of fieldwork in Valletta. Ray was a teacher at a secondary school and Mary worked from home as a dress-maker. Gabriella worked in a government office.

They lived in a large, converted Knights' house close to Grand Harbour, in the parish of St Paul's Shipwreck—the parish of the national patron saint. Over time, I became an integrated member of their household.

It is relatively unusual for young male ethnographers in the Mediterranean to live with local families. It is much more common for them to live in rented accommodation, and for their main points of contact with local people to be restricted—at least initially—to public spaces and public social life (Brandes 1992). I experienced things the other way round; starting off in the domestic space of *Għand Dupont*, and gradually working my way into situations outside the house.

Taking my lead from other urban ethnographers I began initially at the various bars and clubs of the city (Hannerz 1980, Salole 1982). These were meeting-places primarily for men who would gather together to discuss football, politics and *festa*. I also spent time in local churches and grocery shops, which were mainly places that women met. In time I became a familiar face in the neighbourhoods of St Paul's parish, and my notebooks began to fill reassuringly. To give myself an overall sense of the parish from inside as well as outside people's houses, I accompanied the parish priests on their annual post-Easter house-blessing or *tberik*. This enabled me to collect the same demographic data as they did, but also to familiarise myself with the layout and decor of the houses, and with the range of their inhabitants. What emerged was a picture in which different gendered publics lay alongside each other as complementary. This was confronted or resisted, however, by younger Maltese who criticised the rigidities of Maltese gender roles, their resistance leading in turn to public debate over an apparent crisis in the Maltese family.

HOUSEHOLD, FAMILY, GENDER

In Malta, it is expected that household and family be coterminous, and that the simple, nuclear family be a corporate, property-owning unit. However, the housing situation in Valletta made it difficult for newly married *Beltin* to live up to this expectation whilst also maintaining the preference for uxorilocal settlement. Although many properties lay empty and unusued, most of them were run down and uninhabitable, or deliberately kept empty by their owners or tenants. Most property in Valletta was rented, and a forced policy ensured low rentals on older properties (Boswell 1994: 138). Many of the *Beltin* I knew in the early nineties paid annual rents of as little as Lm100 (£200 stg). This compounded the problems of decaying housing stock, as repairs were simply too expensive for owners to undertake. Tenancies were based on a 99 year fixed emphyteutis, with living heirs of a deceased tenant inheriting the rights to a new tenancy. Consequently, sitting tenants were effectively permanent, and many owners were reluctant to rent out their property at all. Similarly, the holders of tenancies were reluctant to give them up, even if they didn't need a property. Several *Beltin* I knew had two or three houses in the city, which they sublet to foreign visitors, used as stores or simply left empty. In many cases, the informal payment of key money was asked of anybody wishing to take over the rental, and this was so prohibitively high that nobody wanted to take it on. For the sitting tenant, it was worthwhile maintaining control of a property with a low rent of, say Lm30 (£60) per year, on the off-chance that somebody would come along who was prepared to pay the asking price of Lm3,000—£6,000—for the key.

The Duponts had had the tenancy of their house handed down to them by Mary's father, who had maintained his claim to tenancy over two separate properties. When they married, one was given to Mary and Ray. Although it was rented, the Duponts were immensely proud of their house, and spent a great deal of time and money on making sure it was attractive and fashionable. The corporacy of the conjugal family as a single household is symbolised by the house itself, *id-dar*, which becomes a significant object of consumption and distinction (see chapter four).

Households are supposed to be single, corporate units, with women and men, wives and husbands, working together in pursuit of the household's reproduction. This corporacy was somewhat individuated, however, because of the prevalence of the dowry, or *dota* which until fairly recently had been considered a Maltese bride's right. It usually consisted of household goods, but among some wealthier families extended to the gift of the house itself (Ciappara 1988, Boissevain 1980). In the case of the Duponts, because it was rented, the house was not considered part of Mary's *dota*, but other, household items were. As Goody and Tambiah have pointed out, dowries tend to lead to an individuation of family relations, because the property passed on to women remains their own, despite being used in the conjugal house (Goody and Tambiah 1973, Yanagisako 1979). Mary Dupont would refer to certain items of furniture and household goods as 'mine' rather than 'ours', to signal their origins in her *dota*. With the 'Family Law' (Act XXI of 1993), the legal status of the *dota* disappeared, confirming that the family and household were now not only ideologically but also legally a single corporate unit.

The segmentary logic of inclusion and exclusion is applied as much to the household as any other area of Maltese life. The threshold of the household is the boundary between the opposed categories of 'inside' and 'outside', *ġewwa* and *barra*, which in turn relate to categories of person. Those *ta'ġewwa*—of the inside—are either members of the household, close kin from outside the household, or particularly friendly neighbours. At a practical level, the category refers to people who can turn up uninvited, and be welcomed into the house, be they members of wider kin-groups, or close friends. The term *ta'barra*—of the outside—logically applies to everybody else, but is seldom used in this context. In time, I became *ta'ġewwa Għand Dupont*: an insider and surrogate family and household member. This gave me first-hand knowledge of Maltese domestic life.

Ideally, the family-household unit is based on a notion of gendered complimentarity, with—broadly speaking—the roles of men and women oriented around public and domestic life respectively. The husband-father is nominally the household head or figure of public authority, who works in the public domain and represents the family at a politico-jural level. The wife-mother provides domestic labour for the household, in the form of cooking, cleaning and nurturing. However, this ideological distinction is frequently transgressed. Women do have a substantive public role, as demonstrated in chapter six, which discusses, among other things, women's role in the political process.

The association of men and women with public and domestic domains has been seen as central to gender relations, and particularly the subordination of women (Rosaldo 1974), often producing a kind of gendered apartheid whereby women are confined to the domestic domain. In this argument, the dichotomy public-domestic is assumed to map onto the division between public and private domains, which means that because women are associated with the domestic, they are also limited to the private—in a Maltese context the *ġewwa* of the house itself. A more sophisticated reading associates the subordination of women with an encompassment of the domestic by the public. Here, rather than opposed to it, the domestic is subsumed within the public, making all domestic relations and activities secondary to the needs of the public domain, and therefore socially devalued. These arguments linking the subordination of women to dichotomies between public-domestic and public-private have been criticised for doing little more than incorporating a Western Industrial gender ideology and presenting it as a universal model (Comaroff 1989). It is argued that anthropologists of gender and household must go beyond this ideology, to take on board indigenous understandings of the roles and positions of men and women in relation to household and supra-household relations (Yanagisako 1979). However, in a context such as Malta, where the gender ideology is arguably the same as that of Western Industrial society, the situation is more complex. Here, going beyond the simple ideological picture takes us not to a vision of local ideology, but to local understandings and particularly local practices which either support or subvert that ideology.

The ideology which links men and women to public and private via the public-domestic dichotomy is consolidated in the Mediterranean situation by notions of honour and shame. The study of gender in the Mediterranean has been dominated by a paradigmatic identification of an 'honour and shame' moral code that has been seen as a defining feature of the region (Peristiany 1965, Pitt-Rivers 1977, Gilmore 1987). This honour/shame syndrome relates gender to household, particularly through the imputation of a gendered division of social space into public and private domains (Hirschon 1981, Reiter 1975). Honour defines prestige or reputation in the public domain, and generally accrues to households via the men who represent them. The honour of a household is inextricably linked to the reputation of the women who live there (Pitt-Rivers 1961, Campbell 1964). This reputation is sealed by their public display of shame, as manifest in a reticense towards appearing in public places. Shame defines a moral obligation to preserve female chastity, ensuring both that men marry virgins and that once they do, they are not cuckolded. Shame is therefore connected to women's association with the domestic domain of the house itself. Honour, on the other hand is connected to men's association with the public domain outside the house. What emerges is a picture of Mediterranean society built up of secluded, female-oriented households linked together by the social ties created by men in the public domain—a situation suggested by the structural equation: women:men::domestic:public. According to this logic, an *ethos* emerges in which men are active and women passive:

> 'Knights are bold and ladies are fair.' Courage and strength are emphasised as male attributes. Beauty and frailty are for women. (Pitt-Rivers 1961: 89).

This view of Mediterranean gender identities has recently been criticised for presenting a stereotype of the Mediterranean that serves to distance the Mediterranean from Northern Europe and North America—a kind of 'Mediterraneanism' akin to Said's Orientalism (Herzfeld 1984, 1987, Pina-Cabral, 1989, Said 1978). It over-generalises the unity of the Mediterranean and thereby ignores the range of different gender ideologies that coexist within the region. More significantly, however, it also serves to sustain, or even promote, the 'official' or 'hegemonic' version of Mediterranean gender, denying female agency, and ignoring the potential and actual contestation of gender identities (Goddard 1987, Lever 1986, Loizos & Papataxiarchis 1991). The notions of male activity and female passivity inherent in the imputation of the 'honour/shame syndrome', it is argued, simply do not conform to the reality of daily life in the Mediterranean.

Like the rest of anthropology, the study of gender has moved since the 1960s from a focus on social structure, to an examination of symbolism and meaning, to one which looks at practice and performance (Moore 1988, Morris 1995, Ortner 1984). This shift has resulted in attempts to highlight the gap between ideological representations or models of gender, and the reality of everyday life, and in attempts to resolve structure-practice dichotomies by focusing on the ways structures are practised. It has become received wisdom that gender identities are not intrinsic to men and women, but are socially constructed (Lacqueur 1990, Ortner 1974, Ortner & Whitehead 1981), and that the symbols and meanings around which people live their gendered lives are in a constant process of reproduction, through people's everyday actions and performances (Bourdieu 1977:

87–95, Herzfeld 1985). As Butler puts it, gender is 'always a doing'—an active performance that constitutes gendered being (1990: 25).

In the Mediterranean context, these developments have had three major consequences, which threaten the legitimacy of the imputed 'honour/shame syndrome'. First, they open up space for recognising and analysing the differences between the hegemonic models of gender and its daily practice. This has particularly influenced ethnographers of women in the Mediterranean, who have repeatedly demonstrated women's substantive public roles, in contrast to their apparent privatisation. Second, they offer up the hegemonic model of gender and its modes of reproduction as itself an object of study. In this context, attention has been drawn to the importance of everyday performance in the production of gender (Cowan 1991, Herzfeld 1985). Third, they permit an adequate theorising of resistance to or contestation of ideological or hegemonic models of gender.

The remainder of this chapter examines these three consequences of the recent 'reconstruction' of the anthropology of Mediterranean gender, for an ethnography of Valletta (Dubisch 1991). Despite access to the demonstic spaces *Għand Dupont,* I lived mainly in a world of male sociability, as is common for male researchers in Mediterranean societies (Brandes 1992). It is for this reason that the ethnography of male lives and particularly male performances is much richer than that of women. Nevertheless, the chapter looks at the active role women take in the production of Maltese society, before moving on to an examination of how men's and women's social roles contribute to the production—through everyday performances—of male and female identities. Finally, it examines some of the gender contestations of the early 1990s, which lead to both critique and reinforcement of the 'traditional' or hegemonic gender ideologies.

It is clear that Malta was at a particular moment in the development of gender identities, where critique of the established gender order led to profound anxiety about the central institutions of Maltese social life: family and household. As with the Maltese predicament more generally, this anxiety revolved around competing notions of 'tradition' and 'modernity', and the extent to which the latter was thought to be obliterating the former. In the context of family and gender, this tension was particularly manifest in inter-generational conflict. Where younger men and—particularly—women were adopting or attempting to adopt more 'modern', 'European' lifestyles, their parents and grandparents saw this as the beginning of the end for Maltese morality. Younger people were more ambivalent. One young Valletta man outlined his vision of the future:

> It's important that Malta moves forward. Things are so old-fashioned here. The church controls too much. The one thing I'd keep hold of, though, is the family. The family is important, and we should keep it so.

WOMEN'S ROLES—FEMALE IDENTITY

Although this is not the case in all Maltese households, female roles within the households I was familiar with—both *Għand Dupont* and the households of the wider St Paul's populace—appeared very much to conform to the image of ideal nurturing motherhood. As the household was considered the unit of a corporate, conjugal family, the woman's role within this was primarily one of domestic labour: cooking, cleaning and nurturing, but also taking care of the family's spiritual needs (Davis 1984). With the man being the primary 'bread-winner' of the household, women's work outside the house was generally stigmatised, although often performed. In one of the interviews I conducted following the *tberik*, I met up with Pawla Sant and Josette Cacciatolo. Pawla was a mother of two in her late thirties. Josette was younger with one child. We sat in Pawla's *salott*, or sitting room—a room habitually set aside in Maltese houses for the reception of visitors. This bracketed the occasion as a visit by an 'outsider'. Likewise, the presence of Josette, who was asked by Pawla to come along because she was 'embarrassed'—*tistħi*—to have a man at her house alone.

I asked the two women to describe their courtship and marriage, from the point of view of employment and economics. Pawla had been working as a tea-packer before she was married and so paid for her own dowry—*dota*. She stopped working as soon as she married, which she declared was 'normal' practice. Josette had never worked, and was vigorously opposed to the idea of married women working:

> It's a matter of personal choice. Not everyone is the same. Some even work after they've had children. But that's not good. If they go out, they might meet other men, and get ideas. Who knows what will happen?

Working outside the house, then, was not only related to the abandonment of responsibility for domestic labour, but also the negation of the family and household as the sole locus of sexual activity: related to sexual morality as much as domestic responsibility. The only way to ensure the maintenance of both was to work at home, either on solely domestic tasks, or on paid work that could be accomplished inside the house.

This latter option was one taken by Mary Dupont, who worked from home as a dressmaker. Compared with paid work outside the house, this was relatively un-stigmatised. In the past she had taken employment outside the house. She had been bored, she said, and lonely, so for companionship and entertainment, she decided to work in a factory. Ray had opposed the move, arguing that the family did not need the money, but the fact he had no objections to her subsequently taking up dress-making suggests that this was not his only objection. Mary explained that he'd been unhappy about the kinds of women she was meeting at the factory:

> Those women, do you know? They would always swear. And the young girls—they'd always swear as well. Every sentence they would swear on something, or even worse. Ray told me to stop going. I don't know. I used to enjoy going there. To do something, do you know what I mean? But Ray didn't like it. And you know how it is in Malta. A husband says something and his wife jumps.

As much as being worried about the company Mary was keeping at the factories, Ray was worried about the effect that her work would have on the reputation of the household. In particular, the fact that it was a public demonstration of his wife's autonomy. It is a view commonly expressed by men that it is dangerous to allow women to get together unless they are kin. Many told me that they would not allow their wives to go to work, because meeting up with other women would 'give them ideas' that might lead to infidelity or the abandonment of domestic responsibilities.

Although clearly oriented to the domestic domain, these responsibilities by no means implied that women were *confined* to the domestic, or 'inside' world of the private house. Indeed, many of the tasks needed to keep a household afloat required daily excursions outside the house—to grocery shops, churches and public meetings. Here they meet with friends, neighbours and kin, to exchange information and 'gossip' about both local and national issues. In these contexts, Maltese women are confident, self-assured, even aggressive. The occasional comments from passing men are met with jocular, even bawdy, rebukes that signal their ability to look after themselves in a public arena. There is no hint here of the kinds of vulnerable, retiring women of the Mediterranean stereotype.

During her fieldwork in a rural Greek village, Dubisch found similarly forthright and confident women (1991). Moreover, she suggests that in their perpetuation of a gendered public-domestic dichotomy, anthropologists have habitually underestimated this public confidence, and consequently ignored the very active role women have in creating Mediterranean public life and social structure. She argues that through their everyday 'kin-work' (di Leonardo 1987), women in rural Greece produce Greek society. By 'kin-work' she means the daily 'tasks that sustain family networks' (Dubisch 1991: 38), such as visiting each others' houses or the local grocery shops to exchange news and gossip. She proposes a 'reconsideration' of the anthropology of Greece, to take account of women's active role and thereby acknowledge the practice of daily life that lies behind the hegemonic model of gender. One might pursue this approach when examining other Mediterranean contexts, not least Malta.

The tasks of rural Greek kin-work are organised around what Dubisch regards as the central unit of Greek kinship—the mother-daughter relationship. Malta, like Greece, is strongly uxorilateral (Mizzi 1981, Sant Cassia pers. comm. 1993), and the mother-daughter bond is such that one might describe it as the 'elementary unit' (Dubisch 1991: 36–38). In the Dupont household, Mary's ties with both her mother and daughter were particularly close. She and her mother would communicate on the telephone several times a day, and see each other at least every other day. This was a common pattern. Despite increasingly neolocal residence patterns in Malta, and even more so Valletta, the maternal household was of major significance in people's lives. Not only daughters, but also sons, would maintain close and frequent contacts with their mothers, dropping in to see them, and telephoning for extended periods. In the taxonomy of social space, such people were demonstrably *ta'ġewwa*—insiders—to the household, a category which revolved around the mother.

Mothers were the primary providers of family kin-work. Knowledge of relations outside the household varied considerably by gender. Both men and women normally generalise kin more distant than first cousins as *kuġini*—cousins—but whereas women generally knew the details of this relatedness, men had a vaguer idea. As well as bearing the knowledge of relatedness, women also organised these social links, and made sure that the family ties were maintained—via telephone and through contact with visitors; by remembering birthdays and organising the household's calendar of attendance at these and other events such as weddings, baptisms and first communions.

Kin work articulated two other types of female work: 'neighbourhood work' and 'religious work'. Neighbourhood work was again concerned with the demarcation and perpetuation of the category 'insider', but this time produced social ties not with kin, but with close friends or neighbours. Moreover, the boundary of inclusion and exclusion was not necessarily that of the household—although this was sometimes the case—but also of the neighbourhood or parish (see chapter five). Religious work represented an extension of kin-work and neighbourhood work into the spiritual domain, where they constitute both nurturing and maintaining relationships with living and dead kin and neighbours.

For women, it was important to strike a balance between purely household-oriented domestic activity and that concerned with kin-work, neighbourhood work and religious work. The average day began early—sometimes as early as 5am, when the first tasks of the day would be cleaning the house and clothes, before preparation of breakfast. Once husbands were seen off to work, and children to school, women would take the first of normally two trips to the local grocery shops, and often attend mass.

Grocery shopping was most often done at the small local shops that served the residential neighbourhoods of Valletta. These grocery shops were also gossip-shops, in that they served as loci for the exchange of information between women. I stress the female gendered nature of these places because men were seldom seen there. Men who did enter were largely ignored, and discouraged from participating in conversation. Although often men, the shopkeepers themselves seemed to conspire to maintain the female exclusivity of their shops, by making sure that men were served and bundled out of the shop as quickly as possible. Grocery shopping was domestic labour, but describing it only as this, is perhaps rather to miss the point. It also performed a significant social function, in that the grocery shops became places where significant local knowledge was exchanged. Women in Valletta generally made sure they went to the shop at least once daily. This trip involved not only entering shops to make a transaction, but also a lengthy conversation with storekeepers and fellow customers. Consequently, grocery shops were often full of people slowly assembling their daily provisions as they talked through the various issues of the day. Daily mass was also a social event. Before, sometimes during, and certainly after the mass, women would exchange gossip and ensure that family/neighbourhood relations were maintained.

After mass, women would return home to prepare lunch—the largest meal of the day—then sleep or watch television in the early afternoon, before a second visit to the grocery shops in late afternoon or early evening. This outing was often supplemented by spending some time in the afternoon sitting or standing at the front door of the house, waiting for friends or neighbours to pass by. In some areas, groups of women would congregate to play cards, or organise informal bingo games. The evenings were largely spent at home, enjoying time with the family, watching television and chatting.

Like much of the 'hidden work of everyday life' (Wadel, 1979), these social activities were largely unrecognised as an act of constituting the social, but were of major importance in the creation of Maltese society. Apparently domestic work, because it both revolved around and produced 'insiders' to the household, it was also of public, political significance because it created the networks of obligation which could be drawn upon for political support, or to motivate political opinion (see chapter six). Through their daily contact with kin, neighbours and friends outside the house, women provided substantive networks of obligation and reciprocity which could be drawn upon in the pursuit of more public goals.

In performing these daily activities, however, women not only produced Maltese society, they also produced themselves as gendered persons. Through cooking, for example, women demonstrate their competence in budgeting, provisioning and preparing for the household—a practical manifestation or performance of the balance between inside and outside that is needed to be a successful woman (see also Goddard, 1996: 205–213).

The visits to mass were also performative events at which women demonstrated their familiarity with and expertise in living up to ideal femininity. Mass is both to do with kin relations with the dead and living and with kin and neighbourhood relations in the here and now. While distant and dead kin will be prayed for, closer kin and neighbours will be met before and after mass, to exchange gossip and maintain relations. Besides this everyday attendance at mass, women have special devotions, often to the Madonna or to Santa Rita, patron saint of lost causes but strongly associated with victims of domestic abuse. Women will sit and pray at their altars, lighting candles and crossing themselves as they do so. Both the Madonna and Santa Rita provide models of suffering in maternal/spousal roles. Through their devotion, women demonstrate a familiarity with these ideal feminine qualities, producing themselves as women in relation to their saintly qualities.

The grocery shop was also a place where everyday women's sociality was played out—where women produced themselves as women. The importance of this activity was emphasised to me by Pawlu and Polly Camilleri. The Camilleri family was well-established in Valletta, and Pawlu and Polly lived with their three adult sons in a part of St Paul's parish that was regarded as its heart. The Camilleri household became a place that I would regularly visit, and through these visits, I got a picture of how domestic life in houses other than the Duponts' was organised. I became somebody who could turn up unexpectedly and be offered a seat in the kitchen, and a cup of tea. In this respect, one could say that I became an insider. On one occasion, I was sitting in their kitchen. Pawlu and Polly had been discussing the fact that he had not been paid for a long time, and was owed several hundred Maltese liri by his employer:

> What can I do. It's not that I'm hard up. That's no problem. I've got money for cigarettes, and a drink sometimes. It's her (Polly) I worry about. It's not fair. Polly's got no money for shopping.

I thought at this stage that he was worried about food, and that he was making the explicit distinction between his responsibilities and hers. By not giving her money to buy food, he was depriving her of the means with which to carry out her domestic responsibilities. I moved to note this down, saying 'I see, you're worried about her not having money to buy the groceries.' Then she interjected:

> No, it's not food that's the problem. We're not going to starve. We've plenty of food. But what am I going to do. Just sit here and stare? If we've got no money I can't go to the shops. I'll just get bored and lonely.

Going to the grocery shops, then, was clearly fundamental to female existence and female identity. Without it, women would simply sit and stare. In other words, they would be denied their personhood: denied the situation in which they become animated, social agents, and therefore proper women. Femininity, then, was dependent on a public context, on producing social ties through the public performance of being a woman.

PERFORMING HEGEMONIC MASCULINITY

If much of women's public performance of identity was achieved in grocery shops and at mass, masculinity was performed in bars, wine-shops and clubs. Here, their activities took place in and produced a public domain in which the production of social ties of a politico-jural significance were more openly acknowledged than with women's sociality. This public activities was carried out in everyday contact and conversation in spaces outside the house. It is therefore associated with the category *barra*—outside.

Locating this sphere of public debate in St Paul's parish begain with finding the right bar/s—the place/s where the male members of the parish interacted with each other. At the time of fieldwork, there were over 20 bars or cafés within the parish. They varied in character, from cafés that attempted to emulate the exclusive atmosphere of the élite Valletta cafés, to lowly wine-shops, where facilities were basic and often rather dirty. The former were places where both men and women could rest from the day's tasks to enjoy coffee and a small snack. The latter were considered more-or-less masculine domains. Women would say they were *tistħi*—ashamed—to enter on their own, and on the rare occasions they did enter, their presence was usually mediated by the men they were with. This was not least the case for the bar which Ray Dupont suggested I frequent, which became a primary field site—a place where information could be gleaned about all aspects of Maltese society.

When I moved into the Dupont household, I explained my intentions were to get to know as many people in the immediate vicinity as possible. In particular, I was interested in the groups of people who involved themselves in the *festa* and other locally-based activities. I was directed to the small bar that stood on the steps of St Lucy's Street, just opposite the parish church. The bar was called *San Paolo Naufrago*—St Paul's Shipwreck—but more commonly known as *Għand Lawrenz*—Lawrence's Place. Here, women tended only to enter on Sunday mornings and during the days of *festa*. At these times, they would sit in a small side-room used during the week for draughts matches, and have drinks brought to them by the men they had come with. Their presence in this public place was therefore mediated by men. At other times, particularly on weekdays, women who worked in the nearby shops would quickly go into the bar, to buy a drink or a sandwich, but seldom stayed there to eat or drink. Whilst they were in the bar, they would strictly avoid eye contact with anybody but those serving. It was clearly an uncomfortable moment, and one which frequently led to them being teased by Lawrence, the proprietor. Some women preferred not to enter at all. They would stand outside the open front of the bar and try to catch the attention of somebody who would buy whatever they needed.

The bar acted as a kind of club-house for the *Pawlini*—Paulites—and particularly members of the *Għaqda tal-Pawlini*—The Association of *Pawlini*. The *Għaqda* was set up in the early 1970s to oversee the administration of St Paul's *festa* (see chapter seven), and met *Għand Lawrenz* on a regular basis. The *Għaqda*, although not limited to men, was dominated by them. It was not until 1991 that the *Kumissjoni tan-Nisa*—Commission for Women—was introduced, providing a seat for one woman on the central *Kumitat*—Committee. The one woman on the Committee during my fieldwork was the wife and mother of two other Committee members. This meant that, effectively, her role was circumscribed, because of her constant association with her husband and son. Although she held office, it was effectively limited by her identification as wife and mother.

This exclusion of women from full participation is true in other spheres of Maltese public office. As public debate was carried out in bars and other male-dominated domains, then women were *de facto* excluded from the process of canvassing opinion, which was a severe handicap to the project of creating public connections, and swaying public opinion in one's favour. Miceli has argued that the character of Maltese politics as a face-to-face business in which men group together to create public opinion, inhibits women's willingness to participate in politics (1994). Such office as women did hold were commonly associated with church organisations—parish councils, Catholic Action, or doctrinal organisations. These were offices that women could achieve by canvassing opinion and gaining support during the daily visits to mass. Moreover, they were offices associated with control over a domain of acceptable 'feminine' activity—the Church—rather than more public concerns more normally associated with men. As Miceli put it, when it comes to political office, '"good" women do not come forward' (Miceli, 1994: 87).

BEING A MAN

As with women, who in the process of acting out their gender roles in public spaces also produce performances that constitute themselves as gendered persons, so men, through their daily sociability, produce themselves as men. These everyday performances constitute a 'lexicon' of masculine practices, which go towards the production and reproduction of the hegemonic male (see Vale de Almeida 1996).

Much conversation in public bars, and more specifically *Għand Lawrenz*, revolved around the notion of masculinity—it was a major preoccupation. In particular, the phrase *tkun raġel*—be a man—was often used, and in a variety of different contexts, as a form of sanction against behaviour or attitudes that were not considered properly masculine. Most often it was used in arguments, when it was felt that one of those involved had lost, and should concede the fact. At this stage, bystanders often interjected: *tkun raġel*—admit that you're wrong. The implication was that to be a man is to be sufficiently resilient—to have fulfilled enough of the criteria for manhood, and for these criteria to be publicly accepted—that defeat on this occasion would not be a threat. This dominant or hegemonic male identity was based essentially on five criteria: heterosexuality; reciprocal sociality; trustworthiness; sociability and fatherhood.

Being a man, first and foremost, involved being heterosexual. A most common and offensive insult, as for the Andalusians of Brandes' 'Like Wounded Stags' (1981), is to question this heterosexuality. This is most often done with the phrase *mur ħudu f'sormok*, which literally means 'go and take it in the arse'. As Brandes has suggested, such an insult implies the adoption of a passive sexual identity, which he associates with a feminisation. However, in Malta, this passivity is not necessarily associated with femininity, but with homosexuality. The two are not the same. Perhaps in contrast to Andalusia, there is an open acknowledgement of different sexualities in the Maltese context, which means that the dominant model of masculine heterosexuality is not only constructed in relation to feminine, but also to male homosexuals—both overt and covert—and a few trans-sexuals. Opinions towards homosexuality varied. Some regarded it as the private concern of those involved. Others were downright homophobic, referring to homosexuals as *imġienen*—madmen—who should be avoided at all costs. Others still were more charitable, including one man who explained the situation as follows:

> *Imsieken*—poor things—I call them. It's not really their fault that they're born like that.

From this spectrum of opinion, it is clear that homosexual and trans-sexual were discrete categories, against which masculinity could be judged. Rather than simply ignoring these divergent or 'subordinate' masculinities (Connell 1995), these differences were openly acknowledged. Not only is this further evidence of the variety of masculinities against which the hegemonic model is judged in the Maltese or Mediterranean contexts, it also demonstrates the role of metaphors such as *ħudu f'sormok*—take it in the arse—in the acknowledgement of such variety. Rather than feminising the man to whom it is addressed, this insult equally implies their homosexualisation. Moreover, at least in this case, homosexualisation and feminisation are not necessarily commensurate.

The use of the term *pufta* is further evidence that homosexuality, rather than femininity, serves as a reference point for masculinity. *Pufta* is the most common term for homosexuals, and although it strictly speaking refers to transvestites, it is used in a variety of contexts where men are seen to transgress the boundaries of acceptable masculine behaviour—particularly when they ignore two further characteristics of the ideal man: reciprocal sociality and trustworthiness. For example, men who refuse commensality, or neglect to reciprocate in the rounds of drink-buying are referred to as *pufta* (see Papataxiarchis, 1991), as in some contexts are men who are regarded as untrustworthy, with either material goods or with information.

Men who betray trust are referred to as well, as *ħaxxej*—lit. 'one who runs after women with evil intent', but can be glossed as 'fucker'. Again, the term has homosexual overtones, implying the same questionable sexuality as *ħudu f'sormok*, but this time portrays the recipient as protagonist—the active agent in a homosexual encounter. This distinction between active and passive partners in homosexuality has been remarked upon in a variety of settings—particularly in Latin America (Lancaster 1997). In these contexts, it has been assumed that although the passive partner is shamed or disgraced—even feminised—the active partner maintains his honour, virility and ultimately masculinity (Loizos 1994). It has even been suggested that an 'active' man is really not too bothered whether his 'passive' partner is a woman or a man—he still maintains his reputation. At the level of the metaphors used by Maltese men, however, this does not appear to be the case. Although being *ħaxxej* implied the strength and vitality needed to 'fuck' one's companions, it was no less questionable than being *pufta* or 'taking it in the arse'. Either way, the activity was illegitimate, because it went against the powerful principle of heterosexuality.

Reciprocal sociality and trustworthiness were not only important in financial matters, but also regarding information. Herzfeld has suggested that there is a common contrast in European thought, between male rationality and female gossip (1987: 96). Where men discuss politics and public opinion in rational terms, women debate reputation. In St Paul's, however, the male trade in gossip was every bit as strong as the female. It had direct political and economic significance. The exchange of male reputation was part of the mechanism by which political allegiance and economic relations were constituted. This political economy of gossip was acute. I was constantly being told by well-meaning acquaintances that under no circumstances should I let them know about my private affairs. To do so would be dangerous, even with particularly close friends.

Different bars in Valletta are associated with different cliques of men, or *klikek*—sing. *klikka*—which are considered by their members to be the smallest and most intimate level of social grouping. Referred to metaphorically as *qaqoċċa*, or artichoke hearts, *klikek* are invoked at a variety of levels, including the political, religious, and sporting. As a category, it encompassed not only the literal, face-to-face friendships created in local bars, but also the relationships between the small groups of 'insiders' believed to be at the centres of political power (see chapters four, six). In general, men who enjoyed the same interests were drawn to each other to form a *klikka* together. Men involved in a relationship of committed solidarity are referred to as belonging to the same *klikka*. Members of a *klikka* spent most of their leisure time together, in one activity or another. Ideally, they would protect and defend each other at any time.

The denizens of *Għand Lawrenz* divided into three *klikek*. The full significance of these distinctions will be brought out in chapter seven. The first *klikka* comprised the older, more established *Pawlini*—*festa* enthusiasts par excellence. The second was a younger group who were also involved in the *festa*, but in a slightly different way. The third were also *Pawlini*, but less interested in direct involvement with the mechanics of the *festa*. Rather, their *hobby* was football, and they played on a weekly basis for various local teams. There was inevitably some cross-over between these three *klikek*, but these were the groups who would refer to themselves as separate *klikek*.

The different groups spent a lot of time together, and I spent a great deal of time with them. In particular, I became friendly with the *klikka* that were most closely associated with the *festa*. At the core of this group was Charlie Zammit, who had not only been on the Committee of the *Għaqda tal-Pawlini*, but was also heavily involved with Confraternities at the parish church, and the Franciscan church of *Ta'Ġiezu*—Our Lady of Jesus. I would meet up with him and the other members of his *klikka* on a daily basis, at the parish church or *Għand Lawrenz*. Conversations would be long and intense, but despite this there was a very clear demarcation of subject matter that meticulously excluded personal matters. One day Charlie had failed to turn up on Sunday morning, which was the most popular time for drinking and socialising. He arrived *Għand Lawrenz* the next day, but made no effort to join in with conversation. It seemed that coming was more of an obligation than anything else, and he was keen to leave as soon as possible. I wondered what was wrong, but none of the other members of his *klikka*, ideally one of mutual trust and support, asked him what the matter was. They simply ignored his uncharacteristic behaviour, and continued as usual, discussing the *festa*. When he had left, I asked what was wrong with him. His assembled friends simply shrugged their shoulders. They did not know, they said, and it was not really any of their business to ask.

Later, I asked about this. What status did the friendships of a *klikka* have, if problems of a personal nature could not be discussed? I was told that this was not the place to discuss such matters. Rather, problems of a personal nature should be discussed with either family members or a priest. Under no circumstances should they be made public amongst a group of male friends. To do so would be to invite its abuse in local gossip. Indeed, there was an almost constant discourse of mistrust within *Għand Lawrenz*. Members of all three *klikek* referred to it as a place where one should not discuss one's private life. Exposed personal knowledge can be used to one's detriment. As one regular once pointed out to me:

> Not everyone who strokes you, loves you. Be careful.

By this he meant that although people might seem to be generous or friendly, trusting them because of this was a mistake. All men, including kinsmen and members of a particular *klikka*, were potentially *ħaxxej*. It would be dangerous to discuss everything inside the bar, as information could get into the wrong hands. Things to be discussed in private between two men were generally taken outside *Għand Lawrenz* onto the street. For example, in the lead-up to the 1994 *festa*, a group of *Pawlini* decided that they would have matching t-shirts printed, with a photograph of the statue of St Paul on the front.

These they would wear during the band marches, and would be entirely original. An appropriate photograph was taken, and a local man contacted to do the printing. They told him to be discrete about the job, as they wanted to be the only group who had such elaborate *festa* gear. Two days after they got their t-shirts back, they heard that other groups in the parish had copied their idea, and gone to the same salesman to get their shirts printed. Rumours began to circulate that the salesman in question had printed up hundreds of the shirts, and was going to sell them during the *festa*. The salesman was quickly dubbed untrustworthy, *ħaxxej*—somebody who had betrayed their contract by letting information flow too freely.

In other contexts, men are referred to as *ħaxxej* if they do not give information freely enough. People refer to manipulators of information as *ħaxxej*. For example, one man who was involved in the annual Good Friday procession habitually referred to its organisers as *ħaxxej*. He had been a *reffiegħ*—statue-carrier—during the procession, until several years previously when he had had to pull out during the procession and go to hospital. He had never been allowed to try again, and was annoyed about this. But his main complaint was the way in which information about the administration of the event was kept away from him. He wanted to help, he told me, but the *klikka* at the centre of Good Friday kept him in the dark:

> They don't tell me anything; they're all deceitful fuckers.

As well as trustworthiness, men are ideally sociable. This property is demonstrated in particular by the ability to take a joke. Once more, the suggestion is that men should be sufficiently masculine to be able to deal with goading either by ignoring it or by making witty retorts. A great deal of time is spent creating the situation where such witty retorts are necessary, and they are framed as a kind of social drama where masculinity was created through performative competence. As things get more heated, and remarks both more cutting and more humorous, all conversation will stop so that people can listen to the entertainment. These spontaneous entertainments mirror the more formal encounters of Maltese folk music, *għana* (see Sant Cassia, 1989, Fsadni, 1993). One form of *għana*, known as *spirtu prontu*—impromptu spirit—comprises song duels between antagonistic singers who try to outwit each other. The same competetive spirit is observable in everyday masculine sociability. Entertainment comes both from the wit displayed by particularly adept adversaries, but also by the reactions of either one of the parties as they become too heated and resort to simple insult, shouting or absenting themselves. At this point, the assembled 'audience' will chide, 'come on, be a man', *tkun raġel*. Some seemed to make it their life's career to goad people and create such scenes. Antonio DeBono was particularly adept at provoking a reaction. He was known as a *xewka*, a 'thorn' whose most common victim was his best friend Michael Gauci. He once said to me with pride that he could get Michael to the point of violence within three minutes, and then proceeded to demonstrate, to the pleasure of all those present.

Finally, and perhaps most importantly, being a man is related to marital status. Here, being a man confers responsibility and authority. Men who were unmarried well into their adult years tended towards a greater public role—seeking office in local religious Confraternities, and/or the organisation of St Paul's *festa*. This gave them a different role in the production of society, and a different set of responsibilities. Some achieved the prestigious position of being chosen to carry St Paul's statue on *festa* day itself. Through this they constituted themselves as performative experts in the process of *festa* (Mitchell 1998c, see also chapter eight).

Married men were responsible for household and family. To this extent, their public performances in places such as *Għand Lawrenz* also defined their domestic role. Family life in Malta ideally involves a complementarity between the genders, centred around a single, child-producing household. For men, this complementarity demands a balance between participation in public activities and those associated with the household and kin. This complementarity was reinforced by both state and religious rhetoric. In May 1994, for example, Archbishop Joseph Mercieca delivered a key sermon on the role of the father, which was reported widely in the media, and became the substance of more intimate counsel from the priests of St Paul's to their male parishioners. One or two of the more involved *Pawlini* were told that they should not allow their enthusiasm for the *festa* to interfere with family life. Others were warned of the dangers of working too hard. This presented a significant dilemma in the context of rising costs of living, in which many householders felt it necessary to take two or three jobs in order to make ends meet.

However, spending too much time outside the home was considered problematic. In another context, a man known as *In-Nono*, a familiar face *Għand Lawrenz* but associated more with the football team than the *festa*, was criticised for not spending enough time at home. In order to raise funds for his children's education, he had started gambling, but the activity had become compulsive. Whenever he saw a gaming machine in a bar or arcade, he would become engrossed, spending many hours—and lots of money—feeding it. To the *Pawlini*, this was a disgrace, not just because the money would have been better spent providing for his family, but also because of the time he spent away from home, as a consequence. *In-Nono* was not living up to his proper masculine role as husband and father.

The husband-father role, then, was associated with spending enough time at home to participate in domestic life. This was the main thrust of the Archbishop's sermon: the extent to which men and women should be seen as complementary parts of the family unit, with the father not only providing finance for, but also supporting, the nurturing role of the mother:

> The father must not mistakenly believe his only role is that of earning the daily bread ... [nor that] ... his responsibility is equal to that of his wife in the work which is necessary for the daily running of the home. (*The Sunday Times (Malta)*, 1/5/94)

Complementarity, then, was framed in terms of men recognising their responsibility in the process of reproducing the family, the household, and ultimately, society. This requires striking a balance between domestic responsibilities and responsibility for organising and administering communal activities such as *festa*. Ultimately, then, it requires a balance between public and domestic sociality that mirrors the equivalent balance required of women, between activities inside and outside the house. This was summed up as follows:

> She is the woman, who, in spite of the currents of our times, is aware that in order to live life in its fulness, she is not inevitably bound to go out to work but can do work in the home itself and dedicate herself fully to her noble mission in the family. (*The Sunday Times (Malta)* 16/1/94)

The balance required of both men and women suggests that the equation of male with public and female with domestic spheres, inherent in the honour/shame model, is an over-simplification. Just as women have important public roles to play, so men must balance their public activities with domestic responsibilities. Focusing on the actual practices of men and women enables us to get beyond the gender ideologies. It also enables us to recognise the productive role men and women have in the constitution of their gender identities. Rather than being defined or interpellated by an over-arching hegemony of gender, men and women actively reproduce gender models. This reproduction often produces a hegemonic model of gender, but also takes place in relation to an openly-acknowledged gender dissidence. This dissidence is observable not only in the homosexuality that defines the boundaries of hegemonic masculinity, but also in the non-domestic paid work taken on by some women. However, it is most visible in the contestations prevalent in early nineties Malta, between men and women of different generations. Here, young men and women actively resist or subvert the prevailing orthodoxy of gender roles and gender identities, to produce their own versions of what 'modern' gender should be.

CONTESTING GENDER AND FAMILY ACROSS THE GENERATIONS

These hegemonic gender roles and gender identities were not unquestioningly adopted by all Maltese. Many of the younger men of St Paul's parish found the requirements of male sociality tedious. Rather than long hours *Għand Lawrenz* discussing the intrigues of *festa*, they would rather be in the resort town of Paceville, where the bars were more lively, had loud music, and where there was a chance of meeting young women. This apparent lack of commitment to the friendly *klikek* and the processes of *festa* drew scorn from the older men (see chapter seven). The younger generation, they argued, weren't men in the proper sense—they were boys, who just wanted to play, rather than taking life seriously. For younger women, too, Paceville was an important place. Here, their activities were seen by older people to transgress the normative boundaries of gendered social space. By entering bars—sometimes unaccompanied—they were entering domains in which the more 'traditional' woman should feel embarrassed—*tistħi*. For their own part, however, the bars of Paceville were not gendered in the same way as those of Valletta. Rather than domains of male sociality, they were places where young men and women could come together in performance of their own gender identities.

The inter-generational tensions about going to Paceville were manifest *Għand Dupont* in the setting of rigid curfew times. On one weekend night, Gabriella was allowed to stay out until 2am, on the others she had to be back by 1.30. On all occasions Ray and Mary would stay up to make sure she came back on time, and any transgressions were marked by a tightening of the regime or a huge argument, or both. Many young people I knew referred to similar tensions in their own households—that were only alleviated by a complex set of deceptions and half-truths that 'protected' their parents from the realities of their evenings out.

In the early nineties, Paceville had become a symbol of all things wrong—even evil—with the younger generations, and 'modern' life. For *Beltin* its growth and success as an entertainments centre was directly linked to the decline of Valletta. It also marked the transformation of the Maltese economy from one based around the British Naval base to one dependent on tourism, which although providing economic stability, was seen as erosive of 'traditional' morality. In particular, the younger tourists who spent their time in and around Paceville were seen as sexually profligate, with a more 'European' attitude to courtship. In practice, this was actually the case, and it was common for young Maltese—particularly men—to strike up temporary liaisons with visiting tourists. There was nothing like the kind of routinised 'hunting' of Northern European women practiced by young Greek *kamaki* (Zinovieff 1991), but there was nevertheless a feeling among young men that female tourists presented an opportunity for sex. They were also seen as an immoral influence on young Maltese women, who—it was feared—would take on these liberal attitudes. In fact, no such loosening seemed to be occurring. Unmarried Maltese women were keen to preserve virginity at least until embarked upon their—usually lengthy—engagement. For the older generations, though, the moral decline was signalled by young local women adopting revealing styles of dress and—even more problematically—sunbathing topless.

Such resistances to hegemonic models of gender have been traced throughout the Mediterranean—both north and south. Cowan (1991) has explored the extent to which young women in Sohos, Greece contest their exclusion from the male-dominated *kafenio* by establishing their legitimate presence within the newly-founded *kafeteria*. Through this transgression, the *kafeteria* becomes a new space in which both men and women can participate in a joint project of constituting the new forms of gender identities. Similarly, by establishing the Paceville bars as legitimate spaces for their own gendered performances, the young women of Malta shaped a new orientation to space and gender. Abu-Lughod (1990) has examined the extent to which young Bedouin women subvert the existing sexual morality by buying exotic and erotic lingerie that is publicly displayed in their wedding trousseau. This overt sexuality mirrors a parallel contestation by young women in Malta, who dress up in such lingerie for a night out in Paceville.

These acts of everyday resistance are not necessarily aimed towards a conscious end, but through their practice led to a transformation in the established patterns of hegemonic gender. This transformation led to concern for the family, and the invocation of an apparent 'crisis' at the centre of Maltese life. Throughout my two years of fieldwork, statistics about the increase in marital separations were published periodically, and became heated topics for debate. By 1994, the number of separations amounted to 60% of the number of new marriages (*The Times of Malta* 13/03/95), and by the time of the 1996 General Election, the introduction of divorce was firmly on the political agenda. At the time of writing, the divorce debate was raging.

The apparent crisis of the family was an issue of concern not only to church and state, but also social scientists. Their conclusions reveal an inherent tension, or ambivalence towards continuity and change in family and gender relations. Of particular importance were two sociologists who were also priests—Anthony Abela and Carmel Tabone.

Abela's work was based on large-scale surveys conducted with Gallup, and attempted to review the 'state of play' in Maltese society. Its conclusions, publicised in the national press, confirmed the dominantly 'traditional' orientation of Maltese gender relations. Under the banner headline 'Maltese women's place is in the home', *The Malta Independent* gave the following summary:

> The Maltese stand out as having the most conservative attitudes in Europe when it comes to women and work ... an international seminar in Valletta was told yesterday. Sociologist Anthony M Abela told the seminar "In Malta women tend to resist the European trend for married women to seek paid work. They are very cautious about the impact of a working mother has on the life of a family." (*The Malta Independent*, 5/12/95)

Tabone's work, by contrast, focused on the contestation of this dominant model of gender relations in the household. He argued that an increase in the numbers of married women working outside the home should not be seen as a negative development in the Maltese family. Rather, he saw it as one of the inevitable changes Malta was going through as a result of modernity. Moreover, he saw it as a potentially positive change, as it marked the beginning of the end of the unequal and exploitative 'traditional' family:

> Current local developments ... suggest a movement towards a new relationship characterised by partnership and similarity rather than patriarchy and difference. Is not this a more faithful representation of the unity and oneness of marriage, and of a new found rationale of stability for the family? (Tabone, 1994: 250)

The contrast between Abela and Tabone neatly summarises the tensions and ambivalences at the centre of Maltese life in the early 1990s. On the one hand there was concern to preserve the 'traditional' family, with its relatively circumscribed division of labour, and the rather rigid demarcation of social space by gender. On the other hand, there was a recognition that this 'traditional' family and the hegemonic gender identities were being contested, and transformed as a consequence.

Gender roles and identities are fluid processes rather than rigid ideologies to which people are forced to adhere. By examining the various ways in which such identities are performed, analysis can be taken beyond a simple description of the hegemonic model of gender, towards examining the practices and performances that go towards the reproduction or subversion of this model. In the context of Malta, this takes us away from the imputation of a monolithic 'honour/shame syndrome' in which men are the active participants in society, and women passive. It enables us to recognise the very real roles women have in the constitution of society, and in the production and reproduction of their own identities. It also enables us to understand the process of transformation in gender identities, by drawing attention to the ways hegemonic masculinity and hegemonic femininity are contested, resisted, and ultimately changed. At the centre of this process of contestation and change in early nineties Malta was a profound anxiety about the future of family, gender, household and ultimately society.

NOTES

[17] The preposition *Għand* means 'at the house of' as in the French *Chez*.

CHAPTER FOUR

Respectability and Consumption

I think our education in the English school and University alloyed what was pure in us. Younger, we talked of love, fear, motherhood; speaking in Maltese as Elena and I do now. But what a language! Have it, or today's Builders, advanced at all since the half-men who built the sanctuaries at Hagiar Kim? We talk as animals might. (Thomas Pynchon, *V*: 309)

3RD OCTOBER, 1993—FIRST DAY IN VALLETTA

On my first day *Għand Dupont*, I was given a ceremonial tour around their house. It was an old building, dating back to the seventeenth century, and Ray Dupont took great pride in revealing that its rooms had formed part of a Knight's Palace. The Palace was far from intact. Like much of Valletta, the block in which the house was situated had been partitioned in seemingly arbitrary ways, giving a higgledy-piggledy plan to the house. Staircases rose and fell from unexpected places, and rooms were encased, on three walls, ceiling and floor, by other people's property. The focus of the house tour was on the refurbishments they had done to turn the rented house into the home that it now was. Emphasis on the age of the house was immediately qualified with references to its comfort. They had invested time and money to make it beautiful.

The house tour, I discovered, was not common among all *Beltin*. Normally when visitors came to a house, they were invited into the *salott* or parlour. This room was generally reserved for special guests such as priests, doctors or politicians, and on many of the visits I made to people's houses was the only room I saw. During the *tberik* or blessing of the houses, it was into this room that priests were invariably invited to give their blessing. In it were displayed precious gifts or family heirlooms, which were shown to the illustrious visitor. The *salott* of even the most humble Valletta house often contained antique items of staggering beauty—and no doubt value. Wooden items such as dowry chests or tables were lovingly waxed, and upholstery was protected with plastic covers that although no doubt doing their job, made summer visiting rather sweaty. As a show-room for wealthy possessions, and place for entertaining distinguished visitors, the *salott* represented the public face of the household. Similar observations have been made by Young and Wilmott (1957) in Britain and Gullestad (1993) in Norway, who have identified the bifurcation of the house itself into a public zone used to entertain 'outsiders' and a more intimate one in which 'insiders' lived. The *salott* operated in a similar way to the *salon* of eighteenth-century French bourgeois society, which was a public room in a private dwelling, demonstrating the extent to which 'the line between private and public sphere extended right through the home' (Habermas 1989: 45). The public was invited into the house, and the household displayed, in the *salott*.

Since the opening up of Maltese markets to imported goods—a process set in motion by the election of the Europe-oriented Nationalist Party in 1987—the concentration on spending for display in the public area of the house has expanded in Malta. This expansion coincided with both the rise of home-ownership in Malta, and the depopulation of Valletta. Many former *Beltin* now live in owner-occupied accommodation outside the city, which is lavishly appointed and decorated to the latest styles. This increase in domestic consumption has expanded the public, display areas from the *salott* to incorporate the whole house. Apocryphal tales were told in the early nineties about Maltese families that had invested all their wealth in creating fashionable houses that effectively stood as show-homes for visitors while on a day-to-day basis, the family lived in the garage. The Duponts' keen-ness to give me a full tour of the house represented an element in this expansion of the public, display capacity of the house, that is tied up with notions of modern respectability and modern domestic consumption patterns. Mary Dupont herself alluded to the importance of showing people the whole house:

> Whenever people come round we always give them a full tour of the house. I'm not sure why—we just always do. It's nice to show them the house.

The increases in domestic consumption and the expansion of display from the *salott* to the whole house combines two important elements in the understanding of early nineties Maltese life. First, it can be interpreted as a response to the anxieties about the family and household outlined in the last chapter. As family appears in increasing crisis, increasing attention is drawn to the prime symbol of the family and household—the house itself. As Gullestad (1993) has argued, home decoration can be seen as a means by which people symbolically construct images of completeness, which confront the apparent fragmentations of modernity. Creating a beautiful and fashionable house, then, can be seen to shore up an otherwise crisis-ridden institution—uniting family and household in house. At the same time, however, the focus on consumption itself creates problems for the family, by increasing the pressure to consume and replacing family values with those of materialism. The Church's concern for the family was often framed in terms of concern about the erosive effects of materialism and the pressure this puts on household finances. Consuming to protect the family, also threatens it, producing a kind of vicious circle whereby attempts to bolster simultaneously undermine.

Second, the expansion of household consumption can be seen in the context of an intricate politics of class distinctions. Clearly, displaying expensive possessions in the public parts of the house is a way of demonstrating wealth. Moreover, displaying valuble heirlooms suggests a genealogical depth of wealth—'old' wealth which confirms social standing. However, the choices of display also implicate a significant politics of taste, within which people demonstrate both distinction and education—their ability both to read and reproduce good design. Aesthetics was a feature of the Dupont house tour. In particular, attention was drawn to the various works of art they possessed. In the *salott* hung two. The first was a sea-scape commissioned by Ray himself, by a well-known artist from Malta's sister island, Gozo. Its presence confirmed the Duponts as not just art appreciators, but patrons to the arts. The second was an abstract, as Ray explained:

> It's an abstract—a very good one. I like it. Most of the people round here wouldn't really understand it—they're not, you know, not educated.

Being 'educated'—*edukat*—was only one of the means by which the Duponts distinguished themselves from other *Beltin*, and other residents of the parish. A variety of other categories were used to distinguish social strata, or demonstrate their own respectability. In ethnographic accounts of Mediterranean societies respectability is most commonly linked to the moral system of honour and shame, in which it is manifest in male-associated honour that in turn is derived from female-associated shame. The last chapter dealt in detail with some of the analytical problems of imputing an honour/shame syndrome in Mediterranean contexts, but there are also ethnographic reasons why honour/shame is an inappropriate metaphor for respectability in Malta.

Honour and shame tend to be viewed moral commodities which must be protected against loss. The Greek *dropi* or Andalusian *vergüenza*, for example, are glossed as 'shame' by Campbell (1964) and Pitt-Rivers (1961) respectively to denote an inherent property of the person, which must be preserved in order to maintain honour. In Malta, however, the moral categories of respectability are processual, rather than commoditised. The word *onor*—honour—is seldom used in Malta to describe social standing. Rather, people refer to those who 'have respect'—*għandu rispett*. Respect is not a property of the person, but a property of relationships with other people—it is something that others give. Thus, when referring to their own social standing, the Duponts said 'We're well respected'—*għandna rispett*—or 'people respect us'—*jirrispetjawna*—rather than 'We're honourable' or 'We have honour'. Similarly, there is no abstract property of the person in Malta that we might want to translate as 'shame'. Wilhelmsen, in his ethnography of Malta's biggest fishing village, glosses *għarukaża* as 'shame' (1976), but in doing so he falls foul of the will to uncover properties rather than processes. A more faithful translation of *għarukaża* is 'disgrace'—a term used not to describe a property of the person, but a property of events. *Għarukaża* is used to describe events which by their nature are deemed to be disgraceful, and was always prefixed by the rhetorical interrogative *xi* or *x'*—what—to refer to specific events as *x'għarukaża*—what a disgrace. Nor was this term used only in the context of sexual morality, but could also refer to other forms of disgrace, at different levels of social organisation: party-political, national or even international. Thus, when Maltese saw pictures of famine from Africa on their television screens, the response would be the same as that towards an unmarried woman becoming pregnant—*x'għarukaża*.

If respectability and disgrace are not inherent properties of the person, but related to a process of ascription, this means that social standing is not determinate. People are not respectable and non-respectable because of their absolute position in a rigid structure of social stratification. Rather, the respect they command is derived from their performance of good standing and avoidance of disgrace—from being a good person in the public eye, and belonging to a good household. Certain categories of person—parents, clergy and one's elders—are expected to automatically command respect. For others it must be achieved, and ascribed by others in a constant process of reaffirmation.

This process revolves around a set of conceptual oppositions between 'educated' and 'ignorant', 'dirty' and 'clean', 'rude' and 'polite', and ultimately 'high' and 'low'—that served to elevate or denigrate self or other. This politics of respectability was a widespread part of everyday life in Malta, and through it social hierarchy and social stratification were both acknowledged and produced. These processes were doubly charged in the early nineties, during which the prime locus of respectability—the family—was under threat. The politics of respectability, therefore, fuelled the escallation of consumption that was itself aimed at maintaining the family.

CLASS, STRUCTURE, CONSUMPTION

The last chapter outlined the extent to which access to and participation in the Maltese public sphere is limited by gender. Women, although substantively participating in social life and indeed actively producing society itself, are nevertheless excluded from the acknowledged public zones of interaction that make up the public sphere, and consequently from achieving political office. Gender is not the only limitation placed on participation in this central area of social life, however. The public sphere is also limited by criteria of social standing.

The significance of social standing has generally been seen by social scientists as deriving from the stratification of society.[18] Society is seen to be built up of different levels, strata or classes of persons who have differential access to resources, and different life chances. The social sciences as a whole were born with the analysis of social stratification, at a time when industrialisation was giving life to a new order of society which needed to be understood. The so-called 'founding fathers' of European sociology were all concerned with understanding this transformation.

The 'classical' tradition (Joyce 1995) derived from these early sociologists, particularly Marx and Weber, sees stratification as ultimately a matter of social class, and class as derived from—even reducible to—economics. For Marx, class position was determined by people's relationship to the means of production (Marx and Engels 1967), whereas Weber linked class to the life chances afforded by that relationship (1978). For Marx, the economic structures of society informed the creation of social structures, which in capitalist society were structures of exploitation. For Weber, social structures were seen as structures of power, with power defined as 'the chance of a man or a number of men to realize their own will in a social action' (1978: 926). He goes on from this to argue that economic power is not necessarily identical with power as such, and that even the economic power of class relations might have its provenance in other considerations—most notably status and what he calls party. While class is reserved in Weberian social theory for situations determined by economic power, status describes the distribution of power by honour or prestige and party its distribution by political association. Class, status and party are applied by Weber to the different strata of social life, such that classes, status groups and parties emerge as the principle phenomena of the distribution of power in society (Ibid). Scott has recently argued that a more helpful reading of Weber's tripartite schema would distinguish class, status and command, with command being the central motivation for party association (1996). Parties realise power through achieving command.

Class status and party—or class status and command—can be seen as the sociologist's classificatory scheme—a means of defining action according to its origins in and consequences for class, status or command, and a means of identifying the contours of social structure. For Weber, they were ideal types, to be used as heuristic tools. It is clear, though, from empirical situations such as that of contemporary Britain, the abstracting out the class, status and command elements of social structure is a messy business. Scott attempts such a task, and in doing so reveals a complex set of inter-relationships between class, status and command that questions such neat abstraction (1996: 226ff). Indeed, Weber is at pains to tell us that there is always complex inter-relationships between the various forms of power, and various forms of social organisation inherent in society. More problematically, though, the sociological project of classifying power situations to identify stratification tends to deny—or at least not foreground—the actors' view of social life. In Malta too, for example, the inter-relationships between class, status and command are complex, and although social actors are aware of the different criteria of power or social stratification, they seldom regard them in isolation from each other. To artificially separate them for the purpose of classification denies this complexity not just objectively, but also experientially.

The abstraction of social structure is equally problematic. The metaphor of structure has been central to analyses of stratification in modern sociology (Crompton 1993, see Dahrendorf 1959), but like 'stratification' has been heavily criticised. The relationship between structure and action is one of the central problems in social theory (Giddens 1979), deriving from the assumption—or implication—behind most accounts of social structure that the former determines the latter. Structure is thus seen as prior to action, and even prior to or outside people themselves. This notion of structure as both determinate and *a priori* derives from Durkheim's vision of society as consisting of durable institutions that exist over and above the people who reproduce them (Durkheim 1982). Chief among the critics of this position is Bourdieu, whose notion of *habitus* attempts to combine structure and action in a kind of dialectic whereby action produces structure, and structure action. In a much-cited and famously opaque passage, he sums up this dialectic as follows:

> ... the structures constitutive of a particular type of environment ... produce the *habitus*, systems of durable dispositions, structured structures predisposed to function as structuring structures, that is, as the principle of generation and structuration of practices and representations which can be objectively 'regulated' and 'regular' without in any way being the product of obedience to rules ... collectively orchestrated without being the product of the organising action of a conductor. (Bourdieu 1977: 73)

This focus on the *modus operandi* rather than the *opus operatum* (Ibid) of social life has led to a new social science that focuses not on structure, but on practice. Such regularities as appear in empirical investigation are the product of *dispositions* rather than rules, and the structure of social stratification is located in lifestyle or everyday life rather than wider, determinate structures (Connell 1983, Thompson 1984). Bourdieu locates lifestyle in *habitus*, a term he inherits from Mauss's work on the body (1979: 97–123). Through *habitus*, structure is seen to reside in the body, as 'patterns of behaviour which are withdrawn from consciousness and which define our way of being in the world.' (Thompson 1984: 55). The differences between different strata of social life are produced and recognised by differences in *habitus*, which combine differences in posture, language, style and taste.

Inherent in this understanding of social stratification is the foregrounding of consumption. Consumption is one of the central metaphors of recent writing on modernity, replacing production as the driving force through which capitalism expands, but also—significantly—establishing the means by which people produce themselves (Miller 1987). For Bourdieu, consumption is both shaped by and produces class *habitus*, combining economic and status elements of stratification. Weber's notion of status had also highlighted consumption, but Bourdieu expanded this to identify the process of distinction—a part-reflex, part-strategic process centred on the accumulation of what he calls cultural or symbolic capital (Bourdieu 1984). According to Bourdieu, consuming the appropriate tasteful and stylish goods is both a product of and produces *habitus* appropriate to a person's social standing. Through consumption, then, social stratification is both represented and reproduced. This process was clear in early nineties Malta, when consumption in and around the house both contributed to an on-going attempt to preserve the family against erosive processes, but also informed a complex politics of social standing.

Naturally, there are limits to people's abilities to consume, which implies not only a status consideration in consumption, but also an element of economics. The idea that social processes set limits on people's behaviour, aspirations or identities is the final contribution the material on social stratification can make to our understanding of the

Maltese social world of the early 1990s. One of the consequences of focusing on practice or action as determinate in social stratification, rather than structure, is the tendency to regard individual action as autonomous from the factors which might limit it. Indeed, this criticism has been levelled at Bourdieu, who in his theory of practice has been accused of both methodological individualism and structural determinism. Either criticism, however, misses the point of his dialectical theory of emergent stratification, which sees the limitations to possible action as inherent in the non-determinate structuring of *habitus*. Through *habitus*, people are aware of the limits to their activities, without these limits necessarily being made explicit. In the Maltese situation, however, the limits are expressed through the metaphors of inclusion and exclusion we encountered in the last chapter when discussing household and friendship. A terminology of 'insiders' and 'outsiders' is used to describe the limitations and inequalities of stratification, with those 'inside' being people who can succeed by virtue of connections with those in government. The politics of social standing, therefore, also informs people's understanding of government and state. The three elements of stratification identified by Scott, therefore, were inherent in early nineties Malta. A class economics informed a status politics of consumption and distinction that defined the contours and influence of command inherent in the state. The interconnectedness of these three elements was complex, and particular social situations defied unequivocal classification.

CATEGORIES OF RESPECTABILITY

The respectability of the Duponts—the extent to which people respected them—was defined by the complex of class, status and party or command inherent in social stratification. The operation of these three criteria does not make sense, however, outside the local classification of social standing. Respectability in Valletta was oriented around a set of opposed categories which are relative rather than absolute. Thus one person's being defined as 'low'—*baxx*—reflects the relative elevation of both the person defining them low, and the people around them. Saying 'you are ignorant' means 'I am educated'. Such statements are strategic, such that Ray Dupont's observation that many *Beltin* would fail to understand his abstract art, was both a way of denigrating his less high-brow neighbours and demonstrating to me—an educated Northern European—that he and I were 'on a level'.

Being the product of strategic practice, such categories are not inevitably linked to particular people, as would be implied by a more structurally-determined stratification. However, through their mobilisation and enactment, they do produce a sense of stratification, conceived as a sense of limitation. This sense of limitation is expressed in terms of the central oppositions *poplu/pulit*—people/polite society—and *poplu/gvern*—people/government. The former denotes a limitation in civil society between the wider population and a 'polite society' at the centre of public life, and the former denotes a limitation that can be understood in terms of Scott's criterion of command. This is dealt with in greater detail towards the end of this chapter. Here, I focus initially on the critieria for defining *pulit* society.

The distinction *poplu/pulit* is also expressed in terms of a division between *għoli* 'high' and *baxx* 'low' society. In Valletta, this is mapped onto the spatial distinction between *fuq* and *isfel*—'high' and 'low' town, which are seen as populated by 'lower' and 'higher' status people. The origins of this association are historical. The design chosen for Valletta by Laparelli—with its strictly regimented grid pattern of streets layed onto the hump-back mound of the Xiberras peninsula—meant that the city is one of slopes. The longer length-wise streets run level along a small plateau from the City Gate and main defensive cavaliers, before falling away towards the end of the peninsula and Fort St Elmo. The shorter, lateral streets have steeper slopes to traverse, on either side down to the two harbours. Some are so steep that they had to be stepped, to allow safe and comfortable passage. The slopes inform a spatial and conceptual distinction between 'lower' and 'higher' areas—classified as one between *il-fuq*—lit. 'the up' or 'high town'—and *l-isfel*—lit. 'the down' or 'low town'.

This differentiation between *il-fuq* and *l-isfel* is not only a spatial one, but also social. *L-Isfel* is not only topographically lower than *il-fuq*, but also socially. The roots of this distinction lie in the development of the city, and the different occupational classes that have lived in these areas. The spatial boundary between the two is rather schematic, although there are more precisely-defined named areas of *l-isfel* that are considered not only geographically 'lower' but also socially. These are the *Mandraġġ*, which lies half-way down the peninsula on the Marsamxett side of Valletta, and the *Due Balli* and *L-Arċipierku*, which nestle behind the bastions on either side of the city's seaward end.

The *Mandraġġ* was created by the Knights, who dug out this low-lying area in an attempt to create a sheltered docking harbour for their barges and caracks. The project had to be abandoned when they hit hard bedrock. Both the *Due Balli* and *L-Arċipierku* are naturally low-lying areas, that became almost enclosed when the bastions were erected. The Knights initially considered the areas uninhabitable, because they lacked air, so they left them empty. As Valletta developed, however, and became a hub of Mediterranean trade, demand increased for—particularly cheap—housing in the city. Property speculators were sold plots in these inhospitable areas to build high-density, low-cost housing. In the *Mandraġġ*, the legitimate building was supplemented by the more spontaneous—and illegal—construction of shantihs and lean-tos, and a small labyrinth of cave-like dwellings that were carved out of the limestone walls left by the Knights' excavations. These areas, and the people who lived in them, contrasted with the genteel splendour of the higher parts of Valletta. There, wealthy merchants and Knights of the Order lived in ornate and decorative palaces with grand fountains and spacious court-yards. In the lower areas, messengers, labourers and galley crew lived in cramped and unsanitary conditions.

During British colonial rule and into the era of Independence, this spatial distinction persisted. High-town was characterised by the wealth and distinction of professional and business classes, and low-town by the relative—and at times absolute—poverty of lower-status manual and semi-skilled workers. By the early nineties, Valletta had ceased to be a fashionable place to live, so that many of the professional and business households had left the city for the wealthy suburbs, to be replaced either by offices or by those from the city's lower areas. Many of these had been displaced by urban renewal or slum clearance schemes during the 1950s, 60s and 70s. The significance of one such project—in *L-Arċipierku*—is explored in the next chapter.

L-Arċipierku is the 'low-town' area of St Paul's parish, and the place of origin of many of the *Pawlini*. It was seen as the 'heart' of the parish, and spiritual home of St Paul. The occupations of those living in *L-Arċipierku* tended to be of a lower status than those of the higher parts of the parish. In Malta, there is a fairly rigid gradation of occupational status, based around levels of education required for the job. Crime is the least reputable mode of employment, followed by long-term unemployment. Thereafter, unskilled labour such as refuse collection, builders' labouring or factory work is closely followed by work as a messenger which enjoys slightly higher status on account of its cleanliness and the necessity of literacy. Following this, skilled workers and shop-workers, then clerical workers, bureaucrats and workplace supervisors. After this, teachers and lecturers, followed by the professions: architects, bankers, doctors, lawyers and priests. Most people in *L-Arċipierku* were engaged in semi-skilled work associated with manufacturing or construction, in government work such as caretaking or cleaning, or in other work associated with the retail trade. Some had their own market stalls, others were messengers or drove delivery vans. Outside *L-Arċipierku* there were a large number of pensioners, many of whom had worked for the British colonial authorities in jobs connected with the harbours. Those still employed tended to be better educated than in *L-Arċipierku*, and either occupied their own position as part of the large shop-owning bourgeoisie or were employed in clerical or other skilled work.

The distinction between *fuq* and *isfel* as determined by occupation, then, was reproduced from the sixteenth to the late twentieth century. The continued tendency of those from 'lower' Valletta to have lower status occupations has resulted in the association of lower Valletta with low status. Indeed, it is thought of as being socially 'low'—*baxx*—with upper Valletta being 'high'—*għoli*. As is suggested by their invocation of a gradient, these terms were not absolute, but a relative means of assessing and ascribing social standing. Moreover, they were not unequivocally ascribed to any particular individuals or groups. People were not fixed as 'high' or 'low', but these categories were used strategically in particular contexts to elevate or denigrate self or other in a constant play of respectability.

Għoli and *baxx*—'high' and 'low'—are themselves translated into distinctions between *pulit*—polite—and *ħamallu* or *pastaż*—'rude', 'uncouth', incorporating elements of what Bourdieu would call *habitus*. Whereas *pulit* people adopt an upright posture, with smart fashionable clothes, speaking quietly and clearly, *ħamalli* speak loudly with grunted syllables, hunch their backs and wear either dirty clothes or those showing no awareness of fashion. These images are broadly stereotypical, but were frequently mobilised in particular situations, to elevate or denigrate. For example, when young women were discussing the relative virtues of different dates, they would often use *ħamallu* and *pulit* to either dissuade or encourage their friends: 'Don't go out with him—he's *ħamallu*'; 'He's so *pulit*—you're really lucky'. *Pulit* and *ħamallu* are evocative of further distinctions, between *edukat* and *injurant*—'educated' and 'ignorant'—and *nadif/maħmuġ*—'clean/ dirty'. The term *edukat*, 'educated' was used both metaphorically and literally as an index of respectability. Being *edukat* meant being genteel and well-spoken in Maltese, English and Italian, which enabled sophisticated inter-lingual word-play to both elevate the self and denigrate the other. It also meant having achieved success in formal education—and particularly having accumulated a large number of 'certificates'. This was a more concrete criterion for the judgement of status, and as such went alongside the gradation of occupation.

Maintaining respectability in early nineties Malta meant avoiding situations in which one could be accused of being *ħamallu*, and therefore adopting appropriate dress, speech and personal body comportment. These practices were strictly maintained by those who considered themselves respectable. By making sure that they were polite and clean in public, and through their education, they demonstrated that they were higher than those around. This demonstration required the cultivation of a certain aloofness. Such aloofness or distanciation is a common feature of social distinction. For example, in Bourdieu's examination of distinction in 1960s France, he observed that higher-status workers tended to distance themselves from popular amusements and pastimes, such as sporting events, circuses or funfairs (1984: 394). This in turn formed part of an overall orientation to the world which saw the bourgeois subject as detatched, objective and contemplative of the world around them (54). The Duponts cultivated just such detatchment. 'We don't get too involved in local things', they had said, when highlighting the 'respect' they commanded.

Ray Dupont avoided involvement in the organisation of *festa*. By many respectable people, *festa* was considered frivolous or even blasphemous, with its focus on statue-carrying, music and fireworks—an element of 'low' or popular culture that led to excesses of drinking and verged on idolatry. For some, those who did involve themselves with *festa* were categorically *ħamallu*. For example, when I discussed the local *festi* with the handful of University students living in Valletta during fieldwork, they said they tended to avoid the city during *festi*. It was too loud, and there were too many drunks, they said. For others it was an object of curiosity. The Duponts themselves were less condemning. They didn't disapprove of the *festa*, but preferred to keep it at arms' length, and simply enjoy the atmosphere on *festa* day.

Ray also tended to avoid the day-to-day administration of *festa*, and was reluctant to enter local bars such as *Għand Lawrenz*, the main centre of *Pawlini* activity. Many of the *Pawlini* who spent their time *Għand Lawrenz* were from *L-Arċipierku*—St Paul's parish's 'low-town' area. They were therefore associated with *l-isfel* and consequently, in the eyes of more respectable Maltese, with the lexicon of 'lower' terms—*baxx*, *injurant*, *ħamallu* etc. As I was told by a local businessman, they were 'basically good people, but ignorant—*injurant*'. Others regarded it as a 'low' place—*baxx*—'where people drink whisky in the morning!'. This was an index of inferior status, and marked off *Għand Lawrenz* as a place to be avoided by the respectable. It was lively and noisy, and this atmosphere often spilled out onto the street. The bar has an open front, and whenever familiar people walked by, the denizens would shout *Aw' Ħabib*—'Hey, my friend!', 'Come and have a drink'. Each time this happened to him, Ray Dupont would turn and acknowledge with a wave, but continue to walk, to not only evade this sociability, but to actively demonstrate his aloofness and respectability.

Għand Lawrenz, Ray was referred to by the polite form of address, as *Sur* Dupont, the term *Sur*—sir or sinjur—being an explicit acknowledgement of respect for rank. As a local teacher, many of the *Pawlini* had been taught by him when younger, so that both his education and occupational class were invoked by the use of *Sur*.[19] He was not the only *Sur* in local life, however, the others being acknowledged as superior by virtue of age, genealogy or occupation. One was an elderly man whose life had been dedicated to the operation of the local religious Confraternity, or brotherhood, of the Sacred Crucifix (see chapter seven). Another the son of a long line of wealthy

Valletta merchants, and also Rector of the Confraternity. The two were *Sur* Gorg and *Sur* Charlie—the use of forename rather than surname ensuring an approachability that cross-cut the attribution of respectability. Ray Dupont, on the other hand, was referred to, from afar, as *Sur* Dupont; a more aloof person, who was nevertheless considered *raġel sew*—a good man.

The attribution of respectability was not only related to class and status, however, but also to party. The Duponts were respected for their work over the years for the Nationalist Party. Ray was a party officer, who had canvassed for local candidates during the difficult 1980s, and had been a representative of the Malta Union of Teachers during the strikes of 1984–85 (see Zammit Mangion 1992: 114). Showing loyalty to the Nationalist cause during these difficult times made him 'a good man' in the eyes of a constituency who were predominantly, and passionately, Nationalist. Links with the Nationalist Party conferred social standing on two counts. Not only was he a 'good man' for helping the party cause, he was also associated with respectability by association particularly with the Nationalists. PN supporters regarded their party as being more respectable than the Labour Party, because of its historical origins in the bourgeois mercantile classes, the professions and the clergy. Their party was therefore more 'polite' than the Labour Party, who were more strongly associated with engineers, architects and dockyard shop stewards. The distinction extended to political style. The MLP were regarded as more populist and confrontational, a characteristic embodied particularly in the rhetorical style of Dom Mintoff, the 1970s prime minister (Boissevain 1994). By contrast, the Nationalists had a reputation for a more subtle political style. They did *kollox bil-pulit*—everything politely.

The maintenance of respectability, then, involved party association, the pursuit of education and occupation as well as the performance of status through politeness and the cultivation of aloofness. Declaring themselves outside, or above, the everyday domains of sociability, however, was a risky strategy for the respectable. Although it conveyed a sense of distinction and social elevation, it also prevented their participation in the everyday performances of gender identity outlined in the last chapter. This often led to a criticism and questioning of gender, sexuality and particularly the sexual morality of the aloof respectable groups. Sexual fantasies were projected onto respectable households, and their moral elevation—the extent to which they were *għoli*—was questioned. For example, in a long discussion concerning the *Casino Maltese*, an elite Valletta club reserved for the wealthiest Maltese, a number of the categories of respectability were turned against the respectable. The discussion involved myself and two younger *Pawlini*, from *L-Arċipierku*, who told me that members of the *Casino* were all cuckolds. It was *każin tal-poġuti*, in their eyes—the club of the cuckolds. One of their cousins had worked there, and seen how married women would be with different men from one day to the next. They were also dirty—they only washed once a month, and although they thought they were educated, they showed their ignorance when they avoided conversations with local Valletta people. Such behaviour was in keeping with the cultivation of aloofness, but led to accusations of being 'cold'—*kiesaħ*. These opinions demonstrated the extent to which the categories of Maltese respectability are labile, manipulable. Although it was acknowledged that the patrons of the *Casino* were elites, they were nevertheless morally devalued, dirty, ignorant and cold. In making these points, the young *Pawlini* were maintaining their own position as morally and physically clean, and at least more polite, if not necessarily more educated than the *Casino* patrons.

This play of categories enabled a kind of structural equality, whereby apparent elites were down-graded and non-elites elevated, through the strategic mobilisation of different criteria for respectability. Boissevain writes of a profound *ethos* of equality in the Maltese villages he researched in the late 1950s. Despite the obvious social ascendancy of politicians, political canvassers, doctors, lawyers, priests, and their strong position as village patrons and brokers, there was, he argued, a reluctance to refer to these people as 'leaders' and a profound egalitarianism prevailed (1993: 40ff). A similar egalitarianism prevailed in Malta of the early 1990s, although the picture was somewhat more complex—the egalitarian *ethos* was maintained precisely through the acknowledgement of social stratification, but also through its simultaneous and systematic undermining by means of the criteria of respectability.

The allocation of respectability, then, rather than mapping onto an absolute social structural division of class, is a strategic process whereby the categories of elevation and denigration are continuously used. Similarly, the assertion of social aloofness is as much strategic as ascribed. Aloofness is produced by, rather than inherent in, the actions of those who consider themselves, and are considered to 'have respect'. Although strategic and therefore not structurally determined, the use of aloofness and the mobilisation of the terms of respect, through their association with particular people nevertheless produce a set of divisions which operate as if they were structural. The distinction between *fuq* and *isfel*, for example, although a relative one, becomes absolute through its usage and association with the other criteria of respectability.

CONSUMPTION AND THE HOUSE

The *habitus* of respectability involved not only demonstrations of politeness and aloofness, but also consumption, and particularly the consumption of household goods. One of the consequences of respectable social aloofness was a focus on the house as an area of sociality, such that it became increasingly important to have a tastefully-appointed house in which to entertain guests. This in turn required an expansion of the 'public' parts of the house from the *salott* to the house as a whole. In this context, the Duponts' insistence on treating visitors to a full house tour can be seen as a further means of demonstrating respectability.

The expansion of consumption in the late 1980s coincided with the increased anxiety about the family, and particularly fears about the effects of materialism on family unity. However, this consumption can also be seen as a means by which Maltese people symbolically expressed the unity of the family to counter the erosion of tradition. Grima and Zammit, discussing the rise of rustic stone-clad house façades in Malta, have emphasised the importance of houses in the symbolisation of family and household:

> People aspire to form strong, durable families ... Our preoccupation with houses is understandable in the light of this desire to create a solid and permanent base. Indeed, in discourse, people often use metaphors drawn from buildings to describe their family. They speak of a 'solid' family and of

> 'building a good relationship'. In this context, the symbolical (sic) value of houses is extremely high, invested as they are with the task of expressing the value and identity of the families who own them ... People in Malta 'say it with houses'. (Grima & Zammit 1996: 46-47)

Saying it with houses, however, can be an expensive business. Expressing family solidity through household consumption, then, creates a kind of paradox or vicious circle, whereby the will to consume is fuelled by a wish to be regarded as respectable members of solid households, but this in turn puts a greater strain on family resources, and therefore further threatens its unity.

The perceived dangers of materialism have already been discussed in the last chapter, in the context of the May 1994 sermon by Archbishop Merceica, which focused on the role of the father. In particular, he voiced concern that increased pressure to consume was leading men to spend too much time outside the home and was therefore threatening the unity of the family:

> God forbid that our workers should be ... enslaved by materialism and consumerism ... The essence of the beauty of family life is not a luxurious house ... [but] ... the parents, united to each other and to their children. (*The Sunday Times (Malta)* 1/5/94)

Here, the Archbishop was focusing explicitly on the dangers of substituting what he regarded as a healthy, harmonious family and household with the symbolic show of family unity inherent in household consumption. His statement was a response to the rise of consumption that took place over the seven years since the election of the Nationalist government in 1987. In contrast to the previous Labour administration (1971–1987), which had been economically protectionist, or even isolationist, the Nationalists believed in free trade, and the liberalisation of the market. This created an unprecedented supply of imported consumer goods, the value of which rose from Lm82.2million in 1986 to Lm147.6million in 1991 (Ministry of Finance 1992). The succession of governments also created the conditions which enabled the expansion of consumption. The Labour government had raised the incomes of lower-paid workers, introducing social welfare and a minimum wage. The Nationalists subsequently ended the wage freeze that had prevailed under Labour, allowing them to rise (Sultana 1994). Per capita expenditure at constant prices rose from Lm494 in 1984 to Lm652 in 1992, whilst private consumption at current prices rose from Lm317.3million in 1984 to Lm417.1million in 1993 (Tonna 1994). Rising prices and the impetus to consume led in turn to an increase in full-time workers taking part-time jobs to supplement their income. By 1995, the number of part-timers holding a full time job was 11,140, or 8.26% of a total 134,832 gainfully employed (Central Office of Statistics 1998).[20] This phenomenon was seen by the Archbishop and others as particularly erosive.

The rise in consumption was particularly centred on household goods and leisure activities (Sultana 1994). A number of commentators have examined the extent to which, in capitalist societies, consumption in the house is a creative act, which in various ways enables people to constitute their identities, as it constitutes the household itself (Gullestad 1993, Madigan & Munro 1996, Miller 1988). In the act of making choices about household decor and furnishings, people appropriate commodities from the mass market, and through them communicate elements of style or taste that in turn demonstrate social attributes such as gender, ethnicity and social standing (Carrier 1996).

In Malta, this consumption focused itself particularly on fitted kitchens and bathrooms, the expansion of which in the early nineties was phenomenal. From 1990 onwards, large and luxurious showrooms began to appear on Maltese high-streets, showing elaborate porcelain and marble bathroom suites, real-wood fitted kitchens and household gadgets including lighting and bathroom fittings (Tonna 1994). Grima & Zammit identified a veritable 'bathroom syndrome' in Maltese household consumption, which they link to a tension between the impetus to consume and a more 'traditional' emphasis on thrift:

> There is a tendency to incorporate as many luxurious bathrooms as possible in a house and to boast about them. Here one can see ... [a] ... precarious balance between a traditional value orientation which dictates that money should only be spent on 'basic needs' such as bathrooms and the new consumeristic trend manifested in the luxurious furnishing of these bathrooms and the often superfluous number of them. (Grima & Zammit 1996: 49)

In houses with more than one bathroom, they were categorically distinguished between those *ta'kuljum*, or 'everyday' bathrooms used by household members or other 'insiders'—those *ta'ġewwa*—and those set aside for use mainly by visitors. This suggests that bathrooms were occupying a similar position in the house as the *salott*—as places of display. If the *salott* represented the public face of the household, however, the bathroom presented privacy or intimacy, although it was no less open to public scrutiny. Clearly, when visitors come to a house for dinner or a drink, they might need to use the bathroom, so it needs to be decorated and appointed in a manner appropriate to the approved, respectable tastes. Above all, the bathroom must be clean—*nadif*. Indeed, because tasteful designs for both the bathroom and kitchen were characterised by marble, tiles, porcelain and chrome, they were both associated with cleanliness. As such, they were particularly appropriate rooms for the representation of respectability through cleanliness. The lack of a bathroom—or indeed an old or dirty bathroom—was interpreted as proof of 'low' status—*baxx*. For example, when I asked a 'high-town' housewife why *L-Arċipierku* was considered 'low', she replied:

> I don't know. They're low—you know ... They live in very small houses; just in one room—with no bathrooms.

In fact, many of the houses *l-isfel* did have bathrooms, and were keen to appoint them in as respectable a fashion as possible. One family, the Camilleri's, who were introduced in the last chapter in the context of femininity and grocery shopping, were in the process of arranging their bathroom in the summer of 1993. These were hard times for this family of five. Two of their three adult sons had recently been made redundant, and the husband, Pawlu was having trouble with his factory employer, who was persistently paying him late. Despite this, the family decided that they needed to modernise their bathroom. Polly, the wife explained the need for a cleaner, smarter bathroom, using both the categories *nadif* and *pulit*. It was partly because the eldest son had recently been appointed to the Committee of the *Għaqda tal-Pawlini*—Association of *Pawlini*—and so might receive visits from its other officers, and partly because the middle son was recently engaged and they could expect visits from her parents. In any case, it was about time the old, scruffy bathroom was replaced—'people would think it's not clean' (Polly Camilleri).

The family pooled its resources, and the unemployed sons started work on the bathroom. They chose ceramic tiles for the walls and floor—they couldn't afford marble, and even if they could, they'd worry that neighbours would think they were getting ideas above their station. Again, this is a manifstation of the egalitarian *ethos*, which sanctions against those who get 'too big'—*jikbru*—or become 'cold'—*jitkesaħ*. They scoured the showrooms for an affordable bathroom suite in white porcelain, that included toilet, bath and bidet. Its installation made the house *iktar pulit*—smarter—and *iktar nadif*—cleaner.

Kitchens were also an important area for the consumption of household goods and decor. They were the main areas for sociability of household members and those *ta'ġewwa*—insiders—but were also increasingly used for visitors, surpassing the *salott* as the primary area for entertaining. In particular, many of the more 'respectable' Valletta women would organise *coffee mornings* which normally took place among groups of friends but would also involve invitations to particuarly respectable guests. For example, Mary Dupont organised *coffee mornings* to which she invited a client for whom she had made dresses, who was also a television celebrity. The invitation had pleased Ray, she said, because 'having her come makes us seem better'.

These meetings were held in the kitchen, which as a consequence needed to be well-appointed and fashionable. More often than not, this meant conforming to the latest European—particularly Italian—styles. Indeed, when Mary Dupont arranged her old kitchen, she had found a local carpenter who could accurately copy the designs from a brochure she had picked up at one of the show-rooms. The actual kitchens had been too expensive, but an accurate copy was just as good. In the terminology of consumption outlined above, Mary Dupont's kitchen was doubly appropriated. A popular mass-produced design had been appropriated from a design brochure, and then placed in the context of the Dupont kitchen. That the new and 'simulated' Italian kitchen received approval was confirmed by Doris Mifsud, one of Mary's closest friends and another *coffee morning* guest, hiring the same local carpenter to fit a kitchen for her.

The significance of consuming European goods cannot be underestimated. Particularly for Nationalists, for whom Europe was also a political project, it was seen as the fount of all things of value in high culture, music, art, and literature. This sophistication was evoked by the repeated use of Beethoven's 'Ode to Joy' on Italian television—the main channels watched by most Maltese. *Għand Dupont*, when this piece of music appeared, with accompanying graphic incorporating the circled twelve stars of Europe, they would turn the volume up, and often remarked on how beautiful the piece was. Not merely composed in Europe, and so somehow representative of Europeanness, this piece of music had become its very epitome, and a stirring emotional reminder of Nationalist aspirations to European entry. The DuPonts clearly bought in to the imagined community of Europe, with its recognisable constellation of symbols of identity (Shore 1993).

The affirmation of European superiority, however, was not limited to the world of high cultural sophistication, but also related to life-style aspirations and *habitus*. Consuming European goods not only conferred European identity, but also distinctions of social standing. European goods were considered higher quality than those locally-produced, a distinction which applied to both food-stuffs and consumer items. In shops, a distinction was made, using the familiar motif of inclusion and exclusion, between goods *ta'barra*—from outside—and those *ta'Malta*—from Malta. In this context, however, *ta'barra* was an affirmation of quality, rather than problematic outsiderhood. *Ta'barra* generally meant European. In 1992, 37.5% of all imports were from the European Union (European Commission 1993), which in turn meant that the high-quality unit of consumption was the European unit.

Alongside the pursuit of European goods was a substantial focus on the originality of household furnishings and decor. In her survey of household consumption in the southern Maltese village of Zurrieq, Cachia notes the emphasis informants placed on the originality of their houses (1998: 163–164). One woman, a school teacher, refused to allow Cachia to photograph its interior in case the style was copied. Indeed, there was a certain amount of friction between Mary Dupont and her friend Doris after she decided to use the same carpenter for her kitchen. Originality confirms a particularly skilful judgement of taste, and a particularly meaningful appropriation.

The Zurrieq school teacher went on to explain the origins of her decor:

> We brought it [the wallpaper] with us from England when we were there on holiday, for we wanted few people to have wallpaper like ours. It turned out to be a good thing for we had more to choose from, unlike here . . . I like houses which seem to be in Europe, in the north. Since we cannot live there, at least I try to make things in a way which remind me of the places we have been to . . . (Ibid: 163)

This demonstrates both the appeal of Europe as a stylistic influence, and its status as a good place to consume, with plenty of choice. It also demonstrates the extent to which the consumption of household goods articulates with that of overseas travel. Like other areas of consumption, overseas travel expanded in Malta in the late eighties and early nineties, and fuelled the pursuit of both European and original items to adorn the Maltese house.

The constellation of influences promoting and enabling the consumption of 'original', 'tasteful' and ultimately 'respectable' European goods, however, were also the elements of European influence seen as most problematic. At an economic level, the impetus to consume led to an erosion of family solidity and household unity. The other influences, of travel, television and advertising were also seen as erosive of 'traditional' morality. Through travelling to—particularly northern—Europe, Maltese were exposed, it was argued, to a different morality, where the family was becoming less important. By watching Italian television they were exposed to its overt sexuality and again to images of eroded and immoral family life—particularly in the frequently-broadcast and very popular soap operas. Many of these were South American, dubbed into Italian, and depicted a sexual freedom that worried many social commentators. There was a profound ambivalence, then, towards the comsumption of Europe, and the expansion of its consumer goods into the Maltese market. On the one hand, household consumption was part of the process of shoring up the beleaguered Maltese family. By focusing on the symbolisation of family unity in the house itself, people were able to demonstrate the maintenance of 'proper' respectability. They were simultaneously able to participate in the pursuit of social status for its own sake, through the pursuit of taste and social distinction. On the other hand, the increase in consumption signalled an increased materialism that was seen as dangerously erosive. It exacerbated financial anxiety, and ultimately caused both unhappiness and social division. Where once households had happily coexisted, they were now divided by arguments about decor and accusations of neighbours copying each others' 'original' styles. As one elderly man from *L-Arċipierku* put it to me:

> In the old days, we had nothing. We were poor, but we were happy. You didn't get all this stress and anxiety. Nowadays, everybody's worried, and it's all because of money. We didn't have anything—we were happy. Now they have everything, and they want more. It's nice to have things, but materialism is destroying Malta.

A SENSE OF LIMITS

Clearly, when it comes to consumption, the brute facts of material wealth are a significant factor. Although consumption can be used to produce and communicate meanings of respectability and social standing, the capacity to do this is not equal for all people. Without the money to do the consuming, the productive appropriation of material goods is impossible. It is a point which has sometimes been overlooked in studies of consumption, but is an entirely pertinent one (Thomas pers. comm. 1995). Such limitations determine that only certain types of person can engage, for example, in the pursuit of originality through travel, or of exclusive and fashionable Italian marbled bathrooms. Others, like the Camilleris, must search for appropriate mass-produced goods. Indeed, in deciding to refurbish their bathroom, the Camilleris were faced with a difficult set of choices. Not only did they have to find appropriately-priced tiles and bathroom suite, but had to make critical decisions about how to finance the refurbishment. Using their sons as labour, rather than hiring in local craftsmen, for example, meant that while they were working on the bathroom, they were not earning. From this perspective, the bathroom was doubly expensive, but a worthwhile choice in their eyes. These kinds of choices were not the only limitations faced by those such as the Camilleris, from relatively low income households in lower

Valletta. Others were created by their lack of education and sophistication, and particularly their lack of connections within 'polite'—*pulit*—or 'high'—*għoli*—society.

Although the categories around which social standing and social stratification are organised are relative, and produced through their everyday mobilisation and the social practices or *habitus* associated with them, this does not mean that they do not produce and reproduce a structural effect. Appeal to a practice-oriented approach to stratification does not imply a transcendent freedom from the limitations of structure. Rather, it locates structure in its production and reproduction, such that structure becomes an abstraction or generalisation of social practices that is available to either the social scientist or the people about whom they write (Bourdieu 1990: 66). This way of approaching stratification moves us away from a vision of the world as made up of automata simply playing out a grand structural scheme, and locates it in people's practices and their own understanding of those practices. This abstraction of social structure expresses and is experienced as a set of limitations to potential practice (Giddens 1987: 61). In Valletta, the limitations are expressed in terms of the same metaphors of inclusion and exclusion we encountered in the last chapter. Thus, the *pulit* or 'polite' strata are thought of as being in some senses 'in', with the rest of society, *il-poplu* or 'the people' being 'out'.

If the *pulit* are 'in' it is because they are thought to be part of a central influential and decision-making group at the centre of Maltese society. Such people are referred to through the same metaphors as those used to express masculine sociability and the solidarity of friendship. The *pulit* groups, then, are *tal-klikka*—of the clique—*tal-qalba*—of the heart—or *tal-qaqoċċa*—of the artichoke heart. Within these groups, as with the *klikek* in bars such as *Għand Lawrenz* favours are readily granted and assistance given, except that because they are more influential, they have more to give. It is therefore assumed that people who have connections in the *pulit* groups are given well-paid jobs, have direct access to government resources, and are protected by the judiciary. This image of clientelism, patronage and even corruption is explored in greater detail in chapter six.

The 'inclusion' of the *pulit* is determined by education and family ties; by employment and links of friendship. Education implies not only the cultivation of taste but also has bound up with it the accumulation of social ties. Malta has a well developed system of private education, most of which is run by the Church. Places at Church schools are limited, and allocated by lottery. Education is free, but schools often request 'donations' which are not only prohibitive to certain sections of the population, but also give rise to rumours about the fairness of the lotteries. The non-Church private schools not only require fees, but are also often selective by social standing. At these more elite schools, only children of particular, influential families will be admitted, allowing them to forge friendships and alliances that can be drawn upon subsequently when these well-educated Maltese go on to become business-people or professionals. These ties of family and friendship are thought by *il-poplu* to produce a kind of closed group or *klikka* at the centre of Maltese society, to which they have no access.

Whilst the category *pulit* society conveys a notion of distinction and taste, *poplu* literally means 'the people'. It has connotations of a 'mass' or 'popular' cultural group, and therefore also connotes what Scott would refer to as a command situation (1996), whereby *il-poplu* are the populace—the plebiscite over whom the *pulit* group governs. Indeed *poplu* is not only contrasted with *pulit*, but also with *il-gvern*—a term which combines both 'Government' and 'State'. The opposition of *poplu* and *gvern* has an historical provenance. In the 1950s, Beeley noted rural Maltese notions of government, which revolved around the anonymous, opaque and threatening image of *il-gvern* (1959: 54). At that time, *il-gvern* was the Government of the British colonial administration, but even before that—back to 1530—the Maltese had been governed by administrations over which they had little control, and must have been regarded as opaque and threatening. Even after Independence, this image of *gvern* as distant, threatening and unaccountable has been maintained, particularly during times when the political party in power is not the party with which one sides. The next chapter deals with just such an occasion—when under a Labour administration, the predominantly Nationalist area of *L-Arċipierku* was demolished.

NOTES

[18] The notion of stratification has been criticised for giving too neutral an account of social division. Where exploitation or brutality occur, 'stratification' seems to suggest a more harmonious co-existence. It has likewise been criticised for implying a relatively static set of relationships between social groups. However, as Scott has argued, such criticisms of the metaphor are born of an ignorance of the complexities and dynamism of geological stratification:
'Strata do not simply lie on top of one another in neat layers like a jam sandwich. they are compressed and distorted into complex shapes that can be understood only through painstaking research and with an analytical imagination that is able to reconstruct the processes through which they have been formed. Indeed, it is precisely the *complexity* of geological formations that makes the metaphor of social stratification so appropriate.' (1996: 192).

[19] The colloquial Maltese for 'teacher' is also *Sir*, which means that in the case of *Sur* Dupont, there was only a slight lexical side-step from teacher to 'sir'.

[20] This figure may well be lower than it should be, because of the prevalence of undeclared employment and income.

CHAPTER FIVE

Nostalgia and Modernisation

> Their compulsion to gather together, their pathological fear of loneliness extends on past the threshold of sleep; so that when they turn the corner, as we all must, as we all have done and do—some more often than others—to find ourselves on the street ... You know the street I mean, child. The street of the 20th century, at whose far end or turning—we hope—is some sense of home or safety. But no guarantees. A street we are put at the wrong end of, for reasons best known to the agents who put us there. If there are agents. But a street we must walk. (Thomas Pynchon, *V*: 323–324)

The demolition of large parts of the low-lying *Arċipierku* in 1972 was seen as a major trauma in the history of St Paul's parish, and of the *Pawlini* as a whole. With this act, as far as they were concerned, a community was destroyed, a neighbourhood dispersed and families displaced. The area was remembered with nostalgia as a kind of Edenic paradise, that was unified and harmonious. Its demolition was seen as a moment when the people of *L-Arċipierku* fell foul of the despotic 1970s Labour Party leader, Dom Mintoff. Although the demolition seems to have been in keeping with the Labour Party's post-Independence modernisation policies, it was regarded by many *Pawlini* as being politically motivated. *L-Arċipierku* had been an area dominated by Nationalist supporters, and this was the reason, they suspected, it had been demolished ahead of other 'low' areas in Valletta.

This chapter examines people's memories of and nostalgia towards *L-Arċipierku,* and people's memories of its demolition. It traces, in the collective and social memory of *L-Arċipierku,* the invocation of an Edenic past that is used as a strategy for criticising the state. In particular, it is used to make the state both culpable for destroying the Edenic past, and responsible for restoring it. In the Maltese context, it is a strategy through which *il-poplu*—those who regarded themselves as 'the people'—criticised the aloof, self-serving and sometimes vindictive clique at the centre of government.

22ND JULY 1972—THE DEMOLITION OF *L-ARĊIPIERKU*

In the 'low-town' area of *L-Arċipierku*, the heart of St Paul's parish and home of many *Pawlini*, the moment had come for demolition. Swinging ball demolition crews were followed up by bulldozers that inched their way round the narrow streets to tidy up the rubble. Demolition began on Old Hospital Street. In other parts of *L-Arċipierku*, people packed up their households onto open trucks, to transport their lives and families to other parts of the city, or to places outside Valletta. Cikku Brincat—known locally as Cikku *tal-Ċekk*—'of the cheque'—hired a truck with a winching rig, to save the statue of St Paul that had stood for as long as people could remember on the street corner where the Valletta plateau ends and dips down into *L-Arċipierku*. As patron saint St Paul had stood there, marking his dominion over the area. Now that the area was being torn down, he had to be saved. When the statue was safely in the back of the truck, Leli Farrugia, a local 'character' posed for his photograph on the pedestal where the saint had stood, himself adopting the characteristic pose—with the right hand held aloft, preaching to the Maltese nation. Then came the bulldozers.

The demolition was part of the then Labour government's post-war, post-Independence modernisation policy. Critical of the British colonial government's *laissez faire* policies, they saw the future in housing and welfare reform. *L-Arċipierku* had been demarcated a 'slum' and fit for redevelopment, although many local people disagreed. They saw scope for refurbishment and rehabilitation, with resources put into improvement, rather than demolition. The people of *L-Arċipierku*, by and large, wished to remain where they were. In the event, their old houses were replaced by a new and modern apartment block, but these apartments were not reserved for people who had previously lived there. Although some managed to obtain housing in the new blocks, and some of the *Arċipierku* houses remained, the majority were dispersed—to other parts of Valletta, or other parts of Malta.

By the early 1990s, the social ties that had been cut by the demolition were largely restored, but memories of *L-Arċipierku* persisted. Social ties were maintained through frequent contact in

Valletta's social spaces—the food market, St Paul's parish church, and local bars—where those who remained in *L-Arċipierku* met up with those who had been displaced. Here, stories of *L-Arċipierku* as it had been, and the circumstances of its demolition, were discussed at length with a profound nostalgia. The memories resembled those of my Maltese tutor, Peter Schembri, whose low-town childhood had involved street football and trips to the red light 'Gut' to spy on sailors and their escorts (see chapter two). Like Peter's of the *Due Balli*, the memories of *L-Arċipierku* painted a picture of poverty offset by communal solidarity. Although times had been hard, claimed my informants, they had been good times, when everyone had been together. These memories lived on in fragmentary artefacts—photographs, press clippings and pieces of masonry kept by those who had been displaced. In Connerton's terms, these were the products of an inscribing practice of social or collective memory, which stores images, texts or artefacts as *aides memoires* to assist future reflection or recollection (Connerton 1989). Such artefacts were brought *Għand Lawrenz*, and taken out from cupboards in people's *sallotts* or sitting rooms, as I sat with them to discuss their lives and experiences. Whenever photos were produced *Għand Lawrenz*, people would huddle round to identify who was on them. Different claims were made about neighbours or relatives in the old *Arċipierku*:

> That's uncle Leli, he used to live by the old well.
>
> No, no . . . that's Guzi Chetcuti—he lived on St Nicholas Street.

A kind of game emerged, in which people would test each other about their knowledge—and memories—of *L-Arċipierku* as it had been. This game of testing each other's knowledge was part of a process of establishing the credentials of people's attachment to *L-Arċipierku*. With that attachment came retrospective neighbourliness, and an acknowledgement of rightful inclusion within *Pawlini* circles. Even younger people, who were too young to remember *L-Arċipierku*, got involved in this process. A pair of twins, who were only fourteen in 1993, and so could not have remembered the area or its demolition, would spend hours testing each other about who had lived where, and which shops had been on which street corners in *L-Arċipierku*. Their accounts were checked against the memories of their parents, who had lived there, with the loser of any disputes having to suffer an inevitable teasing. Their games marked the process whereby the collective memory of a collectively-experienced event became transformed into social memory of an event which still held social significance but was no longer directly remembered. The lengths they went to ensure correct transmission of the memory indicates its significance to them. Demonstrating correct knowledge of *L-Arċipierku* became the means by which they, among others, would confirm their origins in *L-Arċipierku*. With this went not only a pride at originating in a worthy community, but also a kind of 'tough guy' reputation that went along with low-town Valletta.

The lengthy discussions of how *L-Arċipierku* had been always made reference to its demolition, which was a pivotal moment in many people's lives. It served as a reference-point for understanding the relationship between *poplu* and *gvern*—both acknowledging and criticising the sense of limits to action that this distinction defined. Produced through the everyday structuration discussed in the last chapter, this sense of limits pitted 'the people' against an opaque and sometimes vindictive 'government'. Remembering *L-Arċipierku* and its demolition was remembering a moment of injustice where the concerns of the latter over-rode those of the former. However, it was also a means of criticising the particular policies of the Labour government that had overseen the demolition. In particular, memories of the demolition contributed to the vilification of Dom Mintoff, then Labour Prime Minister, who many from *L-Arċipierku* saw as personally responsible for the destruction of their community. This linked a general critique of the state with a particular objection to party politics. Finally, the memories informed an evaluation of modernization and progress. Accounts of the demolition were juxtaposed with those of how the area had used to be. In doing so, they produced a nostalgic account of *L-Arċipierku* which was held up as a model of 'traditional' morality and community values—a kind of Edenic paradise that was destroyed by the impetus to modernize. The old *Arċipierku*, in comparison to early nineties Valletta, was a safe place free from crime, where neighbourhood reciprocity and moral obligations of family and community were assured. This contrasted with fears about present and future, which were characterised by an anxiety about the seeping, erosive effects of materialism and modern life. Memories of

L-Arċipierku therefore juxtaposed not only *poplu* and *gvern* but also Nationalists and Labourites, past and present.

THE NOSTALGIC CONSTRUCTION OF COMMUNITY

This process of narrating *L-Arċipierku* constitutes what I have called elsewhere the 'nostalgic construction of community' (Mitchell 1998a). As such it produced an almost stereotyped account of what *L-Arċipierku* had been like, that constituted a normative statement about what all Maltese neighbourhood communities should look like—with a profound co-operative *ethos* and a strong sense of solidarity. Cohen has suggested that such stereotyped, or symbolic constructions of community can serve as useful vehicles for the critique of state intervention (1982, 1985, 1987). In a statement defining the terms for the then embryonic anthropology of locality, he argued that the purpose of the exercise was to examine 'indigenous views of social association; *and* the impingement of the wider world on local identity' (1982: 2, emphasis in original).

This suggests that rather than seeing stereotypes as incorrect or problematic representations of a more authentic social reality, we should treat them as part of social reality in themselves. Moreover, we should treat them as strategic acts—as practices aimed at resisting the state and wider political process (Herzfeld 1985). Asserting unity makes attachment to locality a powerful political resource, perhaps doubly so when the unity is in the past. By saying 'we used to be like this', people can forge a substantial critique of the present (Mitchell 1998a). However, in the case of *L-Arċipierku,* the image of a positive past is always tempered by the recognition that the past had been difficult—a time of relative poverty. The nostalgic critiques of the state, therefore, were based on an inherently ambivalent attitude towards the past that sees it as both glorious and essentially flawed. Herzfeld (1997) characterises such critiques, based on a form of strategic nostalgia, as 'structural nostalgia', arguing that their effectiveness derives from a discourse on the past that is shared by both 'people' and the state. This shared discourse creates both legitimate authority for, and a means of resisting, the intrusions of the state.

Both the state and those who seek to resist it refer to an Edenic past, before the state existed, or intervened. For the state, this justifies intrusion into people's lives. If the post-Edenic present is characterised by a moral fall, then the state must intervene to maintain order. For those who resist, however, the fall was not abated by the intervention of the state but actually caused by it. This means that the structural nostalgia for a pre-state Eden can be used as a strategic resource to simultaneously emphasise the state's culpability and its responsibility to make amends in the present. Herzfeld uses his time-honoured example of the Cretan sheep-thieves to demonstrate this process. For them, the state should never have intervened in their lives and practices, but given that it did, it can now be held responsible for the difficulties they have, and called upon for strategic benefit.

As with Herzfeld's kleptomaniac shepherds, the former inhabitants of *L-Arċipierku* used their nostalgia as a strategic resource to make the state culpable for the present-day decline. The suggestion was that before *L-Arċipierku* was demolished, its inhabitants could look after themselves—or each other—despite being poor, and despite it being a 'low' or 'rough' area. Indeed, the reputation for being a 'rough' area contributed to what Herzfeld describes as a 'fellowship of the flawed', in which moral integrity is claimed alongside an acknowledgement of imperfection or even moral transgression. In *L-Arċipierku* memory, this manifest itself as a certain pride in the ability of local young men to physically defend the territory, by beating up outsiders. With the demolition of *L-Arċipierku,* however, this fellowship had been eroded, and such physical defence of the neighbourhood was no longer possible. Consequently, what had been unified and protected was now dispersed and vulnerable. Because the state was responsible for demolishing the community, it was therefore seen as responsible for protecting its inhabitants now that they could no longer defend themselves. Paradoxically, then, the criticisms of the state's first intervention led to calls for further intervention to make amends. What emerged were calls for action such as that described in chapter two, when the inhabitants of Valletta asked 'How can we *really* give life to the city of Valletta?'—how can we rehabilitate the city, and recreate the now-demolished sense of community.

Structural nostalgia establishes the terms for a mutual critique of *poplu* and *gvern*. On the one hand *il-gvern* could refer to the 'lowness' of the *Arċipierku*, and the need for housing reform in Malta's post-Independence democracy. From this viewpoint, the demolitions were a triumph of modernisation and social welfare. The state had successfully intervened to eradicate sub-standard housing, and improve the living conditions of its citizens. On the other hand, the people of *L-Arċipierku* promoted the memory of the area as a model of unified community which should not have been demolished. From this viewpoint, the demolition was simply another example of the excesses of the state, and the lengths to which it would go in pursuit of the spurious benefits of modernization. The memories of *L-Arċipierku*, then, contributed to a thoroughgoing critique of both the state and modernisation.

In the context of *L-Arċipierku*, the situation was complicated by party politics, and the fact that the state to which its former inhabitants were appealing in the early nineties was not the same as that which had demolished *L-Arċipierku*. Although *il-gvern* refers to 'the state', it also refers to the government who are in power at any particular moment. This is partly because of the extremely polarised nature of Maltese party politics, and the personalisation of bureaucracy, discussed in the next chapter. This in turn ensures that when one party is in power, its supporters and members have better access to state resources than those of the opposition. The memories of *L-Arċipierku*, then, were not only contributing to a critique of the state in general, but to the particular state—or *gvern*—in power at the time of the demolition—the Labour Party.

L-ARĊIPIERKU—A 'LOW' PLACE

L-Arċipierku means 'The Archipelago', but the origins of the name are unclear.[21] One enterprising informant suggested that perhaps the reason for the name was that just as in an archipelago of islands, in *L-Arċipierku* you had lots of small units close together. The streets had been very narrow, and so there were lots of balconies, lots of dwellings, very close together. So close, in fact, that one could reach out with one's hand from one side to the other. Although perhaps not a correct etymology, this reveals the difference in character between *L-Arċipierku* and the higher parts of Valletta. The latter were characterised by wide streets lined with large, spacious and airy town-houses. By contrast, *L-Arċipierku* is characterised in the memories of people who used to live there, as a crowded, confined space with very narrow streets lined with *kerrejiet*.

The *kerrejja*—pl. *kerrejjiet*—was a kind of primitive tenement building, originally built to house the servants and functionaries who provided service to the city's households and institutions, be they port facilities, religious communities or governmental offices. Built around a central, open courtyard, they comprised a system of small rooms connected by narrow landings. Each floor had between ten and twelve rooms, so that a four-storey *kerrejja* would have over forty rooms. Each room was occupied by a single family, and each landing had a single, communal hygiene facility: a tap and an open chute into which sewage was tipped. Until after the second world war, family sizes in Malta were large, which meant that the *kerrejjiet* must have been extremely crowded. A 1970 report prepared by the church-based Social Action Movement highlighted the overcrowded conditions of Malta *kerrejjiet*. The total of 262 *kerrejjiet* contained 3,159 rooms, 2,636 of which were inhabited. Of the 1,266 households that lived in these *kerrejjiet*, 355 occupied a single room, 574 lived in two rooms, 242 in 3, 70 in 4 rooms, 23 in 5 rooms and only two lived in six rooms (Centre for Social Studies, Malta 1970: 19). This meant exceptionally overcrowded conditions. In Valletta, the situation was the worst of all. In 1945, a Government report had stated that 8,600 people in Valletta were living in overcrowded conditions, this defined as a situation where two or more people lived in each room (Harrison & Hubbard 1945). These overcrowded living conditions entered the national social policy agenda with the publication of this report, which was based on wartime bomb damage surveys. The harbour areas had been a major target for Axis bombing, and much of the housing had been destroyed. Compared to the dockyard towns, Valletta got off relatively lightly, but the surveys nevertheless provided an opportunity to create a strategic building plan that would rid the city of properties described in the report as 'obsolescent'. Among the obsolescent areas were large parts of *L-Arċipierku*, condemned by the Department of Health as 'slums' (Harrison & Hubbard, 1945: 64).

The category 'slum' was borrowed from the English, to become part of the Maltese lexicon. Rather than being a neutral, descriptive term, *slum* is also a moral category—in Maltese as in English. It is an evaluative category, based on the notions of respectability and the axis of stratification between 'high' and 'low', *għoli* and *baxx* outlined in the previous chapter. Slums were thought of as 'dirty' places which lacked proper sanitation. Because they were small and overcrowded they tended to encourage the loud and vulgar behaviour associated with 'rude' or 'rough' *ħamalli*, and perhaps even worse, were associated with a scandalous disregard for—or inability to regard—acceptable norms of personal privacy, and particularly a tendency towards bodily exposure.

The issue of whether or not *L-Arċipierku* was a *slum* was hotly contested both at the time of the demolition and subsequently. Throughout July 1972, the Maltese press was full of debate over the fate of the neighbourhood, and on July 8th a long anonymous letter appeared in its defence:

> Instead of beginning with knocking down the worst slums in Malta, the government wants to knock down some houses in *L-Arċipierku* which in comparison with the rest of the slums are in a good condition. (*In-Nazzjon Tagħna* 8/7/72)

Here, the category 'slum' is explicitly contrasted with 'house', to emphasise the integrity, quality and morality of *L-Arċipierku*—they were 'houses', not 'slums'. In a similar vein, a *Times of Malta* article of 21st July refers also to the quality of the community which is about to be destroyed, and the cleanliness of its houses:

> 'The Arċipierku ... is a stable community ... with strong interpersonal links and friendships and a sense of communal pride. Most houses are kept scrupulously clean ...' (*The Times of Malta* 21/7/72)

This assertion of strong community links is preceded by a defence of the *Arċipierku* people's knowledge of moral issues such as sex and religion. Spiritual cleanliness is reaffirmed by the appeals to physical cleanliness, and contributes to an account of *L-Arċipierku* as a respectable area. However, for many high-town residents, low-town areas such as *L-Arċipierku* were—even in the early nineties—regarded as *slums*, or at least 'low' places. A local banker revealed a significant tension between affirming his own 'high' status through the designation of 'low-town' as a *slum*, and his unwillingness, ultimately, to admit that modern Malta still had 'slum' areas:

> Well, I suppose like any big city, it's got its slum areas ... Mind you, Valletta's not a big city. And it's not really slums. We don't really have any slums here any more. But that area down there—what we call the Archipelago. You'd call it a low class area. It's a low area.

His swift qualification placed the real *slums* of *L-Arċipierku* firmly in the past. Some of the houses were still very cramped, and lacked proper facilities, he said, but it wasn't as bad as it used to be. He asked me to imagine living as a family of six in a single room with no bathroom, and stressed the moral consequences of such a situation. The families of the old *Arċipierku* must have been prone to *skandlu*—the over-exposure of the naked body, particularly to the opposite sex. Such a conclusion confirmed the area's low status, and it was a common assumption that the lower parts of town were characterised not only by *skandlu* but also—in some families at least—by too much inter-marriage. *L-Arċipierku* was said to be *gerfix*—confused—a category that also has connotations of inter-breeding or even incest.

From the point of view of *Arċipierku* residents, however, neither incest nor *skandlu* were prevalent. Whilst it was true that the area had been characterised by a number of large families that frequently intermarried, this was a positive feature of integrated community life, rather than a threat to moral integrity. As argued in the last chapter, it was the elites who were seen as sexual miscreants. David Chetcuti, a man who had lived as a child in an *Arċipierku kerrejja* during the 1960s explained how *skandlu* had been avoided. Every time his sisters and mother wanted to wash, the boys would be taken outside by their father, and they would clean themselves in the corner of their room. Similarly, *skandlu* would be avoided when any of the women wanted to go to the toilet. They would do so behind a curtain and the boys would be told to go onto the landing. The waste was disposed of in a bucket that was poured down the communal drainage point. This way, exposure to both neighbours and family members was avoided. The converse would occur when the men of the family needed to wash or go to the toilet. The women would leave, to let them perform their ablutions without exposure. Thus, despite the potential for exposure of the body to the opposite sex, as suggested by the single-room, quasi-communal existence with its lack of a private bathroom, the potential for *skandlu* had been properly managed in the *Arċipierku kerrejja* in which the Chetcuti family had lived.

As David told me about this, *Għand Lawrenz*, another former *Arċipierku* resident, Charlie Mangion told of similar practices in his family's *kerrejja*. There had been no *skandlu in L-Arċipierku*, he said. Rather, *skandlu* was characteristic of living conditions after the demolition. Conditions in the temporary accommodation provided for the displaced were pitiful, he said, echoing an anti-demolition press report of the time:

> Numerous families that today live in houses suitable for humans, are being sent to indecent places with no sanitation and are being forced to live in a way that is totally immoral for families. The police and soldiers are being sent to bring out the belongings from inside these people's houses, to house them in hutches. (*In-Nazzjon Tagħna*, 17/7/72)

This focus on the morality of the former *Arċipierku* compared to the immorality of subsequent housing conditions fed debates about the demolition at the time, but were also a focus of people's memories. Charlie Mangion went on to describe the consequences of eviction for his family. It had been a particular problem for his sister-in-law. His elder brother, Michael, had married while the family still lived in *L-Arċipierku*, and he and his wife had taken a room close to his parents. However, when the buildings were demolished, the whole family, including Michael and his wife, were moved from separate accommodation to a single dwelling—a small two-room apartment in upper Valletta. In this new house, Michael's wife had no privacy, particularly from her father-in-law. There, she had been scandalised because she had no privacy. No doubt also traumatised by having her familiar environment and marital home destroyed, she had a nervous breakdown, and was ill for many years. Before the move, there had been no problems. Rather, the destruction of *L-Arċipierku* had been the cause of difficulties, and had created the *skandlu* that affected Michael's wife.

Charlie's sister-in-law was not the only casualty of the demolition. Seeing no future for life outside *L-Arċipierku*, David Chetcuti had emigrated to Canada for ten years, only returning when his brother's long-term psychiatric difficulties had become acute. He blamed the demolition for triggering these difficulties, as well as severe anxiety problems in his mother. Others suffered even worse. Leli Farrugia, who everybody remembered fondly from the photograph of him posing in St Paul's place, had died because of the upheaval. As David Chetcuti put it, *kissruna*—'they broke/smashed us'.

These descriptions of trauma and dislocation were juxtaposed to—and justified by—complimentary descriptions of *L-Arċipierku* as it had been prior to destruction. In order to bolster claims that 'they' had 'smashed us', the people of the area must also elaborate exactly what it was that had been smashed. Through nostalgic eyes they presented an image of completeness and unity—of community in an idealised, almost stereotyped form.

ONE FAMILY—ONE HOUSEHOLD

The idealisation of *L-Arċipierku* constituted a 'nostalgic construction of community', that mobilised a variety of symbols to emphasise the unity of the neighbourhood that had been demolished. Among these, the most potent were representations of household and family, themselves embodied in the physical manifestation of the house itself (see chapter four). Linking *L-Arċipierku* with family and household established its moral ascendency over the present. The family is the primary moral unit in Malta, and uncertainty about the future in general is more often than not framed in terms of anxiety about the future of the family (see chapter three). Since the 1970s, there have been various attempts by academic, church and state authorities to trace, deny or decry the 'decline' of the family in Malta (KANA 1980, Tabone 1987). The family is seen as the bulwark of traditional Maltese life, and the main point of comparison between Malta and Europe. European countries with high rates of divorce and separation are seen as morally bankrupt, and potentially polluting. Recent moves to introduce divorce in Malta have caused concern, and rising separation rates are seen as a sign of impending social disaster. In the light of these concerns, the use of family to define *L-Arċipierku* as community of the past produces an image of Edenic purity. Moreover, because family and household are organised around the categories 'inside' and 'outside'—*ġewwa* and *barra*—the association of *L-Arċipierku* with family and household also defines 'insiders' and 'outsiders' to the area.

Of the women I got to know during fieldwork, one of the most friendly and informative was Carmen Brincat. She was born and brought up in *L-Arċipierku*, and was a prominent figure in people's memories of the area. Her family was large and locally influential. Her husband had been instrumental in saving the statue of St Paul from the demolition, and was well-liked. He had organised a youth football team with sponsorship from a wealthy national business. This earned him the nick-name Cikku *tal-Ċekk*—'of the cheque'. Carmen was 69 in 1993, and still lived in her *Arċipierku* flat. She had been lucky during the 1970s, in that her house had been spared demolition. But her neighbours and friends had been displaced, and she would tell me at length about the affects this had had on the local community. Her version of the community stressed family and household. *L-Arċipierku*, she said, had been *bħal familja waħda* —'like one family'.

Her family had been one of four large families which had dominated *L-Arċipierku*, and had frequently intermarried. The Brincats were related to the Chetcutis. Carmen Brincat's husband's mother had married twice—her first marriage being to Censu Chetcuti, David Chetcuti's paternal great-uncle. This meant that David Chetcuti and Carmen Brincat's children were step-cousins (see figure 1). More complex were the relationships between Charlie Mangion and other inhabitants of *L-Arċipierku*. First, Charlie was related to his wife Censina not just by marriage, but also via a marriage in their parents'

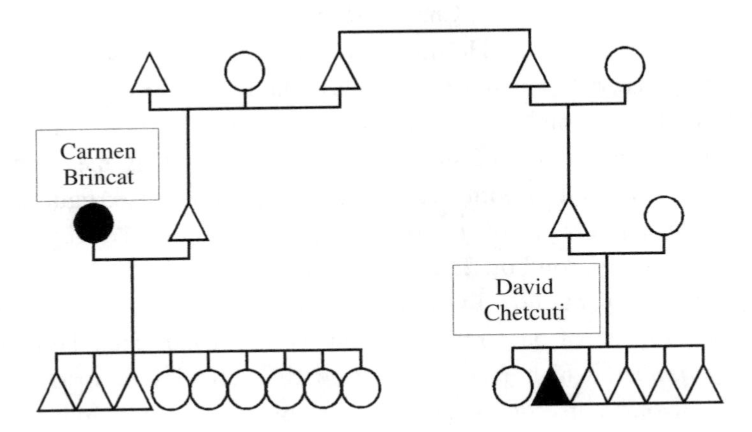

Figure 1 *L-Arċipierku* as *Familja Waħda:* relationships between Carmen Brincat and David Chetcuti

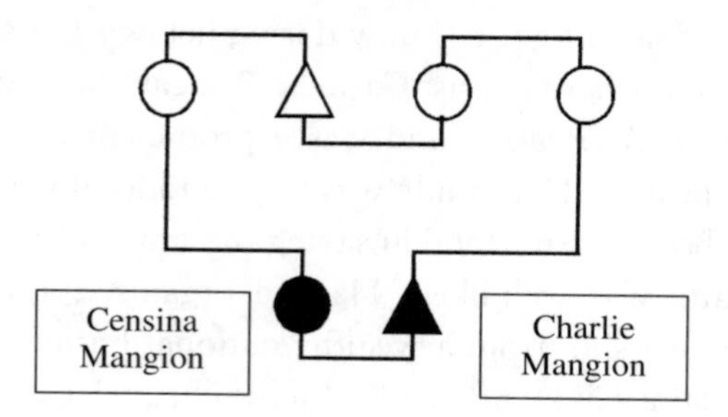

Figure 2 *L-Arċipierku* as *Familja Waħda:* relationships between Charlie Mangion and Censina Mangion

generation. His mother's sister had married Censina's mother's brother. This meant that they shared an aunt and an uncle. For Charlie, Censina's uncle Ganni was his uncle by marriage, or *ziju ta'rispett*—lit. 'uncle of respect'. For Censina, Charlie's aunt Carmen was her aunt by marriage or *zija ta'rispett* (see figure 2).

This is a clear example of two people being related in two ways because of repeated intermarriage. But the Mangions' relations with other families in *L-Arċipierku* were also significant. Charlie was related not only to Censina's family, but also to that of Freddie Cachia, another elderly person who I would visit to discuss *L-Arċipierku*. Through Freddie, Charlie was further related to the Camilleri family who were introduced in the last chapter, in the context of bathroom refurbishment. Freddie was Charlie Mangion's uncle, his sister having married Charlie's father. He was also related to the Camilleri family. One of his sisters had married Pawlu Camilleri's step-brother, born to Leli Camilleri's second wife, Kellina. Moreover, Pawlu's wife Polly was the first cousin of one of Freddie's sisters-in-law. This meant that Freddie was related to both Pawlu and Polly Camilleri (see figure 3).

For the people of *L-Arċipierku*, these inter-marriages were something to be proud of. They confirmed that the area had been not only figuratively, but literally, *familja waħda*. This was consolidated by the extended use of bilateral family nicknames or *laqmijiet*. Through these *laqmijiet*, which referred back to the activities or origins of certain pivotal antecedents, people's attachment to a few influential families was demonstrated. For example, Censu Dalli, a regular *Għand Lawrenz* and former *Arċipierku* dweller, was known as Censu

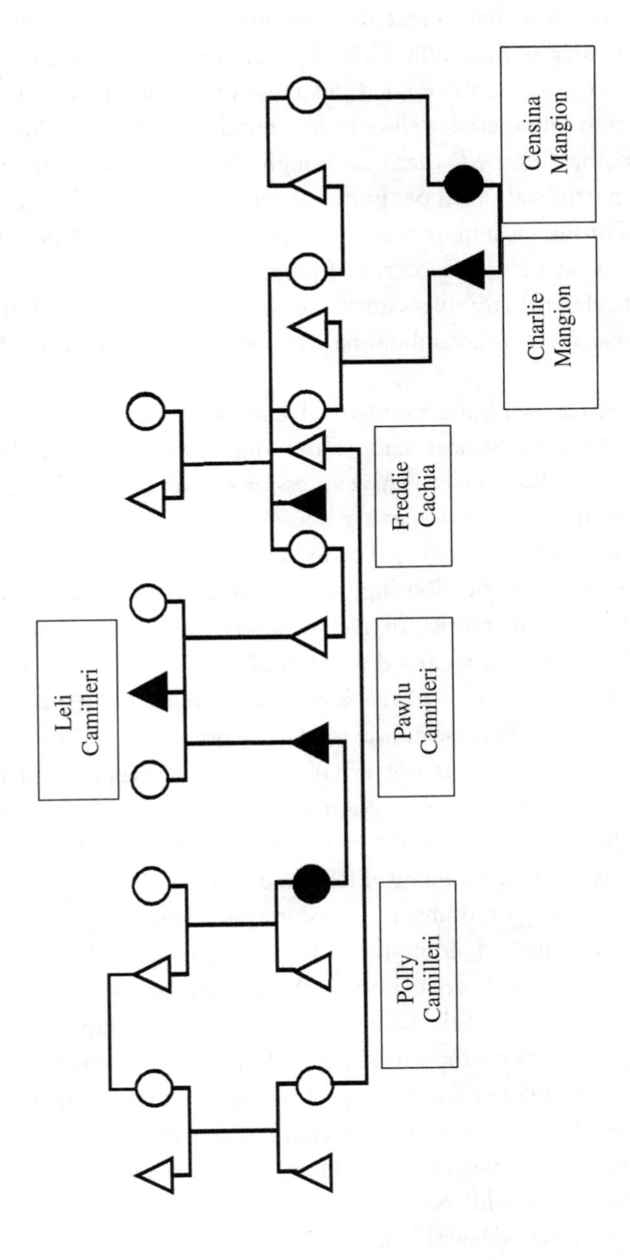

Figure 3 *L-Arċipierku* as *Familja Waħda:* relationships between Mangion, Cachia and Camilleri families

ta'Carabelli—the surname of his father's mother. The nickname extended out from her direct descendents to incorporate all those who were related to the Dallis, either by birth or by marriage, such that the group *ta'Carabelli* was large. Censu was proud of the fact, claiming that his family numbered well over five hundred. When he did so, he referred to the *Carabelli razza*, although this category more strictly refers to patrilineal kin, or more generally those with the same surname. Through a similar process of 'practical kinship' (Good 1981) or transgression of strict criteria of consanguinity, a relatively small number of bilateral *laqmijiet* came to cover most of the population of *L-Arċipierku* further consolidating the notion that it was *familja waħda*.

As well as being one family, *L-Arċipierku* was referred to as one household. Carmen Brincat said of the area *qisna bitha waħda*—we were like one yard/courtyard. This expression conveyed the message that although the area consisted of many households, many dwellings, it was really only one. This was partly dictated by the physical structure of the most common type of housing in *L-Arċipierku:* the *kerrejja*—pl. *kerrejjiet*. People's memories of *L-Arċipierku* were dominated by the memory of the *kerrejja*, regarded nostalgically as a model of communal living. It was the open-ness of the *kerrejja* that made *L-Arċipierku* one yard. The yard, in a Maltese house, is an extension of the inside world of the household proper. It is not usually accessible except through the house, so that access is normally controlled in the same way as access to the house. But in *kerrejjiet* and other types of communal housing, the single yard was open to many different dwellings. The yard is most commonly a place for doing the washing, and thus a place for the outside performance of domestic tasks by women. In *L-Arċipierku*, however, washing was done not in the private yards of individual households but at one of the communal wells. Here, groups of women would congregate to do their washing, talk and sing together. Carmen particularly remembered the clicking of bracelets that accompanied the singing, as washing was scrubbed in communal activity.

On the streets, outside, but conceptually in the yard, the women of *L-Arċipierku* would perform this domestic work, which was categorically associated with the normally semi-private world of the yard. It was the outdoor version of work which women who lived in separate households, would perform in their own, private yards. But the performance of this task in the communal, outside space of the well, was offset by the classification of that space as part of the communal yard, the communal household, that was *L-Arċipierku*. Thus although the washing was done *outside* the house, it was *inside* *L-Arċipierku*.

Carmen Brincat didn't just talk about the open-ness of communal clothes washing, but also the open-ness and safety of the area in general. She remembered, for example, how—particularly in the summer—men and children would sleep outside on the streets, in the cooler outside air, and how the doors in *L-Arċipierku* were habitually kept unlocked. This was a common memory. There was no need to close up the house, because there was no threat of burglary. This was because the single household of *L-Arċipierku* was also a single family—a single moral unit in which everyone was an insider. Being one family and one household meant that there was no threat of burglary or attack. If it was safe to sleep on the streets, then this was because the streets were seen as being inside the boundaries of *L-Arċipierku*. If the doors were kept unlocked it was because they were internal, not external doors. They were doors through which people designated insiders by virtue of being members of the same, larger, household and family, could freely pass.

As one family and one household, *L-Arċipierku* was a single unit of obligation and cooperation. Neighbours would share and exchange goods and services. Even during the war, when a naval blockade had meant there was practically no food, Carmen remembered her mother setting aside a portion from the family's rations to give to the baby next door. Charlie Mangion and David Chetcuti also referred to these obligations to co-operate. 'We were together', they said—*konna flimkien*—and *konna naqbzu għall-xulxin*. This last phrase literally means 'we used to jump for each other', but also means 'we used to help each other out'. It had particular connotations of violence and fighting—defending each other physically against a common foe. It therefore signalled the inherent ambivalence in the Nostalgic Construction of Community. Whilst on the one hand, *L-Arċipierku* was a model of morality and communal solidarity, on the other hand, the justification for this solidarity—the memories of 'jumping' to defend each other—acknowledged the 'roughness', or even 'low-ness' of the area.

THE FELLOWSHIP OF THE FLAWED

Indeed, as with the critiques of 'traditional' household and family discussed in chapter three, there was an inherent ambivalence towards the nostalgic image of *L-Arċipierku*, itself dependent on the symbols of household and family. Just as younger Maltese criticised the rigidities of the 'traditional' family, so they were sceptical about the values of the demolished neighbourhood. For example, after listening to the likes of David Chetcuti and Charlie Mangion wax lyrical about the glories of *L-Arċipierku*, one young man was critical of their traditionalism, emphasising the repressive nature of 'community' life as a regime of social control and surveillance, as much as corporate solidarity. He explicitly linked this critique to his perceptions of life in Northern Europe, which he held up as the epitome of 'modern' life:

> That's the problem with Malta. People always want to know your business. That's how wonderful *L-Arċipierku* must have been—with everybody keeping an eye on you. Not like in England. There you keep yourself to yourself and nobody takes any notice.

David Chetcuti responded by criticising the young man's lack of social responsibility, linking modernisation and individualism with the rise of *egoiżmu*—egotism. Unlike the Greek *eghoismos*, *egoiżmu* was unequivocally negative (Herzfeld 1985). It related materialism to both morality and masculinity in that it was associated with the acquisition of resources at the expense of ties of obligation. As discussed in chapter three, being a 'good man' involved keeping reciprocal obligations, and not exploiting others. With the rise of materialism, *egoiżmu* was seen by David as an increasingly prevalent transgression of these obligations when compared with the unified, solidary *Arċipierku*:

> When we were young, in *L-Arċipierku*, we had nothing, so how could we be greedy? People were together then, and fought for each other, not against each other. That's gone now. There's too much *egoiżmu*.

Paradoxically, this defence acknowledged the negative side of *L-Arċipierku*, in its repeated invocation of violence. Indeed, inherent in the nostalgic image of *L-Arċipierku* as an Edenic paradise was a simultaneous acknowledgement of its negative side. Although the past was in many ways a model of social life, it was nevertheless essentially flawed.

If memories of *L-Arċipierku* contributed to the constitution of *il-poplu* as a category, they also inevitably involved invoking notions of 'low'-ness. There is a hint of this in David's argument, quoted above. If the people of *L-Arċipierku* had nothing, then they were unable to demonstrate their respectability through consumption. But the 'low'-ness of *L-Arċipierku* was further emphasised by descriptions of the toughness of its inhabitants—the willingness of its young men to fight against rivals from other Valletta neighbourhoods, and against British and American sailors. Referring to the violent defence of *L-Arċipierku* effectively acknowledged the 'roughness' of the area. Such roughness was framed in terms of the spatial categories 'up' and 'down' and the social categories *għoli* and *baxx*, associating *L-Arċipierku* with the moral categories *baxx*—'low'— *pastaż* or *ħamallu*—'rude' or 'rough'.

Indeed, Valletta as a whole but particularly the 'low-town' areas had a reputation for violence related to the memory of gangs of young men who used to spend their time on the streets challenging outsiders—young men from other Maltese neighourhoods or sailors—to fights. The image mirrors Suttles' picture of a 'defended neighbourhood' in which groups of young men 'defend' the physical boundaries of the locality (1971). Sandro Mifsud told me of fights he had had, as a member of *L-Arċipierku* youth club, with young men from other parts of town, in defence of his community. *L-Arċipierku's* reputation for rough-ness was carried by men from the area with a certain pride, as tough-guys. If they felt they were being ridiculed, they would reply, *jiena mill-Arċipierku*!—I'm from *L-Arċipierku*—which was seen as a warning—don't mess with me! It conveyed the sense that not only could the speaker look after himself, but he also had friends who would help him to do so. Being 'from *L-Arċipierku*' was at once a personal and a collective statement of tough-ness.

By emphasising the unity of *L-Arċipierku* through emphasising the willingness with which its inhabitants would 'jump' for each other, then, people acknowledged that although a co-operative moral unit akin to a single family or household, and devoid of *skandlu*, the area was nevertheless characterised by activity which might be categorised as *ħamallu* or *baxx*—namely fighting. These descriptions produce a kind of 'diamond in the rough' image of *L-Arċipierku* that simultaneously stresses the positive values of the past, and links the inhabitants of the area to the categories *baxx* 'low' and *ħamallu* 'rude'. It produces what Herzfeld describes as a 'fellowship of the flawed', in which notions of unity and imperfection are simultaneously mobilised in critique of the state (Herzfeld 1997). Claiming that the state is responsible for the destruction of the—albeit flawed—community lends legitimacy to claims for the state's intervention. But these claims were based on two paradoxes. First, that claims to the moral integrity of the former community were based on its rather dubious 'diamond in the rough' character, and second that the destruction of this community, by a problematic intervention by the state, led to calls for further state intervention. However, this second paradox appears less so when we recognise that the state to which the claims were addressed in the early nineties was different from that which sealed the fate of *L-Arċipierku* in the 1970s.

Arguments over the demolition of *L-Arċipierku* had been overtly party political since the time of the demolition itself, when the then Labour government—*gvern*—supported the demolition against the Nationalist opposition's criticism. In this context, invoking memories of *L-Arċipierku* as it had been, and the conditions of its demolition, also involved a critique of party politics. Memories of *L-Arċipierku* pitted not only *poplu* against *gvern*, past against present, but also Nationalist against Labour.

GĦAX FORTIZZA NATIONALISTA

Between the publication of the British government report in 1945, and the election of the Labour government in 1971, *L-Arċipierku* remained intact. Characteristically, the British prioritised military over civilian considerations. Immediately post-war, the Labour Party called for increased investment in housing, and the MLP government of 1955 to 1961 began to implement its policies of urban improvements in the harbour areas, by demolishing and rebuilding the notorious *Mandraġġ* area of Valletta, and inaugurating the new town of Santa Lucia, near Paola. However, by the late 1950s, these social issues were overtaken by arguments about integration and

Independence. The programme of urban redevelopment was halted before *L-Arċipierku* was touched.

In 1964, Independence was granted under a Nationalist government. The opposition, led by Dom Mintoff, campaigned vigorously for the improvement of social welfare and housing, and was elected in 1971 on this platform. Once the Labour government was in place, they quickly made moves to revive the recommendations of the original 1945 report, and turned to *L-Arċipierku*. In July 1971, Labour came to power, and on 2nd June 1972 a declaration was made under the Land Acquisition (Public Purposes) Ordinance that large areas of *L-Arċipierku* were to be requisitioned (Government of Malta, 1972: 1421). On 18th July the first families left *L-Arċipierku*, and on July 22nd the first buildings were destroyed. There was immediate outcry from the residents of *L-Arċipierku* and the Nationalist opposition. The debate became a matter for national concern, as articles were written with claims and counter-claims in the three national daily newspapers—the Nationalist paper, *In-Nazzjon Tagħna,* the Labour paper, *L-Orrizont,* and the English-language *Times of Malta*.

The debate became highly politicised, and led to arguments in parliament between a Labour government in favour of the demolition and a Nationalist opposition against it. Calls for demolition were excessive, argued the Nationalists. Even the Social Action Movement (SAM) defended *L-Arċipierku*. This was the same organisation that in 1970 had argued in favour of 'drastic action—if necessary by eviction—for the elimination of the remaining...kerrejjas (sic)' (Centre for Social Studies 1970: 11). In 1971 the SAM became joint sponsor with the Malta Homes Society, of a new Slum Clearance Commission that conducted a survey of the area. It concluded, and announced at a public seminar in early July 1972, that rather than being a slum, *L-Arċipierku* was an 'area of sub-standard housing' (The Times of Malta, 6/7/72: 10). Under this category, the recommendation was made to rehabilitate, rather than demolish the area.

Debate revolved around the contentious category *slum*, and whether *L-Arċipierku* qualified as one. In early July 1972, the Labour newspaper, *L-Orizzont* carried a feature article on the achievements of successive socialist governments in the area of housing development, concluding with the announcement that:

> The social democratic government of Malta has begun an intensive project of new and comfortable buildings instead of the slums of the city of Valletta. (*L-Orizzont*, 5/7/72)

This appears to have been relatively uncontroversial, except that there was disagreement as to what precisely 'the slums of the city of Valletta' were. The Slum Clearance Commission denied that they were in *L-Arċipierku*, arguing that rather than *L-Arċipierku* being demolished, attention should be turned to the area on the other side of Valletta known as the *Due Balli* (*Times of Malta*, 5/7/72).

The *Due Balli* was and is, in many senses, the local 'other' of the *Arċipierku* self. If *L-Arċipierku* was the heartland of St Paul's parish, then the *Due Balli* adopted the corresponding role for St Dominic's. This opposition was also party political. Whilst the *Due Balli* was renowned as a hot-bed of support and activism for the Labour Party, *L-Arċipierku* was predominantly Nationalist supporting. The *Arċipierku* debate, then, related local rivalry of place to *festa* rivalry between those places' patrons and political rivalry between the parties that were associated with them.

A prominent figure in the Slum Clearance Commission's public seminar of July 1972 was Peter Serracino-Inglott. His family was from close to *L-Arċipierku* and he defended it adamantly. As a spokesperson for the area, his biography symbolises the local and political significance of the *Arċipierku* debate. For just as *L-Arċipierku* was in general a strong-hold of Nationalist support, so Serracino-Inglott went on to become a powerful member of the Nationalist hierarchy. He was also a member of the collegiate chapter at St Paul's Shipwreck church, and therefore associated with its *festa*. These elements in the biography of an influential *Arċipierku* spokesperson sum up the significance of the debate. It was not merely about housing, but also about party politics and the politics of localism. It was therefore not surprising that the Slum Clearance Commission, with Serracino-Inglott as a prominent member, defended the interests of the area against the Labour government. It was equally predictable that they should suggest the *Due Balli* as an alternative site for demolition. The argument was reinforced by a *Nazzjon Tagħna* editorial:

> [The] ... Slum Clearance Commission made it clear that *L-Arċipierku* can be rehabilitated, given a new life, whilst 'slum

clearance' has got to take place in the zone of Valletta known as the *Due Balli*. (*In-Nazzjon Tagħna*, 17/7/72)

Just as the defence of *L-Arċipierku* had moral connotations, so did the denigration of the *Due Balli*. Not only was the *Due Balli* thought of by Nationalists as a substandard and often dirty part of town, it also had a reputation for prostitution and crime. It was close to the part of Strait Street that was famous as a sailors' recreation area. Known as 'the Gut', this area had been lined with bars and dance halls, the facades and signs of which could still be seen in the early 1990s, although the trade was long since abandoned. The Gut was a haven of petty crime and prostitution, and many of its functionaries lived in the *Due Balli*. In contrast to *L-Arċipierku*, the *Due Balli* had a shifting population. No claims could therefore be made for its solidarity as a community. Neither could appeals be made to its moral rectitude, given its reputation.

As will have become clear, the public debates about the demolition of *L-Arċipierku* were suffused with party politics throughout. However, it was not until it was discussed in parliament that the full implications were made public. During debates on 17th July, 1972, the leader of the Nationalist opposition asked the Labour government why *L-Arċipierku* was to be demolished ahead of the *Due Balli*. According to the banner headline of the next day's *In-Nazzjon Tagħna*, the answer had been *Għax Fortizza Nazzjonalista*—because it's a Nationalist fortress (*In-Nazzjon Tagħna*, 18/7/72: 1). This made the links between the government's policies and the political allegiance of the people of *L-Arċipierku* explicit. As far as the Nationalist Party were concerned, the act was pure political spite.

The phrase *Għax Fortizza Nazzjonalista* resonated with memories of the demolition in the early nineties. It cropped up again and again in my fieldnotes as I collected people's accounts of the area, and the events of its demolition. It confirmed that the people of *L-Arċipierku* saw themselves not only as victims of the state in general—*il-gvern*—but also of that particular *gvern* that oversaw the demolition of their neighbourhood: *Il-Gvern Laborist*—the Labour Government. More specifically, however, the accusations of political partiality served to vilify the Labour leader of the time, Dom Mintoff, who many from *L-Arċipierku* saw as personally responsible for the area's demolition. This links memories of the demolition not only to party politics, but also the politics of personality.

THE THEFT OF MINTOFF'S PIPE

Maltese party politics in the 1970s and 80s were dominated by the figure of Mintoff, and the memory of him looms large in those of the demolition, for which he was seen as personally responsible. He was leader of the Malta Labour Party from 1949 to 1983, Prime Minister from 1971 to 1983, and was still an MP at the time of my fieldwork. He had a reputation for being a rabble-rouser, and charismatic leader of the dockyard workers (Boissevain 1994). Roughly half the national population—the Nationalist half—regarded him as a dangerous and vindictive tyrant.

When Mintoff came to power in 1971, his first act was to raise the rental charged to the British for the use of the dockyards. This led to a protracted discussion between Malta and the Admiralty, and the eventual British withdrawal (Austin 1971, Koster 1984). Mintoff also believed that Malta should bridge the gap between north and south shores of the Mediterranean, and developed strong links with Gaddafi's Libya. My Nationalist informants argued that the British withdrawal led to economic decline in Valletta, and the links with Libya made drugs more available, thus exacerbating problems of crime in the city. Making Mintoff personally responsible for not only the demolition, but also these policies which led to economic and social decline, enabled my informants to maintain an image of the 1990s Nationalist government as munificent patrons, whilst at the same time calling on them to remedy a bad situation brought about by Mintoff's abuse of the state.

L-Arċipierku had been razed, they argued, *Għax Fortizza Nazzjonalista*. This phrase linked the demolition not merely to the policies of the Labour Party, but to Mintoff himself. The spitefulness of Mintoff's politics was emphasised by a well-repeated story of the events leading up to the 1971 election. It was told to me, among others, by an elderly man called Pawlu Spiteri, who I interviewed at great length about this and other events. Pawlu was a life-long Nationalist who when I talked to him was 79 years old. He had kept a stall on the Valletta market for most of his working life, and had lived in *L-Arċipierku* until 1972, when his house was demolished and he was displaced. When I asked him about it, he replied that *L-Arċipierku* had been destroyed *Għax Fortizza Nazzjonalista*.

He described how Mintoff had called a political rally in *L-Arċipierku*. Because it was a Nationalist stronghold, the local people had responded with hostility, and showered him with eggs and flour. Mintoff had to take refuge. He was in the habit of smoking a pipe, and when he regained composure, he felt in his pocket to light up. But he couldn't find it. To add insult to indignity, somebody had stolen Mintoff's pipe. I asked Pawlu if he knew who had done it. He refused to tell me, but by the glint in his eye, it could well have been him. The Labour leader was livid, and promised there and then that the first thing he would do when he got into power would be demolish that *Fortizza Nazzjonalista*. The rest, as they say, is history—or memory.

This oft-repeated story links party politics to the politics of personality, and signals an important theme in Maltese political life—the proximity of public, political figures to their electorate. This proximity is central to the political processes discussed in the next chapter, which explores local attitudes towards clientelism and patronage, which are seen as endemic to Maltese life. The story presents not only the Labour Party—and party politics more widely—as responsible for the demolition of *L-Arċipierku*, but particularly Mintoff, a member of the political elite who was able to use his position to pursue an arbitrary and spiteful politics. Such stories—and memories—contribute to a critique of party politics and the state, and coupled with the nostalgic images of pre-demolition completeness also contribute to a critique of modernisation. They are part of the means by which 'the people'—*il-poplu*—come to terms with the sense of limits they are faced with, and turn these limits round to appeal to *il-gvern*. As well as setting up *poplu* against *gvern*, however, they also pit Nationalist against Labour, past against present and *L-Arċipierku* against Mintoff.

NOTES

[21] Aquilina's definitive Maltese-English Dictionary (2 volumes—1989 & 1990) describes *L-Arċipierku* as 'a slummy part of Valletta that was destroyed in 1974 [sic—it was actually 1972]', referring to De Soldanis's 1750 *Damma tal Klien Kartaginis* ... for a fuller etymology. Despite consulting the appropriate volume of De Soldanis in the National Library of Malta, I could find no reference to *L-Arċipierku*.

CHAPTER SIX

All Politicians are *Bastards*

> If there is a political moral to be found in this world . . . it is that we carry on the business of this century with an intolerable double vision. Right and left, the hothouse and the street. The Right can only live and work hemetically, in the hothouse of the past, while outside the Left prosecute their affairs in the streets by manipulated mob violence. And cannot live but in the dreamscape of the future. (Thomas Pynchon, *V*: 468)

As the title of this chapter suggests, Maltese in the early nineties were extremely sceptical of politics and politicians. Nevertheless, politics was—and is—of major importance in everyday life. People were committed in their allegiances to one party or the other, and to particular persons involved in politics and public life. Despite the prevailing scepticism, Maltese elections enjoy some of the highest percentage voting turn-outs in the world.[22] This chapter goes some way towards explaining the apparent contradiction between a sceptical view that 'all politicians are *bastards*' and one which acknowledges that despite this politicians and the political process are both necessary and important.

Maltese party political allegiance is strongly related to place. This spatio-politics is linked to the historical development of party politics in relation to the Maltese labour market. Areas historically dominated by employment in the British colonial service, particularly the dockyards, are now predominantly Labour-supporting. Areas such as Valletta, by contrast, where people were employed by local merchants, or were themselves entrepreneurs, are characterised by strong Nationalist allegiance. This allegiance was consolidated through people's memories of particular prominent politicians and their relationships with local people.

Such intimacy was at the centre of Maltese clientelism and fuelled debates about corruption. These debates were inherently equivocal, articulating a fundamental ambivalence towards 'traditional' and 'modern' political processes. On the one hand, it was argued that such practices should be stamped out, if Malta was to develop into a fully modern democracy. On the other hand, there was anxiety about what would happen, and particularly what would happen to *il-poplu*—the people—if clientelism was abolished. Moreover, there was a sense that such practices, themselves a consequence of personalised politics, and ultimately of the proximity of politicians to 'the people', were a quintessential part of Maltese society and therefore ineradicable. There was therefore a palpable ambivalence towards the processes of reform, which pitted 'traditional' political practices against the 'modernisation' of state and political process. This in turn was both enabled and exacerbated by the particular contours of the Maltese public sphere.

28th OCTOBER 1993: ST PAUL'S SACRISTY

The Sacristy of St Paul's church served as a significant locus for debate and discussion, particularly among men. To this extent, it can be described as part of a sphere of public discussion. The space was used in the main by *Pawlini* men—supporters of St Paul's *festa*—and their associates. I spent a lot of time in the Sacristy, listening to conversations about the *festa* and its administration, local gossip and politics. On this day, the discussion had turned to the issue of clientelism in Maltese politics.

During the months prior to this conversation, which were also the months leading up to Malta's first Local Council elections,[23] public attention had been drawn to the issue of clientelism, or *clienteliżmu*, following the publication of an annual report by the Permanent Commission Against Corruption. This Commission had been set up by the Nationalist Government who had come to power in 1987 and consolidated their position in the elections of 1992 on a platform of anti-corruption and European integration. After a year's work, the Head of the Commission reported that of the several hundred cases that had been opened, not one had been investigated with any satisfaction. The reason, he argued, was that there was a code of silence that stopped the investigators succeeding in their inquiries. He referred to the code as *omertà*, a word that was picked up by the Maltese press to sensationalise his report. *Omertà*, of course, is the code of silence understood to be part of the Sicilian Mafia's mechanism for avoiding prosecution (see Schneider & Schneider 1976, Gambetta 1996). By using the word, the Head of the Commission was not only suggesting that Maltese political life was controlled by a small, self-serving clique, but also that this clique might well have Mafia connections.

This was a common perception, and one which informed the discussion in the Sacristy. The group began discussing a local Valletta politician who had given money for home improvements to people in one of the new *Arċipierku* blocks prior to an election campaign. The assistance was assumed to have been given in return for either votes or political support or both—a clear example of *clienteliżmu*. The case was being put in front of a government tribunal to judge whether or not there had been any serious breach of acceptable practice, and my *Pawlini* informants, who personally knew the politician involved, were awaiting the outcome.

The politician was a Nationalist, as were those involved in the discussion. They referred to the Nationalist Party as simply 'the party'—*il-partit*—seen as a corporate body. One man argued that the miscreant politician should be thrown out of the party. That kind of practice needed to be stamped out. This was the party line—that *clienteliżmu* should be a thing of the past, inappropriate to the nation's European ambitions:

> If we're going to get into Europe, we have to get rid of that kind of thing. Can you imagine that happening in Brussels? If we want to get into Europe, we have to behave like Europeans.

Others were more equivocal, particularly those who had received favours from the politician in the past. They shouldn't get at him, they argued. Isn't that the way all politicians get support? Reference was then made to another local politician—another Nationalist—who had never participated in clientelistic practices. This was admired by some, but criticised by others:

> That's his problem. He's too good. Too pure. He never got involved. That's why he never got very far in politics. If you want to succeed in politics you've got to be *haxxej*—fucker—you've got to be a *bastard*.

The argument was that because he had never been sufficiently self-interested to engage in clientelistic practices, his career had suffered and he had not progressed beyond being a junior politician. Most of those assembled were sceptical. The idea that a politician had *never* got involved was unbelievable. But it was nevertheless a hopeful ideal for the future:

> That's the kind of mentality we're trying to change—the idea that if you want anything you go straight to the minister. Or straight to the office of the government official. That's what we're trying to do away with.

The discussion continued in the semi-heated fashion of political debate in Malta, with each speaker gesticulating and imploring the others to see their point of view. As one man insisted that *clienteliżmu* must be abolished, another tried to shout him down with his views on its inevitability in the Maltese political process. As the debates developed, a third strand of opinion emerged, which saw *clienteliżmu* as not only inevitable, but also in some senses beneficial. The fear was that with the abolition of *clienteliżmu*, Maltese people would be left high and dry, without access to the kinds of resources currently available through such illicit channels. This strand of opinion represented a kind of fatalistic pragmatism born of the acknowledgement of a 'sense of limits' to people's connections with *għoli* or 'high' society and consequently a lack of contact with and access to resources controlled by a central commanding clique. Anxiety about the abolition of clientelism was framed in terms of the needs of 'the people'—*il-poplu*:

> If you get rid of that [clientelism], how are we going to get any help from the government? Those people [in the case discussed above] got their houses improved. And they needed it, too. They were like caves. They're palaces now. How would that happen if they hadn't had some help?

The perception that in order to gain access to the resources controlled and distributed by the state, one must enter into a relationship with a particular person—a relationship of clientelism or patronage—is central to understanding the simultaneous scepticism about and enthusiastic participation in the political process. If the state—*il-gvern*—is not an anonymous bureaucratic institution but one that is populated by particular known people, then who those people are and what relationship one has with them is extremely important. Thus, although politics and the state are seen as fundamentally corrupt, they are nevertheless a necessary and important evil.

PATRONAGE, CLIENTELISM AND MEDITERRANEAN POLITICS

One of the main problems with the analysis of political processes in Southern Europe or the Mediterranean is the confusion—or at least lack of clarity–between evaluative and descriptive categories. Processes described as clientelism or patronage have been seen as an essential feature of political culture in the South, but this description has also contained an evaluative edge that derives from a prevailing model of unilinear state development. As evaluative terms, clientelism and patronage define Southern politics as both corrupt and—consequently—inadequately, or not yet completely, developed. Problematic though this argument is, it is one which is frequently used by Southerners themselves, who adopt a kind of indigenous critique of their own political systems based on a shared understanding of the prevailing model of 'modern' state development and bureaucratic rationalisation. Any practice which diverges from this model is seen as a hindrance to 'proper' development, and as corrupt.

Because of the conflation of descriptive and evaluative categories it is important to distinguish exactly what I understand by clientelism, patronage and corruption. What follows will depend on these definitions. Patronage I see as systemic: it is the abstractable principle or formalisation of a particular political culture—a classificatory category for the system as a whole. As Bourdieu (1990: 66) has observed, such formalisation or abstraction can be performed either by actor or analyst, and this is critical to our understanding early nineties Maltese politics. Both Maltese actors themselves, and myself as analyst, were able to classify Maltese politics in terms of a system, consolidated through long-term ties between persons and politicians that involved an obligation to grant favours and support, and which was consolidated in collective memory. Clientelism complements the systemic features of patronage at a level of practices. If patronage is a guiding principle, then clientelism is what is *done*. I therefore talk of patronage systems and the clientelistic practices through which they are produced. Whilst patronage and clientelism are descriptive categories, corruption is the evaluative gloss placed on either systemic or practical aspects of politics or bureaucracy. Thus although patronage and clientelism are often—were often—seen as corrupt, this was not necessarily so. In other contexts they were seen as moral obligations or simply facts of life.

In the social sciences, patronage has been used to describe a particular type of political relationship between two categories of person—patrons and clients (see Mitchell 1996a). Generally speaking, patrons are considered politically superior to clients, but the relationship has an in-built contradiction between the exercise of power on the one hand, and the assertion of solidarity on the other (Roniger 1994: 4). Accounts vary as to the precise nature of the relationship between patrons and clients, but the basis of patronage is the assumption that the patron has or controls access to political, economic or cultural resources that the client wants or needs. The means by which the client acquires access to these resources is not through appeals to formal bureaucracy, but through the manipulation of personal relationships with the patron. Patronage is therefore seen as non-bureaucratic—perhaps anti-bureaucratic—and therefore marginal to the state.

In his survey of anthropology in and of the Mediterranean region, Davis argues that patronage exists 'whenever men [sic] adopt a posture of deference to those more powerful than they and gain access to resources as a result' (1977: 132). This definition suggests both a voluntaristic tendency in the practices found in patronage systems and an inherent functionality of the relationship. Indeed, patronage has been described as 'a kind of lop-sided friendship' (Pitt-Rivers 1961: 140) that is of mutual benefit to both patron and client. That said, it was acknowledged in the early ethnography of Southern Europe that systems of patronage, although often couched in the terminology of both 'friendship' and 'kinship'—viz. the significance of godparenthood—are frequently neither friendly nor familistic. Pitt-Rivers, for example, highlights the possibility that 'the appearance of friendship be used to cloak a purely venal arrangement, a rich man using his money to attain his ends.' (Ibid).

In the 1970s a broadly Marxist critique of patronage emerged, which railed against the notions of voluntarism and functionality lurking at the bottom of earlier accounts. A number of authors argued that rather than being personal, voluntary relations, patron-client ties were structural, and related to class. Patronage, they argued, was 'myth' (Silverman 1977) or 'ideology', both from the point of view of the relationship itself, and in its elaboration by anthropologists (LiCausi 1975). Gilsenan (1977) argued that the question most frequently asked of patronage systems by anthropologists—'how do the powerless get access to resources?'—should be reversed to query the processes whereby the powerful gain access to or even create subject populations. Behind the ideology of mutual benefit and voluntarism were processes whereby the powerless—those without immediate access to resources—were defined as clients, and therefore dependent on patrons. The voluntaristic idioms of patronage served to conceal an essentially exploitative relationship.

If the cultural idioms of patronage—friendship and kinship—serve at an ethnographic level to emphasise solidarity in the face of unequal power relations, at an analytic level the notion of patronage and its association with clientelistic practice and ultimately corruption has served to contrast the types of political organisation found in 'other' societies from those of the 'West'. Although this opposition is entrenched in popular thinking, however, it does not stand up to empirical investigation. Patron-client relations are just as much a part of 'Western' politics as 'non-Western'.

Patron-client politics were initially identified in the Mediterranean and Latin America, but have increasingly been identified in other parts of the world, where they are seen as part of the faltering development of democracy, or a consequence of a dysfunctional state. This mode of explanation of patronage systems and clientelistic practices has its origins in a particular model of bureaucratic rationality and state development, that in turn has its roots in Weber. Despite wanting to break with the basic assumptions of evolutionism, Weber nevertheless presents a theory in which the modernisation of society comes from a universal historical process of rationalisation. Bureaucracy is part of this modernisation process, which sees bureaucratic authority emerging from the gradual development of legal rationality that in turn leads to the development of a bureaucratic ethic. Habermas characterises the ethic as follows:

> The dominance of a spirit of formalistic impersonality, without hatred or passion, and hence without affection and enthusiasm. The dominant norms are concepts of straightforward duty without regard to personal considerations. (1984: 340)

This clearly contrasts with the personalised nature of patronage politics and clientelistic practices, and led a variety of thinkers to explain these practices in terms of an incomplete or uneven state development (Blok 1974, Eisenstadt & Lemarchand 1981, Gellner 1977). As Gellner puts it, 'where power is effectively centralised, or on the other hand, well-diffused, patronage is correspondingly less common' (1977: 4). The presence of patronage therefore becomes a symptom of incomplete development.

As Herzfeld has pointed out, alongside the oft-cited 'Honour/ Shame Syndrome', the invocation of patronage is one of the means by which intellectuals have created for themselves a sub-discipline of 'Mediterraneanism', to present the region as 'other' and therefore worthy of study (1987). He derives the term from Said's *Orientalism* (1978), and presents it as a particular mode of stereotyping that presents the region as exotic and backward—populated by crafty entrepreneurs and mafiosi, with no sense of bureaucratic correctness and no respect for the authority of the state. According to the logic of the developmental model, 'they' have not 'yet' become sufficiently bureaucratic, sufficiently rational, to organise a 'proper' state apparatus.

Problematic though this argument is, it is nevertheless one that is frequently used in Mediterranean societies themselves—not least Malta. As argued in chapter one, this classification of 'modern' and 'traditional' modes of society is itself based on a shared modernity. It produces a kind of indigenous Mediterraneanism that simultaneously bemoans a lack of bureaucratic rationality and presents such lack as an inevitable part of indigenous political culture. Spencer (1997) has suggested that an anthropology of post-colonial politics should turn to the examination of such cultural features of political process, seen not as essential properties but as features which are nevertheless frequently essentialised as part of politics. Maltese political culture is based on the establishment of essentialised versions of 'indigenous' and 'European' politics, which orient debates about past and future. Whereas indigenous politics is seen as lacking a rigorous bureaucratic *ethos*, 'Europe' is seen as its epitome. As can be seen in the discussion in the Sacristy, Brussels is seen as a model of rational, modern democracy. Given the corruption scandals in the European Commission in 1999, this position is evidently a representation, or essentialisation.

Such 'strategic essentialisms' (Spivak 1987) can be seen as both a product of and a response to the ambivalence of the early nineties Maltese situation, and indeed of modernity itself—between Europe and non-Europe; between 'modernity' and 'tradition'. Spivak coined the term 'strategic essentialism' to describe the processes whereby post-colonial cultures attempt to resist the homogenising tendencies of a particular version of colonial discourse. Al-Ali (forthcoming) has suggested that they are part of the process of cultural decolonisation.

In Malta, they also become tied up in discussions about the possibility of a cultural recolonisation—or at least a reorientation to a broader cultural sphere: a cultural repatriation to Euro-Italian hegemony, as against British colonialism. In many ways, both represent a similar promise and/or a similar threat. The British past is widely viewed as bureaucratically efficient and politically 'clean' when compared to the post-Independence Malta. Similarly, the European future promises to usher in an era of bureaucratic efficiency. Contemporary Maltese debate plays off these idealised versions of politics against the imperfect present, to highlight anxieties about and antagonisms towards the current state of affairs.

In his work on the cultural logic of bureaucracy, Herzfeld (1993) identifies the extent to which indifference is *produced*, using powerful organic idioms of system and pollution to describe the ideals of 'correct' bureaucratic practice and the dangers of heterodox practices. Because they run counter to the system, they are described as forms of pollution. By this logic, Maltese should regard their own politics as 'dirty' when compared to the more rigorously bureaucratic British and Europeans. But Herzfeld's formulation only works if there is an unambiguous notion of 'system'. When asked about 'system', my Maltese informants argued that 'in Malta the system is there is no system'.

As a consequence, the practices associated with clientelism, which in an ideal bureaucratic context would be regarded as polluting and hence corrupt, are regarded more equivocally—the absence of system creates an ambivalence towards its apparent pollution. Thus the opposition between strategic essentialisms of Maltese and non-Maltese politics is used at times to criticise indigenous political culture, at times to defend it as a workable and demonstrably Maltese way of organising society. These different accounts are clear from the discussion in St Paul's sacristy. Those sceptical to reform demonstrated a commitment to the prevailing clientelistic practices of a political system based on the personalised relations of patronage. Those in favour revealed their commitment to the Weberian model of state development, or at least their assumption of its existence in Brussels. That both points of view were vociferously presented by a group of otherwise fairly undifferentiated men demonstrates the particular tensions and ambivalences at play in early nineties Maltese politics. These tensions have their roots in the historical development of Maltese party politics, and particularly the contrasting versions of national history and national destiny upon which they were based.

PARTY POLITICS IN THE 1990s

The single most important issue in 1990s Maltese politics was and is European accession. Party politics is divided between a broadly Euro-sceptic Malta Labour Party (MLP) and a Euro-phile Nationalist Party (PN). The general elections of 1992, 1996 and 1998 were fought around the issue of whether or not Malta should join the EU, with power exchanging hands from Nationalist to Labour and back again. The issue of European accession was not just one of economic or political policy, but also related to issues of moral progress and modernity. European accession was seen as a challenge to 'traditional' practices and institutions such as the family—see chapter three—but also to church and religion.

The conclusions of these two main parties as to the role of the church informed different projections of Malta's correct path into the future, but were also informed by different political orientations in the past. They represented the continuity of certain ideological preoccupations of the late nineteenth and early twentieth centuries. Thus the PN's pro-Europeanism derived from a pro-clerical Christian democratic *Italianità*—Italian-ness—and the MLP's anti-Europeanism from a broadly anti-clerical, socialist notion of *Malta Maltija*—Maltese Malta. During fieldwork, the governing PN favoured EU accession, having tabled an application to join the Union—then the EEC—in 1990. Entry into Europe would, for them, confirm the cultural links with Italy, playing Malta into a Latin Mediterranean sphere that is, above all, European. The MLP opposition were critical of the move, and this was one of the reasons for the rather discouraging—to PN eyes—*Avis* report emanating from the European Commission in 1993. According to the *Avis* there were two main stumbling blocks for Malta's entry into Europe. First, there was the MLP's policy of opposing the accession. The MLP, it argues, accepted that the PN government might enter into negotiations aimed at Malta's entry into Europe, but pre-emptively denounced the outcome of these negotiations. The *Avis* referred to this denunciation in rather euphemistic terms:

> The support of the MLP and the interests it represents for the restructuring measures required for accession, could make easier the success of the reforms and hence the adoption of the *acquis communautaire*. (*The Malta Independent: Avis—The Key to Europe*, 12/09/93: 23)

The second major problem was that of the economy, and particularly taxation. Here the *Avis* was rather more explicit:

> The reforms which imply Malta's adoption of the *acquis communautaire* affect so many different areas (tax, finance, movement of capital, trade protection, competition law, etc.) and require so many changes in traditional patterns of behaviours that what is effectively involved is a root-and-branch overhaul of the entire regulatory and operational framework of the Maltese economy. (Ibid: 25)

The governing PN began work on this 'root-and-branch overhaul' early on in the 1992–1996 Parliament. Most controversial, and politically sensitive, was the introduction of VAT in 1995 that became a major issue during the lead-up to the 1996 election. The anxieties about EU accession, then, involved both morality and economics.

The Nationalists sold VAT to the Maltese public with the promise of Europe. Accession would be coupled with a reduction of the large trade tariffs on imported goods that had previously existed. The result was that an immediate levy of 15% on all goods, and a requirement that all retail outlets be fully registered and issue till receipts with every purchase. This not only caused an immediate increase in the cost of living, but also railed against the prevailing entrepreneurial independence of shop-keepers and market sellers. Much of their economic activity was—and had historically been—carried out on the margins of the formal economy, permitting a certain freedom from state surveillance. This group saw the new legislation as both intrusive and restrictive, preventing them from doing business in the manner to which they had been used.

The introduction of VAT caused a major outcry, particularly from the Labour Party, who used the new tax as an opportunity to criticise the prospect of Malta's entry into Europe. They combined an attack against the increase in cost of living with predictions about the potential influx of legitimate foreign workers to Malta, should it join the EU. They argued that given Malta's nearly 100% employment record over recent years, and the problems of unemployment across Europe, the freedom of movement policies within the EU would mean that the Maltese employment market would be saturated, should the country enter the Union. These arguments about employment were particularly suggestive for a nation in which memories of widespread unemployment were vivid. At several points over the past 150 years, the employment situation in Malta has deteriorated to such an extent that large-scale emigration took place, to other parts of the Mediterranean and the British Empire (Attard 1983, 1989, 1997).

The arguments about VAT and employment were suggestive not only for Labour supporters, but also for Nationalists. Even informants who professed themselves die-hard Nationalists were concerned. For example, David Chetcuti, who I introduced in the last chapter, would frequently ask me whether I thought Malta's entry to the EU was a good idea. He had been involved in Nationalist Party activism for most of his adult life, but was still not entirely convinced of the policy. Other informants were more critical:

> I've heard that joining Europe will mean more taxes. They're talking about introducing VAT next year, because of Europe. I think that's a terrible idea.

This last comment provoked a heated response from those who heard it. It was spoken on the steps outside *Għand Lawrenz,* where groups of men would congregate to drink tea in the mornings. The speaker ran a nearby shop and had stopped to chat for a while, before continuing about his business. He was worried that the introduction of VAT would lead to a decrease in consumption because of an increase in prices. Behind his comments was also the fear that overly-vigilant tax inspectors would limit the scope of his business. The reaction to his statement was partisan. It was Labour talk, his friends replied. How could the speaker be so critical of *il-partit*—the party?

These comments reveal an expectation of unconditional loyalty to the party and party policy. They also demonstrate an assumption of unanimous Nationalist support among *Pawlini* and residents of St Paul's parish. Referring to the Nationalists as *il-partit* was the norm among *Pawlini*, thus affirming collective support. However, in this context it also drew attention to a distinction between the ideology of the party—the fact of being Nationalists, Christian democrats, pro-European—and the organisation in charge of executing that ideology. This, in turn, marked a distinction between specific policy and broad policy thrust, which enabled the speaker to dissent from the party line, without threatening his allegiance. After hearing the response to his comments, he immediately clarified his commitment to the party, confirming that he'd only be critical of party policy in a context such as this, where everybody was a party supporter. Of course, he would never admit to a Labour supporter that their criticisms of the Nationalists might be justified.

Labour's objections to EU integration were not only related to VAT and employment, but also to language. Language was central to Maltese national identity. It was a critical means by which, in everyday life, Maltese maintained separation from the thousands of tourists who flood the island (see chapter three). It was also an important political issue. During the 1920s and 1930s, the 'language question' provoked lively—at times violent—debate. Language also emerged in the 1990s, in relation to the issue of EU membership. The Labour Party argued that the government should only accept the terms of entry stipulated by the European Commission if they included an undertaking to allow the Maltese language to enter the Union on an equal basis with the other languages. To allow any other terms would be an insult to the nation, and would mean a dissolution of national identity. The prominent linguist Frans Sammut, member of the *Akkademja tal-Malti*—The Academy of Maltese[24]—predicted a new 'language question', in which Malta struggled to maintain its cultural integrity without being dominated by Europeans.

This cultural integrity was related not only to language, but also to morality. Although Europe was acknowledged as the home of the Church—this was partly the reason why the Nationalists were so vehemently pro-European—it was also widely considered a source of moral corruption. Fears that entry into Europe would mean an influx of anti-Catholic norms and values, an increase in social problems of drug abuse and pre-marital pregnancy, and an inevitable introduction of divorce and abortion legislation fuelled uncertainty about accession, even among the staunchest of Nationalist supporters. Concern was expressed, particularly in church circles, over the corrupting influence of European television. Although European television, for *pulit*—polite—Nationalists was a desirable symbol of respectability and links with Europe (see chapter four), it was also a dangerous sources of possible moral harm. Such was the paradox at play in nineties Malta—that on the one hand, accession to Europe meant a pursuit of social elevation, but on the other hand it threatened social disaster.

In 1996, the latter assumption prevailed and after a campaign that highlighted the negative elements of European accession—particularly the rising cost of living with the introduction of VAT—the MLP gained electoral victory. They replaced VAT with a government levy, and began pursuing an 'arms length' policy towards Europe. Their term in office lasted only 22 months, and in September 1998, following a bitter internal struggle between the old Labour leader, the inimitable Dom Mintoff, and the new leader, Alfred Sant, an election was called. The Nationalists won, and within days had announced that the Labour government had only been a brief hiatus in the country's journey towards Europe—they would now resume their work towards accession.

PARTY ALLEGIANCE

As suggested above party allegiance, like respectability and social standing, are strongly related to place. Party political allegiance has become consolidated in particular localities through the establishment of long-term ties between particular families or persons and one or other of the main parties. An explanation for this lies in the dynamics of patronage—defined in Maltese terms as a 'system-without-system', in which personal ties become structural ones. Although in some senses regular, this system is not regulated or rationalised and is therefore potentially—and indeed sometimes actually—polluted by corruption—*korruzzjoni*. It is a system that reproduces itself not according to abstract Weberian bureaucratic morality, but a morality based on the establishment of long-term local, familial and personal allegiances based on mutual support and patronage, and consolidated in collective and social memory.

These ties have produced a major conceptual-political division between the broadly Nationalist (PN) north, and the socialist (MLP) south—the frontier between the two being an imaginary line from the inlet of Grand Harbour at Marsa, across through Qormi and to the coast east of Zebbug. The balance of political allegiance can be seen by the percentages of 'first preference'[25] votes given to the two main parties at the 1992 general election in each voting district (see figure four).

The north-south divide has led to local debate about the infrastructural development of each area, and the comparative access of their populations to resources such as power and water, as well as public funding for roads, schools etc. It was said that during Labour administrations, for example, power and water cuts—the latter being frequent during the summer months—were much more likely in the Nationalist-dominated north. With a change of government, this trend switched, and attention focused on the active under-development of the south by a PN administration that was seen by Labourites as spiteful and vindictive.

This partiality—or perceived partiality—of resource-distribution is critical in understanding both the distribution of votes in Malta and the political process more widely. Political allegiance in Malta is related to access to resources, and the two principal resources are employment and housing. Early in my fieldwork I asked a local political candidate what was the principal concern of his electorate, and he replied:

> In general, people in Malta don't vote for any high political principle. Their main concern is to get work, and a cheap

District	PN percentage	MLP percentage	North/South
01	54.78	43.87	North
02	31.93	66.37	South
03	37.01	60.77	South
04	41.88	56.23	South
05	38.48	59.88	South
06	44.17	54.54	South
07	61.62	36.37	North
08	60.33	37.71	North
09	57.12	40.70	North
10	71.24	26.66	North
11	61.27	36.62	North
12	54.58	43.95	North
13	58.94	40.42	North

Figure 4 First Preference Votes as percentages of the total votes cast, by voting district, 1992

> house, but mainly work. If they know that somebody can get them a good job working for the government, then they'll vote for him.

Since the late nineteenth century, there have been two main sources of employment in Malta—mercantilism and the various trades associated with the harbour life, and the dockyards. Both were centred on Grand Harbour but, significantly, on opposite shores. The harbour traders, merchants and marketeers were found to the north, in Valletta. The dockyards were located to the south, in the creeks of Senglea and Cospicua. As employers, the merchants and shop-keepers of Valletta came from a long-established entrepreneurial petit-bourgeoisie. These in turn were the people who became associated with—and sought office in—the Italianate political parties of the late nineteenth century, which in the 1880s became the *Partito Nazionale*, or Nationalist Party (Frendo 1979: 26, 1993). The dockyards, on the other hand, were run by the British Imperial government, which helped develop an upwardly mobile Anglophile middle class to run its bureaucracy (Koster 1984: 57). From this group emerged the Maltese Labour movement, and eventually the Malta Labour Party (Zammit 1984: 52).

Given that these different types of employers operated on opposite shores of Grand Harbour, and that these employers and managers were oriented to different political ideologies and so different political parties, it can be seen how at an early stage, when voters would associate themselves with those who they knew would provide employment, party support became associated with particular localities. In the case of the dockyards, necessity became virtue, as the early champion of Maltese liberty, Sigismondo Savona argued:

> Savona believed those who had come to depend for their livelihood on the British, such as dockyard workers, should make the most of the opportunity; the British presence was grist to their mill in every way, and vice versa. (Frendo 1989: 182)

His pro-British stance, anchored in the realpolitik of dockyards employment contrasted with the anti-British nationalism—and later party political Nationalism—centred on the professional and merchant classes of Valletta (Frendo 1979: 26). The leading light of 1880s nationalism was Fortunato Mizzi, a trained lawyer and leader of the *Partito Nazionale* which by 1885 had established its own national newspaper and a national club in Valletta. The club in particular became a significant focus for political debate, but also for the establishment and consolidation of personal ties and allegiances that were to persist into the 1990s.

POLITICAL MEMORIES

The allegiance to political parties on the basis of place was consolidated by people's memories—collective and social—of such allegiances in the past. Such memories linked not only parties, but also particular persons, with places—an association which, seen at a systemic level, suggests a kind of patronage, whereby well-placed politicians take care of local people's interests in return for political support. The development of this relationship can be seen in the family memories of Charlie Zammit, who I introduced in chapter three as being central to one of the *Għand Lawrenz* cliques, to the local Valletta Confraternities and to the Association of *Pawlini*. He was born in *L-Arċipierku* in the 1960s. His family had moved in the 1980s to a small house on Merchant's Street where he and his parents lived when I met them in the early 1990s. His grandfather, a market trader, had supported the Nationalists in the first decades of this century, attending their rallies and meetings in Valletta and elsewhere. The party had 'looked after' him, according to Charlie. He had never had problems with his trading license, and had developed—through the party—a strong network of suppliers and customers. Charlie told me with pride on more than one occasion how his father remembered an occasion in the 1930s when a Nationalist rally was held in *L-Arċipierku* and his grandfather's balcony had been used by Enrico Mizzi—Fortunato's son and successor as Nationalist leader—to deliver a speech. An entrenchment in party networks, then, was consolidated by association with a particular, prominent politician.

Such collective family memories, articulated to the social and historical memory of the nation, establish not only a sense of continuity in political affiliation but also an intimacy with its processes that is central to the dynamics of the Maltese political 'system-without-system'. The politicians involved were not distant figures observable only in public contexts, but also linked to the private, intimate spheres of the Zammit household and the larger 'household' of *L-Arċipierku*. They were people of whom personal favours could be asked, even if such favours would require their transgressing the official rules of bureaucracy. Through such memories past politicians were personally remembered, and loyalties consolidated.

As well as Enrico Mizzi on the balcony, Charlie's father remembered the Independence celebrations in 1964, overseen by Gorg Borg Olivier, who emerged as a National(ist) hero in the early 1960s and succeeded Enrico Mizzi as Nationalist leader. Like Mizzi, he represented Valletta as part of the First District in Parliament. Prime

Minister at the time of Independence, he was remembered as a friendly and munificent patron, and a figure frequently seen around the streets of Valletta. His memory was evoked and consolidated by the entry into local politics of his nephew in 1994. The dynamics of Paul Borg Olivier's campaign was shaped by the legacy of his famous uncle. Because many of the constituents were much older than Paul, and knew Gorg Borg Olivier perhaps better than he himself, his authority as a local political player was tempered by his uncle's memory. On more than one occasion, I heard elderly Nationalists approach the young aspirant to give friendly, but firm, advice on various aspects of his campaign. The perceived intimacy they'd achieved with his uncle allowed them to intervene to protect the continuity of his legacy.

Gorg Borg Olivier's significance was annually commemorated during the five-day *Independenza*—'Independence'—celebrations held just outside Valletta on a site where mass political meetings have been held for decades. During *Independenza* it is given over to the Nationalist Party as a festival of party celebration. Food-stalls and bars are set up and public debates take place in small arenas erected alongside the main stage, where entertainment is provided, including the party leader's annual *Independenza* speech to the faithful. During the *Independenza* celebrations I attended, Borg Olivier's successor, Eddie Fenech Adami made frequent reference to the legacy left by the signatory to Malta's Independence Constitution. The *Pawlini* with whom I went were also clear about the contribution to national political history Borg Olivier had made. His position was sealed for Charlie Zammit in the memory of his funeral in 1980, which he remembered as a moment of national, local and family mourning.

The links between place, party and family determined a permanent and vehement allegiance to the party. As Charlie Zammit pointed out one day when I asked if he'd ever considered voting Labour:

> Never. Never, never, never. Okay, I don't agree with everything from our side. But you'll not see me voting Labour. I was born a Nationalist—my father's Nationalist and my Grandfather was Nationalist. That's that, I'm a Nationalist. Even if I think the Labour Party are right, and the Nationalists are wrong. In that case, I wouldn't vote. But vote Labour—never.

POSTCOLONIAL AMBIVALENCES

This last quotation suggests a sneaking and covert acknowledgement that despite the rhetorical defence of Nationalism or 'the party'—*il-partit*—Labour's ideas might sometimes be right. A case in point concerns the relationship between Independence and decolonisation. Whilst my Nationalist informants focused on Independence as a key moment in the development of the nation, their Labour-supporting compatriots focused on the final expulsion of British forces in 1979. This event was commemorated in a parallel celebration to *Indipendenza*—Freedom Day, or *Tal-Ħelsien*. Whilst the former attracts Nationalists over five days in September, the latter takes place in March and attracts predominantly Labour participants who celebrate the day on which Malta, they argue, became *really* free from its colonial past.

The withdrawal of British forces came after a series of protracted negotiations between the British Government and then Labour Prime Minister Dom Mintoff. Many of my Valletta informants regarded it as a serious mistake that left Malta not only militarily but also economically vulnerable. Others saw it as a sinister attempt by the Labour Government and Mintoff himself to forge stronger links with the Eastern Bloc and Libya. But despite this overt criticism of the events, and a consequent boycott of Freedom Day, there was nevertheless a deeper commitment to the principle that Malta should not be occupied by a foreign power. It was expressed in terms of access to national territory. As Censu Dalli pointed out, there had been major problems with the British garrison in Malta:

> When the English were here—even after Independence—there were lots of places where we, the Maltese, couldn't enter. Take Ricasoli, for example. Do you know where it is? Opposite Valletta [on the south side of Grand Harbour] . . . Did you know that until the British left, the Maltese couldn't enter there? I remember one time we went swimming across there from Valletta. From where we always go [swimming]—under the bastion. We went across to the opposite side and the English—the soldiers—threw us out. And that was after Independence. That's not supposed to be like that, is it? It's a joke that we're an independent country and we can't go wherever we want.

He was clearly struck by the absurdity of an independent nation which forbids its citizens from entering certain areas. Yet as a committed *Pawlin* and Nationalist supporter, he rejected the ousting of the British as a stupid piece of foreign policy bungling—"Mintoff trying to be George Washington and lead the Maltese against the British". This would never be possible, he argued, because despite it all, the Maltese had a great affection for the British. Indeed, even among the most vehemently pro-Italian Nationalists, there appeared to be a certain nostalgia for the British colonial authorities.

As one rather flippant informant put it, "We liked the British—they were good to steal from". For example, Charlie Zammit, whose allegiance to the Nationalists was based on long-standing family loyalties, had strong links with the British. His father was an ex-serviceman, having worked for the Royal Navy as a cook during his entire working life. They were good employers, he said, and paid well. It was common knowledge in Malta that one of the biggest perks of having been a colonial employee was the British services pension, which he now drew. Well-exceeding the Maltese state provision, this came regularly from Britain in sterling, so could be kept in a foreign exchange account and used to buy foreign goods without incurring importation tax. The British were thought of as even-handed and fair employers, largely responsible for teaching the Maltese a sense of justice. This contrasted with the prevailing Maltese self-criticism at local corruption and lack of discipline. If contemporary Maltese politics was characterised by a system-without-system, then the British colonial period was one in which the system was thought to have functioned according to the most rigorous bureaucratic *ethos*. Moreover, this image of a rigorous bureaucratic past was mirrored by Nationalist expectations of the European future which, it is assumed, will usher in a return to ordered, non-clientelistic politics.

This vision of the external as desirable reveals both the allure of foreign politics and the kind of indigenous Mediterraneanism or 'strategic essentialism' (Spivak 1987) characteristic of early nineties Malta. Such essentialisms were fuelled by an inherent ambivalence towards both past and future, between which the present was seen as disordered and entropic, sandwiched between the ordered rationality of the British colonial powers and that of the European Union. These ordered systems were pitted against the disordered system-without-system of Maltese patronage. The indigenous vision of this system can be seen as an abstraction from the jumble of everyday clientelistic practices, but nevertheless has its own empirical import. Although patronage is not systemic in the way imagined by 1970s ethnographers, it is nevertheless imagined as systemic—albeit in a non-systemic way—by 1990s Maltese.

CLIENTELISTIC PRACTICES

The kinds of long-term political links between families and politicians, and the kinds of intimate relationships that build up as a consequence, led to a personalisation of the Maltese political process. The main form this takes is through the practice of clientelism—*clienteliżmu*—whereby state resources are distributed along personal networks rather than according to a disinterested or indifferent bureaucratic logic. Often it involves the intervention of a politician on behalf of a supporter, to speed up the bureaucratic process or 'jump' an over-lengthy queue. The process operates via the kind of hierarchical networks elaborated by Boissevain (1974), through which agents can manipulate both 'horizontal' and 'vertical' ties in the pursuit of their goals.

Such networks take various forms, combining links of kinship, neighbourhood and club allegiance, solidarity among working colleagues and political allegiances. Pardo, in his analysis of the Neapolitan *popolino* describes what he calls a 'mass diffusion of contacts and favours' (1996: 143). He is at pains to point out that activities associated with this diffusion are based on an entrepreneurial morality which although often lying at a remove from the bureaucratic *ethos*, are no less moral for that distance. This mass diffusion of favours and contacts he sees as strategic practices through which the *popolino* negotiate their lives and relationships. The same could be said of Malta, where practices of a non-bureaucratic nature are morally nuanced. The obligation of a hospital worker to obtain cut-price pharmaceuticals for an ailing cousin, for example, or the expectation that loyal support for a successful politician will be rewarded with a comfortable Government job, signal a moral imperative to act against bureaucracy. Although based on different obligations—on the one hand a principle of obligation to kin and on the other, a reciprocal morality of clientelism—these examples nevertheless demonstrate an attachment to a definitively non-bureaucratic and arguably *Maltese* way of doing things: a system-without-system that contrasts with both colonial British and European sensibilities.

At the heart of the personalisation of politics is the practice of canvassing. In the lead-up to elections, both local and general, candidates personally undertake rounds of visits to bars, coffee-shops, houses and clubs in the electoral districts for which they are standing. Such visits are managed, and the politicians escorted, by local canvassers or neighbourhood officers, who mediate between the politicians and their constituency. The neighbourhood officers are chosen for their connections and influence in the local area. They are opinion-leaders who 'have respect'—*għandu rispett* (see chapter four)—and are often drawn from the groups regarded as 'polite' or 'respectable'.

In the lead-up to the 1996 General Election, Ray and Mary Dupont were asked by a prominent Nationalist candidate to act as neighbourhood officers. Their job was to mobilise local support for the candidate, both by making it clear where their allegiances lay, and by persuading people that their candidate was the best man for the job. This meant establishing his credentials as a trustworthy and 'good man'—*raġel sew*—but also on occasion directly representing people to the candidate in a request for clientelistic favours. They were seen as brokers between 'the people' and the candidate.

Their appointment as neighbourhood officers—narrated by them as an honour confirmed the Duponts not only as people who 'had respect', but also as *tal-klikka*—'of the clique'—or *tal-qalba*—'of the heart': people located within the central influential group to which the broader *poplu* had no access, and which was seen in general terms to command Maltese society. This position was confirmed by their invitation to a drinks party at the candidate's house, at which they met the other neighbourhood officers, but also a number of influential party members. This and subsequent meetings established and consolidated the Duponts' personal links and enabled them to command certain favours from influential policy-makers and bureaucrats, both on their own and on others' behalf. For example, it enabled them to find out about local planning decisions and intervene in negotiations over the conversion of houses into offices, and the building of what they regarded as unsightly extensions to their neighbours' houses. On a more trivial level, it established priority for the replacement of the street lights outside their house, with the addition of a decorative floral barrel to boot. As Mary Dupont put it:

> We didn't ask for much. Some people want jobs or a new house. All I wanted was decent lights outside the house. I spoke to the Minister and within a month we had the new lights *and* the flowers.

The establishment of personal links between politicians and their neighbourhood officers has implications for perceptions of the gendered nature of politics. As discussed in chapter three, it is assumed that although women *can* hold political office, they often don't, because it is not seen as appropriate. This does not mean that women are not important in the political process, however. Indeed, political opinion often centres on women. Although much of the work of political canvassing takes place in bars and clubs—places more often associated with men than with women—it is also taken into the grocery shops and into the house, where women often hold sway on political opinion. In *L-Arċipierku*, for example, there were two or three central female figures who operated as political canvassers. As with the Duponts, they were considered to be people who commanded respect and had direct links with party and bureaucracy. People requiring favours would approach them in the first instance, and politicians wishing to establish support would do likewise.

For example, in the lead-up to the 1994 local council elections, Carmen Brincat—who I introduced in the last chapter in the context of *L-Arċipierku* demolition—became a particular focus. Of her 11 children, 10 had married and of those six lived in Valletta. Given the strongly uxorilateral tendency within Maltese kinship, her house was often full of children and grand-children discussing the various issues of the day. Carmen's opinion, as most senior family member and—perhaps most significantly—mother, was central in these discussions. When rumours emerged that the Brincat family—known as *Tal-Ċekk*, after her husband's nick-name—were planning not to vote, the candidates made appointments to see her, and other neighbourhood officers tried to persuade her to mobilise her family.

In the end, they were convinced, and voted *en masse* for one of the Nationalist candidates, but their objections were registered and recognised as part of the wider anti-corruption movement both within and outside the party. Their objections were based on a critique of clientelistic practices and the apparent corruption of Maltese political and bureaucratic life. It amounted to a principled stand against the immorality of *clienteliżmu*, which stood against the values of bureaucracy and democracy.

Other critiques of the 'system' as constituted derived not from such principled objection, but from those who felt the system worked against them. Such objections confirmed the moral value given to clientelistic practices. As Parkin (1985) has pointed out, morality is most clearly seen in its transgression. It is examples of such morality or obligation withheld that most clearly demonstrate the assumptions behind such practices. A particular case emerged in the early nineties concerning the expectations of supporters and canvassers for a prominent Valletta Nationalist who had stood as a parliamentary candidate in 1987. In the event, he was not elected, but nevertheless rose through the ranks of the party organisation, eventually taking a position at the Nationalist newspaper, *In-Nazzjon Tagħna*. He was an architect by training, and in the early 1990s was chief architect at a large government development in the south of Malta. As such, he was prevailed upon by those who had supported him in 1987 to provide employment. The sons of Pawlu and Polly Camilleri, for example, who were unemployed in the early nineties (see chapter four) approached the architect for work. His response was initially positive, but cautious. The boys should wait until the right openings came. Then after a while, they were given work, but on temporary, unstable contracts. After a few months, they were released from employment, and once more went to the architect only to be told that there would be no chance of further employment. They were angry at this rebuttal. After all the support they had given him, the least he could do was help them out now. Not to do so was a transgression of an implicit morality, but not an atypical transgression. As one of the sons explained to me:

> You can never trust politicians. They always look after themselves. They're all egotistic. They're all *bastards*.

This 'sour grapes' prognosis of an unfulfilled moral obligation reflects a certain fatalistic attitude towards the political process. If all politicians are *bastards*, and 'the people' dependent on politicians, then by and large life is characterised by a series of disappointments. In struggling through their lives people attempt to enlist the help of politicians, well-placed bureaucrats, 'high' society, but with the knowledge that ultimately the well-placed are at liberty to renege on obligations. In the process, what in another context would be considered rights, are turned into privileges, to be bestowed at the pleasure of those in control (Pardo 1996: 154–155). As David Chetcuti, a committed Nationalist put it:

> That's always been the way ... I'll always be a Nationalist, but our party never did anything for 'the people'. They were always on the side of *dawk tal-mustaċċi*—those with moustaches.

Dawk tal-mustaċċi refers to the well-placed, respectable and 'polite'—in this case those supported and protected by the party and government; those *tal-klikka* or *tal-qalba* who had direct and intimate contacts with politicians or top bureaucrats. David's sense of injustice was tempered by the knowledge that if the Nationalists were less than supportive of 'the people's' plight, the Labour Party were directly opposed to it. After all, it was Labour who had destroyed their community, *L-Arċipierku*, and who opposed the emancipatory promise of European accession. But is was also tempered by a pragmatic realisation that despite the problems with politics as constituted, it did bring some benefits. Moreover, there were anxieties about the proposed eradication of clientelism, based on the assumption that even though Malta might aspire to a European-style bureaucratic rationality, the local political culture was so entrenched as to make true reform impossible. Any half-measured reform, it was assumed, would inevitably benefit 'high' society, at the cost of *il-poplu*. 'Those with moustaches' would always win, such was the sense of limits inherent in the conception of the system. What emerged was the sense of a double-bind, in which reform threatens to cut off possible avenues of assistance. This stifled some of the more vehement calls for the eradication of corruption.

CORRUPTION

If the practice of clientelism was regarded as endemic or indigenous to Maltese political culture, as characterised or formally abstracted as an overall system-without-system, a system of patronage, in some circles it was regarded as corrupt. As such, its moral character was questioned, and descriptive accounts of politics became evaluative ones. This was the other side of the double-bind of early nineties Malta, in which aspirations to European bureaucratic rationality fuelled a critique of indigenous practices, which built up an indigenous Mediterraneanism or strategic (self)-essentialism.

At the forefront of such indigenous critique was the small centrist political party *Alternattiva Democratika* (AD)—'The Democratic Alternative'. Formed in 1989 from a coalition of disillusioned former Labour MPs, environmentalists and civil rights campaigners, AD have been largely unsuccessful in achieving political office, but have contributed significantly to the mobilisation of protest against environmentally-damaging development projects, particularly those associated with tourist development (Boissevain and Theuma 1998). Extending the environmental concern with pollution into the political sphere, they focus on both damage to the environment and corruption or suspect practice in the planning system. In particular, they campaigned for the correct implementation of the Structure Plan, which was published in 1990 but not seriously implemented until 1992, when a Planning Authority was established to oversee all planned development (Ibid: 99–101).

Boissevain and Theuma (1998) trace the centrality of AD, in coalition with a number of other environmental groups, in protests against and investigations of a proposed new development by the Hilton group in 1995 and 1996. After a series of mainly non-violent protests against the development, AD gained access to the documents of the Planning Authority, and particularly their own Environmental Management Unit which, they argued, revealed a number of personal links between leading politicians, administrators on the Planning Authority, and the developers (112). These links enabled regulations concerning the appropriation of public land to be waived, and the planned development to be approved despite its threat to the environment. In this case, as with others, the pollution of the environment was linked to the corruption and pollution of the bureaucratic system designed to protect the environment. AD were tenacious in their investigations of this and other cases, and candid in their exposés. Through their links to the European Green Movement, they promoted a move to a more European model of environmentalism and rational, uncorrupt bureaucracy.

For the *Pawlini* of St Paul's parish in the early nineties, the AD activities were somewhat suspicious, as their investigations frequently implicated the then Nationalist government, and constituted a political threat to 'the party'. As Censu Dalli put it:

> A few years down the line we won't be fighting Labour—it'll be *Alternattiva*.

However, there were elements of the AD project for which there was approval—particularly the exposure of injustice in the planning system. This mirrored the assumption that those 'higher' up in society will look after their own interests before taking care of 'the people'. An illustrative case emerged in the latter part of 1993, when the Nationalist government announced that all illegally built beach-huts were to be destroyed. These were small, hand-built buildings that line many parts of the Maltese shore-line, and were used by many Valletta people as store-houses for fishing equipment, beach-huts or even holiday homes during the hot summer months. They were built without planning permission and were strictly speaking illegal, but had been tolerated by the authorities since they began to appear in the 1960s. When it was announced that they were to be demolished, by government order, there was a major outcry.

The government invoked the Structure Plan as justification for the demolition, but there was a feeling that they were chosen because they were a soft target—a way of being seen to act on the implementation of the Plan without disturbing too many influential interests. As the Hilton example suggests, these were not the only Maltese buildings constructed with dubious legality. Indeed, at the time of the government announcement there was another AD exposé of an exclusive housing development being built—against normal regulations—in a secluded valley in the north of the island. The news was received with cynicism in Valletta. Informants pointed out the injustice of their beach-huts being demolished while 'polite' society was allowed to build rural houses and the developers profited. David Chetcuti summed up:

> It's like the Labourites are saying. I saw it in *L-Orizzont* [the Labour Party daily]. They're talking about one law for the big fish and another law for the little fish. We're the little fish, so we have to lose our beach huts, while the big fish get their palaces.

At this point he turned to me:

> You see, the difference between England and Malta is that in England you have public opinion, but here we have no public opinion.

By this he meant that 'the people'—*il-poplu*—conceived as a 'public' had no way of holding the powerful to account. This statement clearly relates to both the 'sense of limits' discussed in chapter four, the sense of injustice discussed in chapter five and the view of Malta as commanded by a tightly-knit *klikka* of people *tal-qalba*, who profited from ties of clientelism and, ultimately, corruption.

This conclusion, promoted by the activities of AD and others, that Maltese public life was inherently corrupt, can be seen as part of a process whereby the image and *ethos* of Northern European bureaucratic rationality becomes internalised as a positive value, thus contributing to an indigenous critique of existing political process. For many, though, the bureaucratic reform associated with European accession was regarded with if not suspicion, then certainly scepticism. After all, if the Permanent Commission Against Corruption could not prosecute any cases, then what was the point in trying? Such was the ambivalent position of politics in early nineties Malta, in which models of indigenous and exogenous political processes competed as rival 'strategic essentialisms' to mediate and in some senses mollify the resultant anxieties. Whilst it was clear that 'all politicians are *bastards*', it was far from clear that reform was a serious alternative. To implement reform would be to deny the reality of Maltese political process, and the strong attachment not only to party but also to particular politicians, that was sedimented in the collective and social memory of places such as Valletta.

NOTES

[22] In the elections of 1987 and 1992, for example, turn-outs were 96.11% and 96.08% respectively (Schiavone 1992).

[23] Council elections took place on 20th November 1993.

[24] Set up in 1920, the *Akkademija tal-Malti* is modelled on the French *Académie Française,* and sees its primary role as defending the integrity of the language. I interviewed Frans Sammut in summer 1992.

[25] The Maltese electoral system is based on proportional representation with a single transferrable vote.

CHAPTER SEVEN

'Because We're *Pawlini*, We're Maltese'—A Contested Commemoration

> She is—if you care for the word—a spirit, constrained to live in Xaghriet Mewwija. The inhabited plain; the peninsula whose tip is Valletta, her domain. She nursed the shipwrecked St Paul—as Nausicaä and Odysseus (Thomas Pynchon, *V*: 461)

The last chapter focused on anxieties surrounding political reform in nineties Malta. In doing so it revealed a tension in Maltese attitudes towards politicians and the political process, between a deeply committed support for particular parties—and personalities—and a prevailing cynicism about politicians' and public officers' motives and trustworthiness. This chapter explores a parallel tension within the organisation responsible for St Paul's *festa*—the *Għaqda tal-Pawlini* (Association of *Pawlini*)—between members of Valletta 'high' society and *il-poplu*; between the clergy and the laity and between younger and older members of the Association.

In the early nineties, St Paul's *festa*, like most other Maltese *festi*, was expanding in scale, attracting more and more attention at a national level and more and more visitors during the days of *festa* itself. What a few years previously had attracted a few hundred enthusiasts now swelled the streets of Valletta with thousands of celebrants from all over Malta, and abroad. In 1993, for the first time, the *festa* was broadcast on national television to supplement the radio broadcasts of previous years. This increased national interest brought with it an enlarged potential for public scrutiny that in turn meant an increased responsibility for the *Għaqda tal-Pawlini* to provide a *festa* that was beyond criticism. Inevitably, the *Għaqda* was unable to please all interested parties, and a number of critical or cynical voices emerged to object to the way the *festa*, the *Għaqda* and particularly its *Kumitat*—Committee—were being organised. Although there was general agreement that the expanded scale of the *festa* was a positive development, demonstrating the strength and continuity of Maltese 'tradition', there was concern over the form the *festa* was taking, and the new ways in which it was publicised.

These arguments over the *festa* exemplify the ambivalence towards 'tradition' and 'modernity' that lies at the centre of this book. On the one hand the expansion of St Paul's *festa,* its televisation and its increasingly explicit national focus were considered positive developments. On the other hand, the innovations at the centre of this expansion, and changes to both form and meaning of *San Pawl,* were causes of anxiety and concern for a number of *Pawlini.* A series of criticisms were levelled at the *Għaqda Kumitat* that revealed tensions between 'high' an 'low', between clergy and laity and between older and younger *Pawlini.* These tensions, although emerging at a new historical moment, were continuous with similar tensions apparent when the *Għaqda tal-Pawlini* was created, and which the *Għaqda* was intended to alleviate.

FEBRUARY 10th 1970, ST PAUL'S *FESTA* DAY—ST PAUL'S SACRISTY

On the day of the *festa*, as with all Maltese *festi*, the statue of the patron saint is taken out of the parish church and carried in procession around the streets of Valletta. It is the high-point of the *festa*, and one which holds particular emotional significance for all those involved. For *Pawlini* it is vital that this climactic event occurs, the problem being that because *San Pawl* occurs in February, it is often threatened by bad weather. Because the statue is antique, it cannot be taken out of the church in the rain, so in order to complete the *festa* properly, there must be good weather on February 10th. Conversation in the lead-up to *festa* always revolves around the weather, with rather anxious assessments made of long-term weather prospects. The debates often become heated, as anxiety for the *festa* translates into vociferous argument.

On this day, the debate became particularly acute. It looked as though the clergy were not going to allow the procession to take place, because the weather looked bad. The decision lay in the hands of the parish chapter, and more specifically in those of the Archpriest. An argument began in the church sacristy, that was eventually to lead to the formation of the *Għaqda tal-Pawlini*:

> Everybody was anxiously waiting for the person who took it upon themselves to ring . . . the Meteorological Office to get the official weather forecast. Others began shouting their own forecasts. Some people shouted. Everybody had their own version. Everybody wanted Paul to go out and bless the unique Valletta streets, but in circumstances like those you had to consider your decision. On occasions like those everything begins to get confused with everything else. One argument leads to another. Everybody thinks they're right. When all is said and done, [the decision] wasn't everybody's responsibility. In a word, it was the kind of situation that not for the first time became heated. (St Paul's Parish 1995: 8—my translation)

Rev Carmel Muscat—known as *Dun* Karm—was one of the parish vice-priests. He was generally a placid man, but was prone to explosions of temper. The argument was getting increasingly confrontational. The laity were criticising the clergy, for their suggestion that the procession might not take place, but what they did not understand—according to *Dun* Karm—was that the clergy had a responsibility to preserve the statue, which was the property of the Church, but also an important national artefact. Frustrated with the responsibility of calming down this tense situation, *Dun* Karm snapped. He grabbed the bench-top of the huge mahogany chest used to store damask drapes, and lifted it two feet from its normal position, letting it drop into place with a huge bang. There was immediate, stunned silence.

Pawlu Spiteri was walking up the hill to go and have a *festa* drink at La Valette band club when his brother-in-law came running up:

> You've got to come—there's a huge argument in the sacristy—*Dun* Karm has gone crazy.

By the time he got there, the argument had finished. The procession never took place, but a few months later, Pawlu got a message from Censu Galea, a well-known opera singer and committed *Pawlin*, inviting him to a meeting at the Anglo-Maltese Union, a small club on Merchant's Street. At that meeting, the decision was made to form a new association—the *Għaqda tal-Pawlini*—that would take care of administering the *festa*, and take responsibility for decisions about the procession.

The new *Għaqda* was to incorporate members of both clergy and laity, and aimed to thereby alleviate tensions between the two. Historically, the clergy had adopted a patron's role, mediating between 'people' and state by helping parishioners in legal disputes or other matters that required literacy (Boissevain 1993: 42–44). Drawn from 'polite' families that 'had respect', they were members of 'high' society and therefore considered not entirely trustworthy. As with much of Catholic—and indeed Orthodox—Southern Europe, a distinction was made between Church and Religion that permitted the coexistence of devout Religious faith and profound suspicion of the Church and its officers (c.f. Christian 1972, Herzfeld 1985, Kertzer 1980, Pitt-Rivers 1961). Such suspicion or even anticlericalism was most notable among Labour Party supporters, but also discernible among the predominantly Nationalist *Pawlini*. Most prevalent among men, the suspicion derived partly from anxieties about the exposure of intimate knowledge as local gossip. Some men told me they preferred to give confession to priests outside Valletta, whose knowledge of their lives could not compromise their local reputation.

There were also enduring tensions surrounding authority over Church property, particularly property that the laity considered to be theirs—the property of the Church's Confraternities (see below) or associated with the *festa*. Many of the treasures held at St Paul's Church were purchased by public subscription or individual bequest, and attempts by the clergy to establish administrative authority over them were treated with suspicion. Likewise attempts to modify *festa*. Ruth Behar (1990), analysing the consequences of the Vatican II reforms on popular religiosity in rural Spain, shows how the laity responded with hostility to clerical attempts to change religious practices. A similar hostility was evident in St Paul's parish, where a broadly conservative *ethos* led most *Pawlini* to defend the 'traditional' *festa*. When in 1993, the parish Archpriest decided, at the request of the television company broadcasting the *festa* mass, that the Eucharist would be celebrated on a table altar facing the congregation rather than on the main altar as usual, there was a major outcry. When he was overheard saying to the programme director that he'd 'whip' the

Pawlini if they didn't agree, the argument nearly came to blows. What had no doubt been intended as a flippant comment was interpreted as a cynical attempt to assert control and command not only the shape of the *festa* but also the *Pawlini*. It seemed to make stark what many suggested about the nature of clerical authority—that behind the rhetoric of the Church belonging to the people, it was actually controlled by a clique of self-serving priests.

The *Għaqda* was intended to allay some of these suspicions, and clarify lines of authority over the *festa*. It also represented a union of 'high' and 'low' town St Paul's. Prior to 1970, just as the parish as a whole was divided along a spatial gradient, so too was the *festa*. Whilst the St Paul's Chapter and a few well-placed members of 'high-town' society organised the procession and festivities occurring in and around the church, a small group of men from 'low-town' organised their own festivities in *L-Arċipierku*. The *Għaqda* brought together the *festa ta'fuq*—'high-town *festa*', lit. '*festa* of up'—and the *festa t'isfel*—'low-town *festa*', lit. '*festa* of down'.

Pawlu Spiteri had himself been instrumental in organising the *festa t'isfel*, along with his brother-in-law Guzi Mangion, Charlie Mangion's brother (see chapter five). They had collected money door-to-door and worked on street decorations for *L-Arċipierku*. They had even hired bands for the neighbourhood festivities, and organised band marches, an important feature of any *festa*. Censu Galea, on the other hand, had been central in organising the *festa ta'fuq*. He was a well-connected and 'polite' member of Maltese society, an opera singer from a well-known and well-educated Valletta family. The new *Kumitat* brought together these two men, who were to become the first two Presidents of the *Għaqda*. In doing so, it brought together the 'high' and 'low' *festi*.

This union was not approved by all *Pawlini*. In particular, Pawlu Spiteri's friend, Pawlu DeGiorgio—a brother-in-law of Polly Camilleri, and helper with the original *festa t'isfel*—objected. He refused to go to the initial meeting, and effectively dropped out of organising the *festa*. This was indicative of the tensions between 'high' and 'low' influences at the time of the *Għaqda's* creation. The 'high-town', 'polite' *Pawlini* were seen as allied to the clergy, who often made what were considered bad decisions regarding the *festa*, and ignored the suggestions of 'the people'—particularly those from

L-Arċipierku. Such tensions, like those between clergy and laity, were still evident in the early 1990s.

RITUAL, COMMEMORATION, PRACTICE

Ritual has occupied something of centre stage in Social Anthropology (Douglas 1966: 65). A number of scholars have attempted definitions of ritual, but behind most theories is the assumption that it communicates things—ideas, values, practices—that are necessary, or presented as necessary, for social life (Leach 1968, Lewis 1980, Turner 1967). The communication inherent in ritual is sometimes achieved through a direct linguistic mode—through oratory (Bloch 1974, 1975, 1977)—but more commonly through a more indirect, symbolic mode. Indeed, the presence of symbolism in ritual has become part of the definitional framework, so much so that Kertzer, paraphrasing Geertz, has described ritual as 'action wrapped in a web of symbolism' (1988: 9).

Such action is considered different from other types of action, if not necessarily in form then certainly in meaning. For Catholics, for example, eating bread during holy communion is different from eating bread at any other time. Humphrey and Laidlaw have even suggested that ritual action can be distinguished from other types of action because of an absence of meaning—the 'action' of ritual is partly that of imbuing action with meaning (1994: 2). Such an argument turns the tides on the received orthodoxy that rituals act on persons. Rather, it suggests that persons produce rituals, through a process of 'ritualisation' (Ibid, Bell 1992) that involves them as subjects, rather than objects.

The assumption that rituals act on persons derives from the principally Durkheimian assumptions behind much anthropology of ritual (Lukes 1975). For Durkheim, the central function of ritual is to strengthen the bonds attaching people to society. It achieves this by concentrating attention around a central symbol, or totem, which is a material expression of both god and society (1915: 236). It is the main medium for the inculcation of the collective representations that are the stuff of *conscience collective*—at once a precondition for and a constituent of society itself. Ritual in this sense produces society—or certainly social cohesion. Behind this theory, although not made explicit, is the assumption that ritual ensures social continuity. It is in acknowledgement of this Durkheimian legacy that Connerton identifies ritual as one of the ways societies 'remember' (1989: 103).

Connerton elaborates two levels at which what he calls communal memory can be 'conveyed and sustained by (more or less ritual) performances' (40). The first is through commemorative ceremonies,[26] the second through bodily practice. Commemorative ceremonies differ from bodily practices in that they are explicitly not everyday practices, but extraordinary practices that are formalised and standardised in particular ways. Such ceremonies, he argues, are uniquely capable of transmitting social, historical, collective memory:

> [in commemorative ceremonies] a community is reminded of its identity as represented by and told in a master narrative. (70)

Their effectiveness is assured by their performative nature. Commemorative ceremonies are above all performed, enacted—a point to which I return in the next chapter. For the moment, though, I want to concentrate on the assumptions of collectivity inherent in Connerton—and indeed Durkheim. Both assume the effectiveness of collective rituals in doing the work they attribute to them. For Connerton, this effectiveness is guaranteed in part by the power of re-enactment—either explicit or 'rhetorical'—that serves to bring the past into the present (61–70). It causes the reappearance of that which has disappeared, and enables—or even forces—people to participate in their own histories. However, what Connerton seems to forget is that commemorative ceremonies are planned, organised and performed by people who are agents of this process. Moreover, they are often agents with different agendas and different interests in the particular ritual or ceremony.

Recent work in the anthropology of ritual has paid increasing attention to the various groups or 'constituencies' (Baumann 1992) involved in any one ritual, suggesting a move away from the Durkheimian assumption that rituals produce collectivity. Rather, it suggests that while ritual might overtly aim itself at the production of collective unity and social harmony, it is very much a domain of contest (Aull Davies 1998, Kelly and Kaplan 1990, Cohen 1993).

Baumann, working in multicultural Southall, West London, suggests a rethinking of Durkheim to argue that rather than being inwardly-focused, on the project of creating cohesion and community, rituals often look outside to other, competing groups (1992: 99). Further to this, he suggests that rather than being performed by unified, cohesive and uniform 'congregations', they may also be performed by 'competing constituencies' (Ibid). His material shows this competition in at least two senses. First, the same ritual can assume a different form and different meaning when performed by different groups. For example, Christmas is different among Sikh Jats and Hindus in Southall (102–103). Second, and most relevant here, the same ritual event can be used by different 'constituencies', in different ways and to different ends. Baumann discusses the opening of a local sports centre at which 'a loose alliance of ritual constituencies, each us[ed] symbolic forms to stake mutual claims' (101). Cohen, in his analysis of Notting Hill Carnival, has demonstrated that such varied ritual constituencies can just as often stake diverse claims (1993).

Such work has emerged from the general move in anthropology away from theories of structure towards theories of practice (Ortner 1984). It is in this context that scholars such as Humphrey and Laidlaw (1994) and Bell (1992) suggest we focus not on ritual *per se* but on 'ritualisation'—on ritual as action or practice, rather than a 'thing'—something people *do,* rather than something people have done to them. Bell in particular argues that we should look at the various ways in which actions are produced as rituals, and identifies a number of strategies in this process of ritualisation:

> strategies of differentiation through formalization and periodicity, the centrality of the body, the orchestration of schemes by which the body defines an environment and is defined in turn by it, ritual mastery, and the negotiation of power to define and appropriate the hegemonic order. (Bell 1992: 220)

Leaving aside the question of the body, to which I return in the next chapter, it can be seen how *festa* involves the strategies of periodisation, formalisation and standardisation of the hegemonic order that Bell identifies. The activities of *festa* became 'set aside' as special, ritual, through a series of ritualised acts—band marches, fireworks, the procession—that are overseen by the *Għaqda.* Indeed such ritualisation was partly achieved by the setting up of the *Għaqda* as an 'official' entity. This officialised and legitimised a degree of control by the *Pawlini* over what had hitherto 'belonged' to the Church, and created an institution dedicated to organising the ritualisation of *festa*. In particular, it established the relatively spontaneous celebrations of the *festa t'isfel* as part of the standard order of the *festa* proceedings. In doing so, it also established an official domain in which matters of ritual propriety could be discussed, contested. The *Għaqda tal-Pawlini* was, above all, concerned with ritual mastery and negotiating the formal hegemonic order of *festa*, the significance of St Paul's shipwreck and indeed the importance of religion and the Church in contemporary Malta. To this extent it was an organisation set up with the express purpose of managing and administering the ritualisation of *San Pawl*.

REREADING *FESTA*

Since Boissevain's pioneering work in the 1950s and 60s, *festa* has always been thought to be as much about talking to 'others' as it is concerned with creating unity within. Boissevain describes how different class, locality and party-political factions present their antagonisms—*pika*—in the form of *festa partiti*—'*festa* factions' (1993). These *partiti* compete with each other, in ever-escalating demonstrations of their ritual ascendancy, which are aimed primarily at the 'other' (1984). Indeed, St Paul's *festa* has been involved in such a relationship of *pika* with its neighbouring parish *festa*, St Dominics, for as long as anybody can remember but certainly since the establishment of the two rival Valletta band clubs—the Kings Own and La Valette—at the turn of the twentieth century.

The development of brass band clubs went hand in hand with the emergence of modern *festi* and *festa partiti* in the mid- to late-nineteenth century (Boissevain 1993: 75ff). Nowadays, most *festi* involve numerous band marches played by hired bands from all over Malta, but the most important march is that performed by a *festa*'s 'own' band club—normally in the early afternoon of *festa* day. For St Paul's feast this is played by La Valette, for St Dominic's by King's Own. As argued in chapter five, the antagonism between St Paul's and

St Dominic's parish, and hence the *pika* between their two *festi* and band clubs, is informed not only by parochial concerns but also by politics. This is true of the relationship between *festa partiti* in other parts of Malta (Ibid: 83). Just as most *Pawlini* are Nationalists and members of La Valette band club, so most *Duminikani* are Labourites and King's Own members. Each club has a club-house in one of the grand *palazzi*—palaces—in the upper part of Republic Street, where decorative plaques commemorate past Presidents, Secretaries and Treasurers. The La Valette plaque reads as a role-call of promient Nationalist politicians, whilst the King's Own has an equally prestigious litany of Labour officials.

This almost binary opposition has led in the past to violent attempts by the rival band clubs to disrupt each other's *festi,* and tallies with Boissevain's observations that *festi* have for some time been aimed precisely at 'others' as much as 'ones own'. However, Boissevain tends to see a one-to-one relationship between *festa* and faction, such that each significant group becomes its own *festa partit*. Although central to his analysis are the antagonisms between clergy and laity, and disputes *between* different *partiti* are emphasised (eg 1993: 84–91), he focuses less on disputes *within partiti*—particularly among the lay groups associated with *festi.* Thus whilst his theorisation of *festa* incorporates part of Baumann's entreaty to 'reread Durkheim'—by examining the 'other'-focus of ritual—it stops short of a detailed analysis of the 'competing constituencies' within any one *festa*. Indeed Boissevain sees the role of *festa* in generating solidarity as central to its contemporary significance, and particularly the recent trend of escalation.

In a range of publications, Boissevain has charted the development of Maltese *festa*, and particularly its—to him unexpected—escalation since the 1950s (1984, 1988, 1991). Most recently, he has located this escalation in a wider European context (1992a). The widespread critique of post-war industrialisation, and consequent valorisation of 'tradition', coupled with increased affluence and leisure time, he argues, have freed resources to enable the organisation of rituals, and an overall climate of state tolerance towards popular cultural forms has meant that they have been free to expand. The increased demand for 'traditional' and 'authentic' rituals from tourists and migrants has been fuelled by their unprecedented exposure in the mass media, and particularly television, revitalising what he had initially thought would become increasingly anachronistic religious practices in an increasingly secular world. Boissevain traces this trend in the Maltese village of Naxxar, where he sees the expansion of St Lucy's *festa* and the development of a Good Friday procession as new modes of identifying, strengthening and asserting the uniqueness of the local, in the face of increasing tourist numbers (1992a: 11, 1992b). Here, the *festa* is seen to create a kind of Durkheimian solidarity that Turner (1969) has more subtly glossed as *communitas:*

> Maltese celebrations have been growing because they express the desire of people buffeted by waves of radical change and political divisiveness to play and so re-establish their identity and contact with one another and to achieve, momentarily, the peace of communitas. (1992b: 152)

Indeed, the production of solidarity or *communitas* is becoming an increasingly conscious aim by those involved in the organisation of *festa*. The functionalist reading of ritual as a source of social cohesion is no longer the preserve of the social scientist. If people express a desire for unity, it is a self-conscious desire, and one which they know all too well how to satisfy. This is no less so for the *Għaqda tal-Pawlini,* whose President explained to me in my first interview with him:

> The *festa* is nice, you know. It's a tradition. But it's good because it brings people together. Especially nowadays, many people live outside Valletta, and many people are busy. It's nice that everybody comes together for *San Pawl.*

This self-consciousness of the *festa*'s sociological purpose on the part of those organising the event lends credibility to an interpretation of ritual as practice. Rather than a cultural reflex performed automatically and uncritically in the unthinking reproduction of tradition, *festa* is a conscious activity undertaken for a particular reason. Rather than simply happening, *festa* is something people *do,* with particular objectives in mind. Of these, the production of unity is an important one, although paradoxically, such self-consciousness about the purposes of *festa* leads to fragmentation and tension between different ritual constituencies, over how best to achieve this end. Among *Pawlini,* such tensions reinforced and exacerbated prevailing antagonisms between 'polite' and non-polite, high-town and low-town, younger and older *Pawlini*. They were manifest as disagreements over the appropriate forms of ritualisation—the appropriate forms and practices the *festa* should involve.

For the *Pawlini,* the imperative to 'get it right' (see Humphrey and Laidlaw 1994: 111f.f.) was doubly contentious because *San Pawl* was a national feast as well as a local one. It establishes a continuity of national ritual tradition and national Catholic identity that mirrors the national significance of Valletta as a whole, and although not one of the official national celebrations such as Carnival or Independence Day, it is *de facto* a national *festa*. It is marked by a national holiday, and a day of religious obligation,[27] and is also the only *festa* at which the attendance of the Archbishop, the Prime Minister and the President is habitual, if not obligatory. Links between the parochial and the national are further cemented by their constant reiteration during *San Pawl* itself. St Paul is referred to as *Pawlu ta'Malta*—'Paul of Malta'—*L-Apostlu ta'Malta*—'the Apostle of Malta'—*L-Appostlu Missierna*—'the Apostle, Our Father'—*Missier il-Maltin*—'the Father of the Maltese'—and *Pawlu Tagħna*—'Our Paul'. This national significance put the *festa* in the national public eye, to the extent that the nation as a whole was regarded as a ritual constituency in itself, with a vested interest in ensuring appropriate ritualisation.

PUBLICITY: THE IMAGE OF THE *FESTA*

The responsibility for the form of *festa* was given over to the *Għaqda tal-Pawlini*. Membership of the *Għaqda* was open to any people considered earnest supporters of the *festa*, who were practising Catholics and who were committed to the apostolic legacy of St Paul. In practice, this meant it was open to any Maltese who expressed an interest, although they tended to be people with direct connections to the parish. Its principal activities involved the organisation of fund-raising, through door-to-door collections and fund-raising activities such as bingo evenings, plays and song contests. It also involved managing and administering the expenditure of these funds, on street decorations, band marches, fireworks and publicity. *Għaqda* membership entitled people to vote in the annual election for the *Kumitat*—Committee—who were responsible for running the *festa*, administering funds, booking and getting police permission for fireworks and band marches, and making decisions about changes in the form or content of the *festa*.

In general, the election of the new *Kumitat* was relatively uneventful, but controversy periodically emerged, making the election discussions quite volatile. There was almost limitless scope for criticism of the *Kumitat*. If new street decorations were considered badly designed, hired bands did not play well, or fireworks were set off at the wrong times, there was criticism. These arguments were, in Bell's terms, concerned with the appropriate forms of ritualisation for St Paul's *festa*—what should *San Pawl* look like and how should it be celebrated? Moreover, they were concerned with negotiating authority over these hegemonic forms—who was to decide on what these forms would be?

In the early 1990s these arguments in many ways replicated those which had led to the formation of the *Għaqda* in the first place. Tensions persisted between a 'high-town' *klikka* seen in general as 'modernisers' and a 'low-town' *klikka* who saw themselves as representing the 'traditional' interests of 'the people' and the spirit of the old *festa t'isfel* in *L-Arċipierku*. For the latter group, the maintenance of a 'traditional' *festa* was linked to the perpetuation of *L-Arċipierku* as a nostalgic community. It was therefore not only concerned with the commemoration of St Paul as historical memory, but also that of *L-Arċipierku* as social and collective memory. For the former, the importance of commemorating *L-Arċipierku* was less important. Rather, their agenda revolved around the *festa* as a national commemoration. The tension between these two groups was born out in a debate that emerged in 1993, concerning the publicity poster for the *festa*. Such posters were an important artefact for committed *Pawlini*. Not only did they advertise the *festa*, but they also became objects of aesthetic appreciation that were pleasing souvenirs.

On one wall of the bar *San Paolo Naufrago*—'St Paul's Shipwreck' known more commonly as *Għand Lawrenz* or 'Lawrence's Place'—was a small notice-board on which were pinned advertisements and timetables of local events—particularly religious events. *Għand Lawrenz* was an important field site, as it acted as a kind of unofficial club house for the *Għaqda tal-Pawlini*. Most *Għaqda* meetings ended up there, and most policy decisions were discussed there. It was a focus for political canvassing and for activities during the *festa* of St Paul. As such, like the parish church sacristy, it was an important site for public discussion.

Early in January 1993, the newly-designed poster for the forthcoming feast of St Paul was pinned to the notice-board for the first time (see figure five). It was an innovative design. Against a black background was a black-and-white line drawing of St Paul standing with a muscular right arm raised high in the air. This is the familiar stance of the saint as most commonly represented, preaching to the Maltese. Above his head was a large Maltese flag, signifying the national importance of St Paul, and to the left of the saint the blue waves of the sea and the triangular prow of the boat that brought him to the island. Onto the dark area of sky were printed the programme of *festa* events, and at the top of the poster, picked out in yellow, were the words *San Pawl '93*—St Paul '93—and the motto: *Għax aħna Pawlini, aħna Maltin*—'Because we're *Pawlini*, we're Maltese'.

Designed by two members of the *Għaqda* Committee, the poster was circulated to local businesses and shops to advertise in their shop-windows. Given Valletta's centrality as a financial and commercial centre, this advertising encouraged a *festa* audience that went beyond the immediately parochial. As a form of advertising, the poster needed to contain necessary information concerning the *festa* schedule, but it was also considered to be an important representation of the spirit of the *festa*, and of the *Pawlini*. It was particularly important that this representation should be inclusive, rather than exclusive. While other *festi* were primarily concerned with a kind of local patriotism or factionalism *San Pawl*, as the national *festa*, was explicitly inclusive of the whole nation, not just local people.

As a consequence, the events which surround *San Pawl,* and the image given to the *festa* through publicity material, must successfully convey an inclusiveness that takes it beyond the merely parochial to include the national, and even international. As far as *Pawlini* were concerned, it commemorated the central agent in the spreading of the gospel and hence the production of the Church as an international institution. It also incorporated national and international figures into its ritual practice, involving national state dignitaries and leaders of the international churches that have congregations in Malta—Roman Catholic, Greek Catholic, Greek Orthodox, Church of England,

Figure 5 Poster for *San Pawl 1993*

Church of Scotland and Methodist. The main events of *festa* day are broadcast on national television, making the whole event an object of national public scrutiny. Such scrutiny led to controversy when the new poster was criticised *Għand Lawrenz*.

Giovanni Gauci, an enthusiastic *Pawlini* man from *L-Arċipierku* began the critique. He was a carpenter, and had had training in the art of religious representations. He was responsible for much of the wooden street furniture that was erected in the lead-up to the *festa* (see below)—the ornate marble-painted columns and statue pedestals that provided a classical back-drop to the *festa's* outside proceedings. The picture of the saint on the new poster was ugly, he said, and not close enough to the ideal provided by the monumental *vara*—statue—that occupied centre stage during the *festa*.

Here, the existing representation was being set up as a model of orthodoxy against which the innovations of the poster were judged. As with debates concerning the refurbishment of Valletta as a whole, this orthodoxy was predominantly Baroque. The monumental *vara* was carved from wood by Melchiore Gafà (1635–1667), an associate of Bernini, who according to church historians was 'the greatest exponent of the Baroque' (Ciarlò 1995: 42). The poster's line drawing, on the other hand, was more modern in style, and as such appealed to a more 'challenging' bourgeois aesthetic than the high Baroque *vara*.[28] It was criticised for being too obscure and modern—going against the traditional aesthetics of *festa*.

A further criticism, which came not only from Giovanni Gauci, but from others, was that the poster was too political:

> It's like the Independence [Day posters] ... Oh, so we're from 'the party' now are we?

Here, they were referring to the use of the Maltese flag in the poster, which is seldom seen in a religious context. Rather, it is most commonly associated with rituals of state, and the Independence Day celebrations which, as we saw in the last chapter, serve as not only a national, but also a Nationalist feast. The use of this political imagery in the religious context was considered objectionable, partly because in a general sense it was considered wrong to mix religion and politics—this despite the historical intertwining of religion and politics throughout Maltese history (Koster 1984). However, it was considered particularly problematic to publicly associate *San Pawl* with the Nationalist Party.

Although my informants agreed that most *Pawlini* were Nationalists, and *San Pawl* as a *festa* was strongly associated with *L-Arċipierku*, a 'Nationalist Fortress', it was nevertheless wrong to publicly advertise the *festa* as a Nationalist event. To do so would not be in keeping with the inclusive *ethos* of the *festa* as a national event. Indeed, because it was a national event, and therefore an object of public scrutiny, its organisers were usually at pains to down-play its political overtones. To its critics, the poster represented a significant gaffe. It left the *Pawlini* vulnerable to accusations of exclusivity.

Coupled with this criticism at the overly-political implications of the poster, was a wider complaint about the motto, 'Because we're *Pawlini*, we're Maltese'. This was intended to be the motto of the *festa* as a whole, and presumed to show the linkage of local and national interests that *San Pawl* embodies. However, when the poster was circulated, a number of people complained that what had intended to imply an inclusiveness actually suggested the opposite. To state that 'Because we're *Pawlini*, we're Maltese' implies that the only true Maltese are *Pawlini*. In order to work, the motto should have been written in reverse—'Because we're Maltese, we're *Pawlini*'. The point was made by a local shop-keeper who worked in St Paul's parish but had lived all his life in Floriana, Valletta's neighbouring—and rival—town:

> People will take offence at this. [The *Pawlini*] always say they have a *festa* for everyone. How is this for everyone? It says that if you're not *Pawlin* you're not Maltese. People in my neighbourhood will take it to heart.

Within a few days, his prediction had materialised and the motto provoked a major debate that went on not only in small bars and clubs such as *Għand Lawrenz*, but also in the media. I heard it discussed over coffee at the University, on the radio and in the press. These public media discussions were then themselves discussed *Għand Lawrenz* and elsewhere. The speed and efficiency with which the criticisms voiced *Għand Lawrenz* appeared in the public media suggests that despite the complaints expressed by David Chetcuti in the last chapter—that there is no public opinion in Malta—there is nevertheless a functioning sphere within which public opinion is discussed, at least about *festa*. The dynamics of this public sphere in many ways coincide with the dynamics of Maltese politics more widely, with 'the people' and public figures enjoying a certain intimacy of relationships that is nevertheless cross-cut with divisions based on respectability and a sense of being either included or excluded from a central, influential *klikka*.

The Committee that had designed the poster for *San Pawl 93* were regarded by many *Pawlini* as part of this influential *klikka*. Indeed, the President had been involved with the Nationalist Party, and was later elected as Nationalist mayor of Valletta. This may have been one of the reasons behind complaints about the political nature of the poster. If *San Pawl* became explicitly linked to the Nationalists, then his political career could only benefit as a result. However, the complaints also referred back to previous arguments over *San Pawl*, that focused on the form of *festa* itself as much as its image.

COMPETING *KLIKEK*—COMPETING CONSTITUENCIES

San Pawl 1991 took place during the Gulf War. It had been suggested by the Archbishop that, because of the situation in the Gulf, it was inappropriate to have a full celebration of *festa*. He suggested that the more lively external festivities, such as band marches and fireworks should be excluded, turning the *festa* into a 'pilgrimage'—*pelegrinaġġ*. The Archpriest was in favour of this, and after much discussion, the *Kumitat* eventually agreed to cancel all external festivities except for the main procession, which would take place in solemnity, with no brass bands present.

The decision involved cancelling the inaugural 'Demonstration' with a new statue of St Paul's conversion that had been planned two days before the *festa*. The Demonstration amounted to a procession with the new statue, which was to be carried around the streets of the parish before being mounted on a large pedestal in Valletta's central square—in front of the law courts. Its cancellation marked the outgoing *Kumitat* as 'traditionalists'. Not only had they reverted to an acceptance of the Church's authority over *festa* decisions, they had also delayed an innovation that many were looking forward to, but which had attracted criticism beforehand. Some *Pawlini* had argued that it would take people's attention away from the main *festa* events, and its cancellation by the *Kumitat* seemed to endorse this view.

There was a major outcry. The *Kumitat* was accused of bowing down too easily to the wishes of the Church authorities. After all, hadn't this been the reason for setting up the *Għaqda* in the first place? At the Annual General Meeting that followed the *pelegrinagg*, the existing *Kumitat* was deposed, and replaced by another. It was widely believed that the new *Kumitat* would be stronger in its dealings with the ecclesiastical authorities, partly because of the new President, who had been a powerful political campaigner for the Nationalist Party. He was a well-connected man from 'high-town' St Paul's parish. As such, he was thought to have influence and be able to manipulate situations to the benefit of his constituents. He was an innovator, thought to have a more 'modern' outlook than the outgoing *Kumitat*. He was responsible for the controversial publicity of *San Pawl* 1993. The outgoing administration, and their supporters, were suspicious of this 'modern' outlook, the association with 'high-town' and particularly the links with party politics. There was a worry that he would use the *Għaqda* as a vehicle for his own political projects. They, on the other hand, saw themselves as more attached to the traditions of *festa*—more attached to its popular roots in *L-Arċipierku*.

The tensions between the older, low-town *Kumitat* and this newer, high-town *Kumitat* became consolidated in two groups, or 'cliques'—*klikek*—comprising members of the two *Kumitati* and their friends. Although seldom made explicit, there was an air of antagonism in relations between these two *klikek*. The tensions were played out *Għand Lawrenz*, where members of the different *klikek* sat in different parts of the bar. Those associated with the new *Kumitat* would congregate behind the bar itself, passing the occasional comment about the 'old-fashioned' former *Kumitat* that itself sat in front of the bar, grumbling about the declining standards of *festa* and its organisation. Occasionally, arguments would break out, that invariably concerned the form and content of the *festa*, and the responsibilities inherent in its administration.

The schism was consolidated in 1992, in an argument that involved one of Charlie Zammit's friends (see chapters three and six). Charlie had been on the outgoing *Kumitat* of 1991, and was committed not only to St Paul's *festa*, but also to the religious confraternity at the local Franciscan church of *Ta'Gieżu* ('Our Lady of Jesus'). Indeed, when he lost his office in the *Għaqda* he began to concentrate his attentions on the confraternity, eventually becoming its procurator. His friend, Manwel Grima was a prominent member of the *klikka* associated with Charlie. He was a jovial figure with a passion for the Church and *festi*.

In 1992, Grima—as he was habitually known—was in charge of ordering and administering the fireworks for the *festa*. Every *festa* is accompanied by periodic bursts of fireworks, in the form of loud petards set off each day in the lead-up to the *festa*, at mass times. On the eve of the *festa*, a display of ground fireworks—flares and rotating 'Catherine Wheels' attached to complex wooden scaffolding—is organised, and the culmination of fireworks is the *kaxxa infernali*—'infernal box'—set off when the saint's statue leaves the church. This is a one- or two-minute burst of rapid fire aerial fireworks, including decorative flourishes and plain petards. It is the moment when the saint is greeted to the outside world, and was Grima's favourite part of the *festa*.

Determined to make a good show of this, his first year as commissioner for fireworks, he rather over-estimated the needs of the *kaxxa*, and underestimated its cost—the result being that he overspent the fireworks budget by some Lm300 – £600stg. When this came to the attention of the rest of the *Kumitat*, it was placed on the agenda of the Annual General Meeting. At the meeting, Grima was suspended from office, and an inquiry instigated. The events caused a great deal of argument among the *Pawlini*, not least between Grima and his assistant, who was brother to the new President. The case sharpened tensions within the *Għaqda*, between the outgoing *Kumitat* and the new one.

Fireworks are one of the main ways the events of the *festa* are 'set aside' or 'ritualised'. They provide an important aural back-drop against which *festa* is performed. A necessary part of *festa*, they are also one of the main media of competition between rival *festi*, both in terms of sheer scale and aesthetic value (Boissevain 1993). Rival *festi* will attempt to exceed either the quantity or quality—or both—of their neighbours, and great pride is taken in having the better fireworks. Arguments about the scale of expenditure on fireworks can be seen as arguments over this important aspect of ritualisation. Similarly, the debates about introducing the Demonstration, and cancelling it in 1991, revolved around who had authority to make decisions about ritualisation. In the case of Grima's fireworks expenditure, the debate quickly condensed into one between the *klikka* associated with Charlie Zammit and the old *Kumitat*, and that associated with the new *Kumitat*. In the event, Grima was found guilty of no more than over-enthusiasm, but the case left him cynical about the workings of the new *Għaqda*. During my fieldwork, he declined to participate in any of its meetings, regarding them as pointless. He was a major source of complaint about the way the *festa* was going. Along with his other friends, Charlie Zammit, Censu Dalli and David Mangion, he would bemoan the lack of attention to 'tradition' in the policies and activities of the new *Kumitat*. At least he had tried to expand on a 'traditional' practice of ritualisation—fireworks. The new *Kumitat* would *jivvintaw*—'invent'—new things, seemingly for the sake of doing so.

These disputes recapitulated the divisions of 'high' and 'low' town *festi* that the *Għaqda* had brought together, focusing attention and concern on the relative ability of each group to properly organise the ritualisation of *festa*. However, the anxieties expressed by Grima and his friends were not only aimed at distinctions of respectability, but also at differences between the different age-groups within the *Għaqda*. As they had become increasingly side-lined from the organisation of *festa*, their roles had been taken over by a younger group of *Pawlini*. As with the concerns examined in chapter three, concerning the morality of younger Maltese, this created tensions between the different generations of *Pawlini*. These tensions were particularly evident in discussions about the preparations for *festa*, and particularly the organisation of street decorations.

PREPARING THE *FESTA TA'BARRA*

All Maltese *festi* are divided conceptually and administratively between events *ta'ġewwa*—'inside' the church—and those *ta'barra*—'outside' (see figure six). The former are those practices which occur inside the church, are associated with the solemn liturgical elements of the *festa*, and are organised by the clergy. The latter occur outside the

Inside Festivities

Saturday 21st January, 6pm

Hrug of the statue of St Paul

Wednesday 25th January, 5.15pm

Feast of St Paul's Conversion: Rosary, followed by sung mass

Thursday 26th January, 5.45pm

Mass for children, followed by play about St Paul performed by children

Friday 27th January, 6pm

Mass celebrated by local Franciscan community

Saturday 28th January, 7pm

St Paul's song contest

Sunday 29th January, 6pm

Mass celebrated by invited priest from St Paul's church, Rabat

Monday 30th January, 6pm

Mass celebrated by the Charismatic Group

Tuesday 31st January, 6pm

Mass celebrated by all Maltese nuns

Wednesday 1st February, 6pm

Mass celebrated by Neo Katekumenali community

Thursday 2nd February, 6pm

Feast of Candlemas

Friday 3rd February, 6pm

Mass for the Apostolic Groups

Saturday 4th February, 6pm

Mass for all committee members of sporting and other organisations in Valletta

Sunday 5th February, 6pm

Mass for all men, women and children with a devotion towards St Paul

Monday 6th February, 5.15pm

Mass, followed by *Tridu* sermon and *Antifon*

Tuesday 7th February, 5.15pm

Mass, followed by *Tridu* sermon and *Antifon*

Wednesday 8th February, 5.15pm

Figure 6 *Festa* Schedule, 1995

Mass, followed by *Tridu* sermon and *Antifon*

Thursday 9th February: *Lejlet* – 'eve' – of the *festa*

10am – Mass for the sick and aged

5.30pm – Translation of the relic of St Paul

7pm – Sung mass

Friday 10th February: *Festa* Day

9.15am – *Pontifikal* Mass, with *Panegyrku* to St Paul

11.45am – Mass

4pm – Mass in English

5.15pm – Procession of Statue

9.30pm – Re-entry of Procession, Celebration of Eucharist, *Antifon*

Outside Festivities

Sunday 5th February

10am – Band March

7.30pm – Band March

Monday 6th February, 7.30pm

Band March

Tuesday 7th February, 7.30pm

Band March

Wednesday 8th February, 8pm

'Demonstration' with statue of St Paul's Conversion

Thursday 9th February: *Lejlet* – 'eve' – of the *festa*, 7pm

Band March, followed by Fireworks

Friday 10th February: *Festa* Day

12.45pm – Band March

5.30pm – Band March

6.30pm – Band March and Procession

Figure 6 *Festa* Schedule, 1995 (*continued*)

church and are associated with the popular celebration of *festa*. These events are the responsibility of the laity, and in St Paul's, of the *Għaqda tal-Pawlini*. The administration of the external festivities involves skills associated with male sociability. Thus, the *Għaqda* spend their time convening meetings among themselves or with other organisations, at which they must be able to negotiate, argue, compromise. They must also be able to mobilise sufficient manpower to make sure that not only are the *armar*—'street decorations'—correctly maintained throughout the year, but also that they are correctly and efficiently put up in the weeks leading up to *festa*.

Every street through which the outside festivities passed was decorated. The main items are: flag-poles from which were suspended decorative fabric arches—*pavaljuni*—that turned the uniform beige streets into colourful avenues; the *pavaljuni* themselves, which are suspended from large wooden beams with ornate brass end-pieces; the wooden columns that are erected the length of St Paul's Street, topped with large brass bowls in which palm leaves are arranged; the brass chandeliers that are suspended from hooks along St Paul's Street; the plain green tinsel that is suspended in festoons with hired lights; and finally, the huge wooden pedestal on which the statue of St Paul's conversion sits, after it has been carried on its Demonstration. These items take up a lot of room, and are secreted in various parts of the parish—in Church- or *Għaqda*-administered buildings. For example the *pavaljuni* are rolled up around the beam from which they hang, and stored in a loft above the sacristy of the parish church, the wooden columns and brass paraphernalia are stored in the basement of the Union of St Joseph on St Paul's Street, where the *Pawlini* Youth used to meet, and the flag poles and pedestals are stored in the small workshop, or *maħzen*, rented by the *Pawlini* on East Street.

The *maħzen* is also the place where maintenance and restoration work was carried out on the *armar*. This was a considerable task. Most of the more decorative items were wooden, painted ornately to resemble marble. Because they were stored in often very humid conditions, and taken out only once a year into the cold, wind and rain of early February, they would warp, crack and chip. Making sure they were presentable during *festa* was a major task, involving considerable skill, organisation, and above all work.

Much of this work had been provided by Charlie Zammit, Censu Dalli, David Mangion and Manwel Grima—the *klikka* I have identified as more traditionally-oriented than the new, post-*pelegrinaġġ Kumitat*. They were regarded as true *dilettanti* of the *armar*—a term that connotes respect for a passionate enthusiasm and genuine expertise, rather than the rather pejorative English dilettant. They would work long hours in the *maħzen*, an activity that involved as much sociability as industry. On virtually every occasion they got together to work on the *armar*, they would also have a drink, either *Għand Lawrenz* or in the *maħzen* itself.

However, just as the events of the 1991 *pelegrinaġġ* and the 1992 case against Grima caused a rift in the organisation of the *festa* so too it seemed that a line had been drawn between different *klikek* involved in the maintenance and restoration of religious and *festa* artefacts. The task of maintaining the *armar* passed on from this *klikka*, and one of their major concerns was the extent to which the standards they had met were being maintained. The standards related both to workmanship and the degree of commitment shown by the new men involved in the *armar*. In particular, criticism revolved around the state of the *maħzen* itself. When this group had been in charge, I was told, the *maħzen* had operated like a kind of club. Going there was not considered a chore, but part of normal, sociable existence. As David Chetcuti put it:

> It was just like a club. We used to go down there every day, and even if there wasn't really any work to do we'd go and play around with something or other. And girls would come there too—it was really like a [community] centre. We had a fridge there and a cooker. We'd take a case of wine down and have big meals outside on the parapet overlooking East Street. It was like our own place, and we kept it clean, you know. Not like now. The floor was as clean as a glass, you could eat off it. Now look at it. It's closed virtually all the time—and dirty.

As Anton Grima had written in the *festa* programme for 1992, 'for those involved at the *maħzen*, the *festa* begins on the 11th February every year and ends on 10th February' (St Paul's Parish 1992: 18). David's criticism, from 1994, was that this spirit of year-long work had disappeared. It clearly reflected a nostalgia for the times when he and his friends were more central to the *festa* preparations and the maintenance of the *armar*. During that time, commitment was unquestioned. Those involved would turn up every day, and if younger men were courting, women would come too. This comment was a direct reflection on the apparent lack of commitment by the younger men who had taken over the *maħzen* and the administration of the *armar*. They had become too 'flighty', and too preoccupied with courtship.

An oft-cited example of the slip in standards was that of the flag-poles that normally lined the streets during *festa*. They had become cracked and chipped, so that in 1993 they were unusable. The *Kumitat* made an agreement with the *festa* committee of St Dominic's feast, to borrow their flag-poles. This was regarded as little short of a scandal. Not only did it not make sense, given that the *Pawlini* had their own flag-poles, but it also sullied their reputation for being able to stage a *festa* in an efficient, self-sufficient manner. The fact that it was the Dominicans, the *Pawlini* rivals, from whom the poles were borrowed, rankled even more. It was evidence that standards had sunk to such a degree that even age-old rivalries had to be put aside.

After the change in *Għaqda* administration, responsibility was taken over by Michael Camilleri—the son of Polly and Pawlu Camilleri, introduced in chapter three. The Camilleri family were and had been heavily involved in *San Pawl*. In 1993 and 1994, two of the three sons were elected to the *Kumitat*, and Polly was involved with fund-raising activities. The family's involvement was significant. They had been through some difficult times, I was told by Michael, but prayer and devotion to St Paul had pulled them through. For this reason alone, Michael and his brother were enthusiastic in their involvement, which centred around the organisation of the *armar*. They were both in their mid twenties and unmarried, and therefore in a position to devote time and energy to the *festa*. But they were constantly frustrated by the unreliability of their peers. On countless occasions I met Michael *Għand Lawrenz*, waiting for friends to turn up and perform some task or other. I would talk to him as he got more and more frustrated, and eventually storm out, leaving a message that things had been called off.

For the older *klikka* of Charlie Zammit *et al*, this was indicative of the changing priorities of young *Pawlini*. David Chetcuti was sympathetic, referring to him as *miskin*—'poor thing'—for having to put up with this kind of unreliability:

> He really wants to work for St Paul, but what can he do when he's got nobody but those children to help.

Referring to the younger helpers as children, David was signalling two things about their abilities. First, that they lacked the skills to perform the necessary restoration work involved in the *festa*. Restoration involves skill in carpentry, electrical repairs, plastering and painting. This involved techniques which most men learn as part of their training for a particular occupation, or when they become householders. Because a necessary condition for being a householder is to be married, the attainment of these skills depended on marriage—one of the central criteria for 'being a man' (see chapter three). However, second, and more significantly, David was implying that the young men lacked commitment or reliability to form a single *klikka* around which the *armar* could be organised throughout the year.

Rather than a unified *klikka*, the group that took over the *armar* was a loose association of young men with various concerns—courtship, football, billiards or other pastimes. They came together only as a temporary group, around *festa* time, and to this extent were a contingent, rather than a committed *klikka*. This sharpened the distinction between putting up the *armar* as a work activity, and its character as leisure—a *hobby*. What for David and his friends had been simply a pleasurable and rewarding part of their daily lives, became for Michael's contemporaries a chore which took time and effort to administer.

The sense of decline in the standards of *armar* maintenance was seen by the more 'traditional' *klikka* as symptomatic of the erosive effects of modern life, and particularly the influence of Europe on young people's activities and aspirations. It encouraged them to be increasingly materialistic, they argued, only interested in going to Paceville, driving their cars around with loud music blaring out and trying to meet young women (see chapter three). Alongside this materialism went an increasing secularisation that threatened to take young people away from the Church, and away from *festa*. With these concerns, it was impossible for them to maintain the high standards of *festa* preparation necessary. In their defence, the younger men would emphasise the innovations that had been made by the new *Kumitat*. New band marches had been introduced, extending the *festa* from five days to a week, but there had also been innovations in the *armar*. In 1994, a new set of *pavaljuni* were hung on St Paul's Street, which were the pride and joy of the new *Għaqda*. For the older group, such innovations were pointless if the older *armar* were not maintained properly. It was important to build on the 'traditional' materials already in existence, which were regarded as a legacy—or patrimony—of those who had organised the *festa t'isfel.*

The sense of responsibility for maintaining the *armar* can be traced back to the overall sense of responsibility for the *festa* itself—for commemorating the national patron and the patron of *L-Arċipierku* in a way that befits the saint's status. The perceived drop in standards was linked to a feeling of ritual entropy that derived in part from the fact that the former *klikka* of true *dilettanti* had been displaced from this responsibility, and partly from a general sense that Maltese society was not going in the right direction. Although Europe, and modernisation, was a principal aim, it nevertheless held a certain threat for Maltese life—not only in the increased materialism and irresponsibility of the youth, but also, and consequently, in the threat to 'traditional' ritual forms such as *festa.*

If the more directly micro-political arguments concerning the relationship between the older *Kumitat* and the newer one, and the different *Pawlini klikek*, are related to the struggles and negotiations to establish hegemony over the correct order of *festa* ritualisation, then these latter arguments about declining standards and the entropic effects of Europeanisation and modernisation are linked to the inherent ambivalence towards such processes. Although the *Pawlini* were predominantly Nationalist—and the *klikka* associated with Charlie Zammit vehemently so—they were nevertheless anxious about the party's European ambitions, and did not wish to see progress occurring at the cost of 'tradition'.

PREPARING THE *FESTA TA'GEWWA*

The tasks associated with the outside festivities are related to ideas of solidarity and sociability among men, and of male responsibility and capability to maintain and erect the *armar* efficiently and with responsibility. They are tasks which David Chetcuti had glossed as being those of 'real men'—not the 'children' who were performing the tasks in the early nineties. By contrast, the tasks associated with the inside festivities, of the *festa ta'gewwa*, are ones which in the domain of the household would be considered the responsibility of women. Rather than the productive pursuit of masculine craftsmanship, they involve a more decorative aesthetic, involving acts of caretakership rather than production. This distinction between female caretaking and male production is discussed in the context of the Greek house by Pavlides and Hesser (1986). In Malta, there is a certain homology between the division of *festa* into *barra* and *ġewwa* and the division of the household along the same lines (see chapter three). As with the household, *ġewwa* in the *festa* refers to a domain of intimacy, when compared to the open, public nature of the *barra* events. The *ġewwa* events—or 'insider' events—are open primarily to members of the local community, whilst *barra*—'outsider'—events are open to all (Boissevain 1992a: 12–14). Because of the national nature of St Paul's *festa*, however, this distinction is slightly skewed. Certain of the 'insider' events are also explicitly for 'outsiders'—in particular, the pontifical mass, which is celebrated on *festa* day, and broadcast on television to the whole nation. Nevertheless, the distinction is still maintained, and particularly among local *Pawlini* there was a certain irritation when people turned up to the 'inside' functions to find the church full of outsiders.

Although the 'inside' preparations involve what might appear to be 'feminine' tasks, these tasks are nevertheless also performed by men. In the lead-up to *festa*, elaborately embroidered damasks are hung on the church walls; all the *festa* silverware is taken out of its cupboards, polished, and placed on the altars; carpets are laid on the steps before each altar; and the entire church is cleaned. This latter task is undertaken during the year by a group of dedicated women who spend one morning each week cleaning the church, but in the lead-up to the *festa*, it is done by men. Hence, the *festa* emerges as a special context in which activities more commonly associated with female domestic chores are undertaken by men. This suggests, further, that the acts of ritualisation are themselves considered male activities, just as the institution in charge of ritualisation—the *Għaqda*—is.

The only task which remains the preserve of women is that of flower-arranging. The normal displays produced by local women, however, are surpassed by the ostentatious sprays that are commercially produced for the occasion. These are placed in front of the saint's statue for the duration of the *festa*, and bear the names of organisations, families and persons that have donated them. These include the local Nationalist Party club, La Valette band club, the leader of the Nationalist Party—during fieldwork also the Prime Minister—and other local politicians or prominent public servants. The elaborate garlands give these public figures further reputation, as patrons of the *festa*. The practice resembles those observed by Foster in Mexico, where political leadership was both demonstrated and enhanced by direct sponsorship of ritual occasions (1967: 203–204).

The decoration of the church is managed by the various Confraternities to which the side altars of the church are dedicated. The church itself is built to the same design as most, with a central nave flanked on either side by small chapels, each with its own altar, and altar-piece. The Confraternities fall into two broad categories—guild Confraternities and religious Confraternities. The guild Confraternities, as many *Pawlini* were keen to tell me, were the original trade unions. This was, of course, a loaded statement, given the broadly anti-socialist opinions of most of their number. Claiming the original trade unions for the Church, the *Pawlini* and through them the Nationalists, served to undermine the Labour movement, that saw itself as heir to the trade unions as introduced in the early twentieth century dockyards (Zammit 1984). The Valletta guild Confraternities predated these unions, having developed in the seventeenth century as mutual aid groups looking after the well-being of artisans from the different trades. Each guild was dedicated to its own patron saint, and contributed to establishing a side-altar in the church of St Paul. Before the twentieth century there were seven guild Confraternities (see figure seven). By the early 1990s this number had reduced to four, with the chapel and Confraternity of St Eligius being taken over by the chapel of the Blessed Sacrament, those of St Helen being given to the religious Confraternity of Our Lady of Charities, and the Confraternity of St Agatha dying out to leave its chapel in the hands of the Church.

Religious Confraternities centre not around the patron saint of a profession, but around a particularly effective object of devotion or source of intercession. Arguably the most important in St Paul's parish was the Miraculous Crucifix housed at the Franciscan Church of *Ta'Gieżu*. Its Confraternity had a large Oratory from which was organised the annual Good Friday procession. It was this Confraternity to which Charlie Zammit turned after being ousted from the *Għaqda*

Guild Confraternities

St Michael – Patron of Grocers and Retailers

Sts Crispin and Crispinian – Patron of Cobblers and Harnes-Makers

St Eligius – Patron of Blacksmiths, taken over by the **Blessed Sacrament**

St Agatha – Patron of Oarsmen and Port Workers, died out

St Helen – Patron of Goldsmiths, taken over by **Our Lady of Charities**

St Homobonus – Patron of Drapers and Tailors

St Martin – Patron of Merchants

Religious Confraternities

Our Lady of Charities

Blessed Sacrament and the Sacred Heart of Jesus

Figure 7 Confraternities of St Paul's Shipwreck Church

Kumitat. At St Paul's church, the Confraternity of Our Lady of Charities was the most important and influential. It had three chapels: Our Lady of Charities, formerly the chapel of St Helen, St Theresa of Avila and St Joseph. It also had a large Oratory adjoining the church, in which the relic of St Paul himself was kept. Our Lady of Charities, or *Tal-Karitas*, was regarded as a Confraternity of the *pulit*—of the wealthy and well-placed. Equally influential, though rather less exclusive, was the Confraternity of the Blessed Sacrament and the Sacred Heart of Jesus, based in the chapel of the Blessed Sacrament. This also had an Oratory, above the sacristy. Members of this Confraternity were widespread throughout the parish of St Paul, and participated particularly in the processions at Corpus Domini and Easter.

A Confraternity—*fratellanza*—is open only to men, although the wives and families of its *fratelli* benefit from its activities. The guild Confraternities in particular used to operate as trade organisations, defending the interests of a particular trade. All Confraternities acted as charitable donors to members who had run into financial difficulties. However, as the numbers of members dwindled in the middle of the twentieth century, they became increasingly oriented to the dead. Their main function in the early nineties was to ensure that all their members had a decent burial on consecrated ground. They held tombs either at the national graveyard in Paola, or other, local graveyards and managed their funds in the maintenance of these tombs. Money came primarily from legacies or bequests, many of which were left on the understanding that the interest from the sum endowed be used to fund masses said for the soul of the departed in perpetuity.

The figurehead of each Confraternity was a Rector—*Rettur*—who was usually the most influential member of the *fratellanza*. However, his role was mainly symbolic, and it was the Procurator who was responsible for the day-to-day running of the Confraternity, the organisation and administration of money, the commissioning of masses and the maintenance of the tombs. They were also responsible for the maintenance of the Confraternity's altar, and its decoration in the lead-up to *festa*. This involved laying out the riches—ornate silverware and expensive carpets—conferred on the Confraternity by previous generations. By and large, in the early nineties the different Procurators were friends. They were *dilettanti*, and *festa* experts, taking care to consult the older *fratelli* who remembered how *San Pawl* used to be organised, and the parish archivist, who would tell them the history behind the different artefacts—who had donated them, how much they had cost, where the money had come from. Their responsibility was to make sure their part in the *festa* lived up to the legacy of this history—a responsibility magnified by that towards the souls of the past *fratelli*. To shirk in these duties was not only to dishonour the Confraternity of the present, but also its past.

As with Valletta as a whole, the *festa armar* and 'tradition' in general, there was a profound sense of decline of the Confraternities. Numbers were dwindling, but maintained by a small group of enthusiasts, who thought that their legacy was important. As Charlie Zammit pointed out:

> People paid their money and trusted the Confraternity to look after them—even after they died. We have a responsibility to them.

David Chetcuti's reasoning was more linked to familial ties, and particularly memories of his father. His father had been a shoe-maker, and a member of the guild Confraternity of Sts Crispin and Crispinian. When he died he had left money for a mass to be said in his memory on the saints' feast day. Every year, David would make sure his family were at the mass, to commemorate his father, and pray for his soul. In 1992, he decided that he should continue his father's commitment to the Confraternity, and on its feast day that year he was initiated into the *fratellanza*. It was a small ceremony that took place in the side alter of Sts Crispin and Crispinian. Afterwards, David had funded a small reception with pastries and whisky, in the church sacristy to celebrate. I had not been long in the parish, but was invited because, as I was told, it was an important 'tradition'. David was clearly very proud at having been admitted to the Confraternity and circulated through the reception receiving words of congratulation from his fellow *fratelli*. Towards the end of the reception he turned to me:

> This is what you should write down—before it all disappears. The younger people, they're not interested in maintaining these traditions. I try to make my sons [they were in their early teens] come along and join in, so that it won't all disappear. But most of the time, the others are just interested in football and going to Paceville.

This sentiment was echoed by others I talked to throughout my two years in St Paul's. While the older people—David was in his early 40s—complained about the youth's lack of commitment to the traditions of *festa* and family, the young people grumbled about the restrictions of 'tradition'. Yet the tensions at play were not only between old and young. There were also antagonisms between high and low town, between clergy and laity and between the old and the new *Kumitati*. These different constituencies with contrasting positions vis-a-vis the central commemoration competed over the terms of ritualisation—over the forms the *festa* would take, and over the innovations that were introduced.

The arguments revolved around a sense of declining standards and the erosive effects of modernisation—that made young people less interested in *festa*, and more interested in the pleasures of consumption and materialism. It therefore relates back to the sense of declining morality explored in chapter three, but also to the nostalgia for community expressed in chapter five. For the older *Pawlini*, the *festa* was as much a commemoration of *L-Arċipierku* as a commemoration of St Paul. The two were inseparable. The arguments also related to the enduring tensions between 'high' and 'low' town St Paul's and of 'polite' society and 'the people'. As the former increasingly turned towards Europe and modernity, there was a fear that the more 'traditional' elements of *festa* would disappear, leaving it as a celebration not for the people, but for *il-pulit*—for politicians and other public figures to use as a vehicle for self-publicity.

NOTES

[26] Connerton is not principally concerned with the various attempts to classify different types of ritual (see especially Gluckman 1962, Leach 1968). By 'commemorative ceremonies' he simply means rituals which—like *festa*—are oriented to the past.

[27] All Maltese are obliged by the Church to attend mass.

[28] Bourdieu (1984) discusses the importance of 'challenge' in the articulation of artistic 'taste' (260ff).

Chapter Eight

Viva San Pawl!

> The Situation is always bigger than you, Sidney. It has like God its own logic and its own justification for being, and the best you can do is cope. (Thomas Pynchon, *V*: 483)

St Paul's *festa*—known as *San Pawl*—takes place after months of planning, and comes as a great relief to the *Pawlini*. Despite the conflicts and disagreements inherent in these preparations, over the forms of ritualisation the *festa* is to take, *San Pawl* nevertheless succeeds in its central aim of unifying the *Pawlini* in collective commemoration of the saint. *Pawlini* from all over Malta travel in to Valletta, to join in with the euphoric celebrations. It is an opportunity to renew and consolidate friendships and acquaintances. *Festa* is a family occasion, that brings together women and men, young and old, to celebrate and commemorate. In the case of *San Pawl*, it is also a national event, that attempts to unify all Maltese. Because it is primarily a Nationalist event, not all Maltese are willing—nor feel able—to participate fully, but those who do are drawn into Valletta to participate in an event that produces a sense of unity—of what Durkheim would have called 'collective effervescence' (1966: 241)—in its invocation of collective history and of collective religious tradition.

This sense of unity is achieved through the creation of particular experiences associated with the *festa*. By *being there* and participating in the *festa's* sensory feast, people achieve an intimate engagement with their patron saint, that in many ways parallels the intimacy of people's connections with politicians and other public figures. Indeed, the link is made metaphorically, in a popular proverb that compares politicians and patrons to saints.[29] Like politicians, saints are both distant and immediate, both public figures and personal associates.

The saint is represented in the monumental statute—*vara*—that serves as the focus of attention during *festa*. But more than mere representation, the *vara* is a substantive embodiment of the saint himself, that becomes animated during the *festa* days, and engaged with as if it were a person, on an intimate basis. The presence of the saint, in the form of the *vara,* and the intensely emotional atmosphere that surrounds his commemoration, produces salient personal and collective experiences that become sedimented in people's memories. Such memories complement the quotidian memories of Valletta and of *L-Arċipierku* discussed in chapters two and five, reinforcing the significance of the city and its neighbourhoods in the national imagination, and particularly that of the former St Paul's residents and their offspring. For them, the *festa* was particularly important. For example, one group of non-Valletta residents—all called Paul—would meet up each year to go to *festa.* Their families all came from the parish, but had moved out either when they were young or before their birth. They had all gone to the same private school outside the city, and had developed a pride in this collective origin, particularly given the 'tough guy' implications of coming from *Il-Belt*—'the city'.

The effectiveness of the memories produced during *festa* derived from their polyvalence—their invocation of the national, the local, the familial and the gendered. The experiences were particularly salient for the men at the centre of the *festa*, who carry the monumental statue during the final procession—*purċissjoni.* For them, the *festa* is an almost magical moment of physical engagement not only with the statue, but with the saint himself, and all he stands for—the national and Nationalist histories, that of *L-Arċipierku* and of Maltese religious 'tradition' more generally.

The impetus to maintain this 'tradition' derived from the prevailing sense of anxiety about present and future that was characteristic of early nineties Malta. With the need for rehabilitation of Valletta came a call for ever-increasing attention to the maintenance of *festa* as a means of bringing together the people of the capital, and uniting its dispersed inhabitants. The performance of *festa* brought the nation together in celebration of its past. For *Pawlini,* the *festa* was a significant moment in the maintenance of *L-Arċipierku* as a nostalgic community, forged in the collective and social memory of the neighbourhood and its demolition. *Festa* was also an important family event, bringing together women and men, young and old, in commemoration of the saint.

10th FEBRUARY 1993—ST PAUL'S FEAST, VALLETTA, MALTA

After the main *festa* procession, at which the monumental statue, or *vara,* of St Paul is carried at shoulder-height around the streets of Valletta, the men who had done the carrying—the *reffiegħa,* or 'statue-carriers'—retired to have a drink *Għand Lawrenz.* Their exertions had exhausted them, and they sat wringing their shoulders in between sips of whisky. The more experienced among them had developed large calluses on their shoulders and necks, that served as bodily traces of the physical exertion—the physical engagement with the statue and saint (see Mitchell 1998c). As they sat, they compared these calluses—known as *ħobża* or 'bread-buns'—examining the new bruise marks that would add another layer of scar tissue to the fleshy build-up.

Anthon Dalli had not yet developed a *ħobża,* though his shoulder was red raw from the exertion of the procession. This was his first time as a *San Pawl reffiegħ,* and he had taken the place of a more experienced *reffiegħ* who had fallen ill a few weeks before the *festa.* There had been an immediate search for a suitable replacement. Many men came forward, but most had neither adequate physical strength nor sufficiently good reputations as reliable and trustworthy *Pawlini* to be considered. Being a *reffiegħ* was linked to the processes of masculinity discussed in chapter three. It required being *raġel sew*—a 'good man' who was well-connected and well respected. The ability to perform masculinity in this extraordinary context was therefore dependent on the more everyday performances that conferred such reputation (Mitchell 1998c: 70). Eventually, Anthon was chosen because of his family's long-term connections with the *Pawlini* and *San Pawl.* His father had been a good a reliable *reffiegħ* during the 1960s and his cousin, Censu Dalli, was currently responsible for choosing the *reffiegħa* team. Moreover, he had previously shown himself to be a good *reffiegħ,* carrying statues during the annual Good Friday parade when he was a teenager.

He was now 26, and had recently returned to Malta after five years in Australia, where he had emigrated along with numerous other Nationalists during the politically tense 1980s. This had interrupted his statue carrying but not his enthusiasm for *festa.* Despite a large Maltese expatriate community, there were no *festi* on the scale of *San Pawl.* As he explained:

> It's not that they didn't have *festi* in Australia. We always celebrated *San Pawl;* and there was even a procesion. But it wasn't the same. The statue wasn't very big, and there weren't many people there. In any case, there's only one St Paul.

The 'one St Paul' was carved by Melchiore Gafà (1635–67), a student of Bernini. Its curved lines and elaborate gilding are characteristic of the Baroque orthodoxy that dominates Maltese religious art (Ciarlò 1995: 42). The statue was commissioned by the Maltese aristocratic family Testaferrata, and subsequently donated by their heirs to St Paul's Church. It was first carried in procession in 1690, and is now only removed from its niche in St Paul's for the *festa.* The *Pawlini,* and particularly the *reffiegħa,* are extremely proud of the statue, one of the oldest *festa* statues in Malta. As a *Pawlini* church historian put it, 'The Maltese cherish a special devotion and tenderness towards this highly artistic statue' (Ibid). *Pawlini* have no doubt as to the importance of the statue, referring to it habitually as a national treasure—part of the national patrimony. The *reffiegħ's* engagement with the statue, therefore, is an engagement with an important artefact. The form of *festa* serves to embue the statue with value—it serves as a focus of celebration, becoming a tangible embodiment of the saint himself, rather than mere representation.

His first opportunity to carry the statue, and engage physically with it was clearly an important occasion for Anthon Dalli. As he sat *Għand Lawrenz* he tried to explain how he had felt when asked to carry the statue, and how it felt when carrying it:

> It's like coming home properly. I've been away from Malta for so long, and now I'm right back home. It makes me feel proud. Because when I went away, I as just a boy, really. Now I'm a man.

He therefore saw his engagement with the statue as a form of home-coming. As with the other dispersed *Pawlini,* the return to *festa* was a return to the fold—to *L-Arċipierku,* St Paul's parish, and Malta. Moreover, it was a confirmation—or even constitution—of his masculinity. In performing the procession, he confirmed that he was a 'good man' and well connected in *Pawlini* circles. However, he was also aware of the unifying role of *San Pawl.* It was not only an occasion of personal significance for himself, but also a collective event. Indeed, the significance of *festa* in the constitution of masculine reputation is dependent on the collectivity, which acts as an audience to the *reffiegħa's* activities. However, it is the role of the *festa* as a unifying ritual that Anthon emphasised:

> It makes you feel proud because you can bring everybody together. *San Pawl* brings people together. That's good, especially nowadays.

RITUAL, ARTEFACT, EXPERIENCE

Based on ethnographic evidence primarily among Aboriginal Australians, Durkheim's foundational work on religion and society—*The Elementary Forms of the Religious Life*—sees ritual, and particularly totemic ritual, as central (1966). The totem, he argues, is a representation of society—the totemic species being the sacred emblem of the clan or lineage—so that the worship of the totem during ritual activity is also the worship of society. At such ritual events, the participants are whipped up into a highly emotionally-charged state of 'collective effervescence' that convinces them of the power of the sacred, and of the social. In one of the most important passages of the book (240ff), Durkheim offers a comparative elaboration of this elementary example, examining the implications of collective effervescence for the understanding of larger scale societies. At this point above all others he offers a general, universal theory of religion, ritual and society.

This section of Durkheim's argument has been—often only implicitly—central to anthropological understandings of ritual and its role in producing collective identity. Turner, arguably the next scholar after Durkheim to offer as coherent an account of ritual and its social role, focused on the moment of *communitas,* which produced a kind of horizontal comradeship or solidarity that stood in formal structural opposition to but ultimately sustained the social order (Turner 1967). *Communitas,* like 'collective effervescence', describes the emotionally charged atmosphere of ritual and its capacity to produce solidarity:

> It is that 'sentiment for humanity' of which Hume speaks, representing the desire for a total, unmediated relationship between person and person (1969: 111)

One of the problems with both Durkheim's collective effervescence and Turner's *communitas* is that neither give a coherent theory of the cognitive or phenomenological processes behind their effectiveness. Both assume that at the centre of religion—or even society as a whole—lies a series of intense emotional experiences gained during important rituals, but neither manage to explain how these experiences work. More recently, however, a number of scholars have forged a more rigorous account of religious experience, locating their explanations in theories of memory and embodiment. Such theories are vital to understanding the effectiveness of *festa* in mitigating the anxieties of early nineties Malta.

At first sight it might seem legitimate to adopt a Durkheimian, totemic reading of Maltese *festa*. Like the clan emblem of Durkheim's theory, the patron saint represents the collectivity—the parish of St Paul's, the *Pawlini,* the nation. The saint's statue, or *vara*, could be seen as a concrete manifestation of this representation—a symbol of the symbol of the collectivity. However, the *vara,* to *Pawlini,* is more than mere representation. It is a concrete manifestation, or embodiment, of the saint himself. As such, he invokes powerful emotional responses, through a process described by Miller as the introjection of a projection (1987: 178).

Miller's aim is to construct a theory of consumption, through a rethinking of Hegelian phenomenology, and particularly his notion of 'objectification'—the process by which human subjects are produced, involving an awareness of the externality of something they themselves have created, and which they feel inevitably moved to reincorporate as themselves, thereby transforming themselves in the process (21). Hegel's theory of objectification, argues Miller, resonates through a series of works by subsequent scholars, not least himself:

> Hegel represents only one source for the meaning of [objectification], which was later transformed through its

> exemplification in a variety of studies of human development and cultural relations, all of which were concerned with the development of a given subject through its creation of, or projection on to, an external world, and the subsequent introjection of these projections. (Miller 1987: 178)

The result is a theory of culture that amounts also to a theory of praxis—a dialectic of the external and the internal that reflects the human propensity to construct themselves a history that is itself the product of historical conditions (Marx 1959: 320). Miller's argument is as useful to the study of *festa* as it is to consumption, because it explains the processes by which objects such as the St Paul *vara* acquire value, to be then engaged with, experienced or consumed as valuable.

Central in this process are the 'framing' mechanisms by which objects become set aside as special. These may involve particular activities associated with the object, or just as often other objects, the sole purpose of which is to 'frame' the main object or artefact. As in the ornate frames given to works of art, their function is to draw attention to the work itself, whilst nevertheless constituting valuable artefacts in themselves (Miller 1987: 100–101). Such 'humble objects' operate at a subconscious level, sacrificing their own value to that of the main artefact. Complementary to the overall processes of ritualisation, such objects abound in the *festa*. The main focus, the *vara,* is framed throughout the year by the prominent niche in which it is housed, in St Paul's church. In the lead-up to the *festa,* it is taken from this frame, and placed on an ornate wooden pedestal in the main body of the church, awaiting *festa* day itself, when it is removed and processed around Valletta. Such framing animates the *vara,* giving it value as an embodiment of the saint himself, and enables *Pawlini* and other *festa*-goers to engage at a physical level with the saint.

Physical engagement with objects is central not only to the ritual process, but also learning more generally. Alongside the experience of special objects that are set aside or framed, goes the more everyday, mundane engagement with the world around us that for Piaget is central to the learning process (1977). Piaget focuses on childhood learning, but there is evidence that this spatio-visual cognition persists beyond childhood, remaining central to human sociality or 'culture' (Arnheim 1986, Bourdieu 1990, Csordas 1994, Mitchell 1997, Toren 1990). This is nowhere more clearly demonstrated than in Bourdieu's celebrated example of the Kabyle house (1990: 271–283), that is not only a concrete manifestation of a particular conceptual framework, but also the means by which that framework is learned. This dialectical movement of object-production and internalisation—inherent in people's engagement with the physical world—suggests that objects or artefacts play a 'bridging' role, between concrete and abstract, percept and concept:

> the artefact ... does not lend itself to the earlier analysis of symbolism which identified distinct abstract signifiers and concrete signifieds, since it simultaneously operates at both levels. Instead ... the object tends towards presentational form, which cannot be broken up as though into grammatical sub-units, and as such it appears to have a particularly close relation to emotions, feelings and basic orientations to the world. The artefact may be used to promote fine distinctions through its relation to extremely sophisticated mechanisms of perceptual discrimination which tend to remain outside of consciousness. Finally, its physical presence exemplifies the concept of praxis, in that this materiality is always an element in cultural transformation. (Miller 1987: 107)

If I have quoted Miller at length it is because of the eloquence with which he asserts the centrality of the material in understanding the human condition. This centrality is clearly evident in the *festa,* which offers a unique opportunity for engagement with the central artefact of *Pawlini* life—the *vara* of St Paul. The *festa* operates through people's engagement with him, and the bodily experience that surrounds their engagement. As such, it works through a process of substantive incorporation, not merely introjection. Whilst the latter term suggests a purely cognitive operation of internalising the conceptual implications of a particular artefact, the former suggests also a bodily accommodation *to* the object and so reaffirms the transformative properties of such engagement. For the *reffiegħa* this is evident in the *ħobża* calluses that are worn with pride, as physical traces of their intimate engagements with St Paul. For other *Pawlini* it is inherent in the genuflection and adoration of the saint's *vara*—the saint himself.

A number of anthropologists have recently attempted to account for this experiential element of ritual, focusing on the relationship between ritual, experience and the body (Bell 1992, Bloch 1992, Humphrey and Laidlaw 1994, Strathern 1996). The most significant of such new accounts of ritual experience comes from Whitehouse's examination of the Pomio Kivung cult in Papua New Guinea (1995). Whitehouse identifies two distinct 'modes of religiosity' among adherents to the cult—a 'doctrinal' mode that rests on regular ritual occasions centred around textual and verbal communication, and an 'imagistic' mode that involves more sporadic rituals that are primarily experiential. Whilst the former mode is practised by the mainstream cult, the latter is employed by a break-away cult, and Whitehouse is interested in how each of the cult groups transmits its knowledge effectively, despite doing so in different ways. In examining this problem, he also addresses questions asked by Barth about religiosity among the Baktaman (1987). Barth's puzzle was how religious cults among the Baktaman remained effective despite long periods between the ritual occasions that were supposed to sustain them. The answer provided by Whitehouse (1992) lies in an understanding of the cognitive significance of the ritual occasions, which he would classify as 'imagistic', and how they are remembered. What he presents is a theory of the effectiveness of ritual that hinges on the evocation of powerful and long-term memories.

Whitehouse's theory centres on the phenomenon of 'flashbulb memory'—a particularly vivid memory evoked by sensorially stimulating and emotionally intense events—see chapter two. Such memories are very intense, and there is even evidence to suggest that they become more intense over time, rather than fading (Whitehouse 1995: 195). A number of scholars investigating Melanesian ritual have explained them in terms that approximate the theory of flashbulb memory (Herdt 1989, Poole 1982, Whitehouse 1996). Focusing on the violence and emotion of ritual, and the effects of music, smell, taste, they have suggested that the significance of these rituals lies in the experiences they produce. For Whitehouse, a critical element of these rituals is the role they have in highlighting a sense of unity:

> One of the marked features of memories encoded in these sorts of conditions, whether or not they have the character of flashbulb memories, is that people are very likely to remember central details, such as who else was there at the time ... [In the context of the Pomio splinter cult, they] ... create and express

> … solidarity among particular people co-ordinated in time and space, but it impressed on memory the unity of a particular community of people. (Whitehouse 1995: 195–196)

Whitehouse offers this sensorially-intense, 'imagistic' mode of religiosity, based on intense events that become internalised in a similar way as flash-bulb memory, as an alternative to the more routine 'doctrinal' mode. However, there seems no reason not to suggest that some ritual forms could contain elements of each mode. Indeed, this is what I wish to suggest for *festa*—that it combines an imagistic mode of religiosity inherent in the intense, sensory experiences associated with the lively external festivities, with a more doctrinal mode of religiosity in the internal festivities, that revolve around preaching and texts.

Whilst the external festivities provide a more spectacular, sensorially stimulating mode of commemoration, the inside festivities are more reflective. The boundary between the two, however, is transgressed by the statue itself, which starts off inside the church as a focus for the *festa ta'ġewwa,* but is then taken outside during the final *festa* procession—*purċissjoni.* Throughout, the statue as an object can be engaged with, but this engagement is particularly intense during the *purċissjoni,* which brings together inside and outside festivities in a final climax to *festa.*

THE *ĦRUĠ:* 'FRAMING' THE STATUE

San Pawl begins on a weekend two weeks before February 10th, with the first function, the *Ħruġ tal-Vara*—'taking out of the statue'. The *Ħruġ* is the first stage in 'framing' the statue as a meaningful object, an embodiment of St Paul. It also marks the moment at which the inside-outside distinction is instigated, setting in motion a chain of events that is finally completed on *festa* day itself, during the *purċissjoni.* During the *Ħruġ,* the statue of St Paul is taken from the glass-fronted niche in which it is normally housed, and carried shoulder-high to the main altar, where it is rested for a few minutes. Here, a prayer is said by the parish Archpriest, and the hymn of St Paul is sung by all those congregated. It is then carried down the church, to a side apse, where it is placed on a large ornamental pedestal. Here it will rest until the final day of *festa.*

The *Ħruġ* is well-attended by *Pawlini*, and is a moment of great emotion. As the towering figure emerges from its niche, the shouts begin—*Viva San Pawl, Viva L-Għaxra ta'Malta*—'Long Live St Paul', 'Long Live the Tenth [of February] of Malta'. This is the opening of the *festa,* and the first opportunity for a year, for people to have a proximate engagement with their saint. It is poignant. As the huge—probably 10 feet tall—solid wood statue is walked down the central aisle of the church, faces look up in awe, and tears begin to well up—*Viva L-Għaxra ta'Malta.*

The *Ħruġ* is important in that it makes the statue, and the saint, available to everybody for a more totalised experiential engagement than is possible throughout the year. It can be walked around, and touched—experiences of the saint which cannot be gained at any other time of the year, when the saint is behind glass in his niche. As an object, it becomes framed by the pedestal, by the church, and by the events of the *festa.*

After the *Ħruġ* the statue sits on its pedestal in the church for two weeks, awaiting *festa* day proper. The space in front of him is decorated with flowers and candles, and becomes a space where both men and women will congregate, to chat, pray or simply sit and stare in wonder at the presence of *L-Apostlu ta'Malta*—'The Apostle of Malta'. During this time, the statue and the saint occupy what one might call a 'liminal' position, between inside and outside—inside the church but outside the niche. In this respect, the *festa* resembles the classic three-part structure of ritual developed by van Gennep (1960) and expanded by Turner (1969) and Bloch (1992). According to this structure, participants in ritual—most classically initiands in rites of passage—are taken away from their everyday lives, and placed in a liminal position, either spatially or metaphorically, before being reincorporated into society at the end of the ritual.[30] Clearly, the *festa* is an inversion of this classic scheme. Whereas other rituals involve the removal of human subjects from everyday, mundane life to be placed in a liminal position that allows them an engagement with the transcendent or sacred, *festa* involves the removal of a sacred subject—the saint—from its normal position in the transcendent—the closed niche in the church—and placing it in the everyday, mundane space of the church, and then later the streets of Valletta. The characteristics of the liminal period are also inverted. Whereas other rituals involve a liminal period that negates the identity of participants, *festa* involves a saintly liminality that animates the statue, producing identity through the process of objectification discussed above.

During the period of *festa,* from *Ħruġ* to *festa* day, people change their way of relating to the statue. It becomes animated—something or somebody to whom one can talk directly, rather than simply offering a tribute, as is the case throughout the rest of the year when St Paul is behind glass. When the statue is here, people avoid turning their back on him, and when they do they will apologise—*Sorry Pawlu.* These are days when special prayers can be offered to the saint, with the possibility of direct physical engagement implying also a more direct spiritual engagement that assures or assumes an increased possibility of intercession. It is also a time when young children, and particularly boys, are taken to visit the saint. Babies are taken to visit the saint throughout the year, but particularly during *festa,* when the statue can be viewed from all angles, even touched, and therefore better engaged with. As one parent explained to me:

> This is the nicest time to take your children to see Paul. This way they can really understand.

I saw several children being encouraged to recognise St Paul, with the question, *Fejn hu San Pawl*—'Where's St Paul?', after which pre-speech children would point to the statue, to the pleasure of those present. The trick was even tried in other contexts, where small models of the statue, photographs of it, or even paintings that did not resemble the statue, were treated as the objects to be acknowledged. Older children were encouraged to mimic the apostle's stance—with right hand held aloft, preaching to the Maltese—once more rewarded with a smile, a kiss or a sweet.

The *Ħruġ* marks the beginning of a period when the whole family of *Pawlini* can appreciate and engage with the apostle. Before 1992 it had taken place on Sunday mornings, after the final mass at 11.45. This meant that it would get caught up in the usual Sunday morning sociability, and end up with an excessive drinking binge *Għand Lawrenz.* In 1992, however, it was moved to a Saturday night, after which a fund-raising dinner dance was organised by the *Pawlini.* This was a more family-centred event than the previous male-oriented drinking session. Indeed, *festa* as a whole is a family-oriented ritual. Even families whose parents had separated would come together for the occasion. Given the tensions that prevailed in early nineties Malta, surrounding family and gender, and between younger and older generations, the maintenance of *festa* was considered important, as it united an institution that was thought to be in crisis (see chapter three). The union of the family was matched by the union of inside and outside festivities that *festa* entailed. In achieving this union it also succeeded, albeit momentarily, in suspending the tensions between clergy and laity, between 'high' and 'low' and between 'polite' and less polite society. This is not to say that all sections of Maltese society participate in *festa*. For some it is a vulgar pursuit that should be curtailed. Others are simply indifferent. For those who do participate, however, it represents—and creates—a valuable unity.

INSIDE FESTIVITIES: THE *TRIDU*

Inside festivities revolve around what Whitehouse would call a doctrinal mode of religiosity. In contrast to the experiential focus of the external *festi ta'barra,* these *festi ta'ġewwa* are oriented around the verbal transmission of familiar textual material—particularly the story of St Paul's shipwreck itself. On 6th February, after evening mass, comes the first function of *festa* proper—the first of the inside functions, and the first day of *Tridu.* The *Tridu* is a three-part sermon delivered on consecutive days by an invited, 'celebrity' priest. They focus on a particular aspect of the saint's life, drawing out the implications of this for followers of the saint, and the Maltese as a whole. In 1993, for example, the *Tridu* focused on Malta's destiny following the saint's arrival. It should not be seen as a fortuitous accident, argued the priest, but as part of a greater plan for the Maltese people.

The *Tridu* sermons serve to consolidate communal ties between *Pawlini,* by reinforcing the common knowledge of St Paul's life and significance. Annual attendance at the *Tridu* builds in the audience a stock of expert knowledge about the saint. The *Tridu* therefore creates a distinction or disjunction between *festa* insiders and outsiders—those who attend the external festivities, but who do not have the same knowledge of or commitment to the *festa* as the *Pawlini*. During the *Tridu* the church is packed with local people, many of whom are aged inhabitants of *L-Arċipierku*. During the year, they are often unable to climb the steep hill to the parish church, but make the effort for the *Tridu*. They regard *festa* as theirs, particularly if they come from the low-town 'heart' of the parish. As Pawlu Spiteri, an elderly informant who had remained in *L-Arċipierku* despite the demolition of his house, put it:

> The *festa* is ours. Ours. The people from *L-Arċipierku*.

This possessive orientation was particularly evident in relation to the internal festivities, which were regarded by some as being the exclusive preserve of local people. Although the *festa* as a whole was inclusive, and the external festivities seen as enhanced by the thousands of visitors who thronged the streets, there was a certain antagonism towards outsiders who turned up to the inside festivities. As locals sat waiting for the *Tridu* to begin, they would look around and nod acknowledgement to neighbours and friends. Unfamiliar faces were remarked upon, leading to conspiratorial chatter about their origins and legitimacy for being there. *Pawlini* who are not seen throughout the year are also greeted with a certain hostility. Such people are known as *fatati*—'ghosts'—who only haunt the parish to enjoy *festa*, but do not contribute financially or practically to its organisation.

The sermons themselves contain well-known stories about the saint and his life, slightly recast to make new points about his important relationship with Malta and the Maltese. As the priest for the 1993 *Tridu* told me, it was all about playing to the gallery:

> You have to give people what they want. Tell people what they already know, but make it sound like you're saying something new.

As performance, the *Tridu* sermons are judged by the congregation on the basis of existing knowledge. From an early age, *Pawlini* children are taught the story of the saint's arrival, through locally-produced picture and story books that are read at school or during the doctrine lessons they attend from the age of four. During one Valletta doctrine lesson, just before *San Pawl* 1994, a lengthy quiz was organised, in which children were to learn the answers to a variety of questions about the life of the saint, and then prepared to repeat them *verbatim,* if asked. This childhood knowledge is supplemented when they begin to attend the masses and sermons of *festa,* such that by the time they reach adulthood, they have built up considerable expertise, with which to judge the annual *Tridu.* This doctrinal transmission of religious knowledge complements the more imagistic, experiential transmission associated with the external festivities.

Not all *Tridu* performances are equally praised. After each of the three nights, the congregation will gather to discuss the merits of a particular year's preacher, often congratulating him on the sermon, or questioning particular elements of his story. This period of conversation is significant, in that it enables the *Pawlini* to demonstrate their common knowledge of the aesthetics of the *Tridu.* Outsiders, without the stock of knowledge about St Paul to draw upon, cannot join in with this critical assessment, which therefore serves to delineate insider from outsider. This character of the *Tridu* as exclusive insider festivity aimed at local *Pawlini* clearly contradicts the assumption that *San Pawl* should be an inclusive, national celebration. However, it does succeed in bringing together the competing constituencies of *San Pawl* in appreciation—or criticism—of an outsider. The priests invited to deliver the *Tridu* are always from outside the parish.

Each night, after *Tridu* finishes, a band march begins, marking the contrast between inside and outside festivities. As the congregation walks out of the church, and into the streets, they are met by large crowds of *festa* visitors, ready to enjoy the exuberant band march. The initial closure of the internal festivities contrasts with the open-ness of these parallel external *festi,* to which I now turn. These are public celebrations to which everybody is welcome, whether *Pawlini,* other Maltese or tourists. The most numerous of these *festi ta'barra* are the band marches, which take place on each day of the lead-up to *festa,* and again on *festa* day.

OUTSIDE FESTIVITIES: BAND MARCHES

In contrast to the doctrinal focus of inside festivities, the outside celebrations involve a more imagistic mode. They are visual, aural, olfactory feasts, involving fireworks, balloons and flags, brass bands and more fireworks. Following the *Tridu* sermon, the congregation sits to listen to the rousing *antifon*—antiphon—of St Paul, before filing out through the sacristy to the start of the first band marches. Marches are followed by groups of men and women, who treat the occasion as an opportunity to meet friends and neighbours, and enjoy the rousing music. The routes the marches take vary slightly, so that most streets in the parish have a march passing through at some stage. Many of the marches also leave the parish boundary, to move along Valletta's central street, Republic Street. This confirms *San Pawl* as a *festa* oriented to Valletta as a whole, not merely St Paul's parish.

Usually, just in front of the band, there is a group of young men, who keep ahead of the march, moving from bar to bar, getting progressively drunker, dancing and singing along to the marches. In the *festi* I saw, this was the group of younger *Pawlini* who came together as a temporary *klikka,* to facilitate the street decoration or *armar*. As well as decorating the streets they would also create props for themselves to carry during the band marches, and wear matching t-shirts with images or slogans of St Paul—*Viva San Pawl, Magnus* ('the magnificent'). In 1993 they painted umbrellas with alternate sections of red and white. Picked out onto the white background was the insignia of St Paul—a snake emerging from a fire. The colours were significant, in that they are not only those of St Paul, but also of Valletta and Malta as a whole. They also made large poles out of plastic piping, to which were attached red and white balloons, and flags with *Pawlini* written on them. All these props were carried during band marches, and added to the atmosphere of *briju*—'merrymaking', 'brio'—as they were swung around in time to the music. The band march *briju* often became rather boisterous, as participants danced drunkenly, shouting, singing and chanting along to the rousing band music.

For many *Pawlini,* the band marches were the first time they got drunk. The pattern is to follow the march route in front of the band, moving from one bar to the next, so that as the band approaches, the drink is finished, and the march rejoined. As participants become tipsy, the timing gets more difficult, and drinks are taken out into the streets. In 1993 and 1994, imported Heineken beer was a popular drink, and during the band marches, it was not uncommon to see young men with two or three bottles held between the fingers of one hand, and a fourth in the other hand being drunk. As levels of alcohol rise, so does the intensity of *briju*. The 'rucks' that develop in front of the band can involve several hundred people who sing, shout and sway to the music. They frequently cause delays in the proceedings, as scores of young men fall to the floor, hugging and laughing in a kind of collective ecstasy. This behaviour raises eyebrows in some circles, particularly among the more 'polite' *Pawlini,* who see it as vulgar and uncouth.

On one particular occasion, this behaviour became the subject of special concern. It was the day in 1993 of the inaugural *Marċ tal-Ħadd Filgħodu*—'Sunday Morning March'—that was one of the innovations of the new *Kumitat*. They were proud of the new march, and had even negotiated with La Valette, the *Pawlini* band club, to play the march without charging their normal fee. This Sunday morning march was a popular innovation, because it effectively incorporated the normal weekly Sunday morning social occasion, into the *festa*. Instead of congregating in the parish bars to drink and talk, *Pawlini* now had a band march to attend.

The incorporation of the Sunday morning socialising placed what was normally a purely male occasion into a family context in which women and children were also involved. While the younger men followed the *festa* from bar to bar, dancing and singing at the head of the march, women, children and older men would follow the march from the sides. They too would get drinks from bars along the way, but would more commonly enter the bars to sit for a while, before returning to rejoin the march further along. Not prone to the excessive drunken-ness of the younger men, women and older men nevertheless sanctioned the *briju* by maintaining a spectator's presence. They would walk alongside the energetic 'ruck', laughing at the drunken abandon and passing the occasional comment. They would also join in with the singing that accompanied most marches. Inventive rhymes would be sung to the band's tunes, most of which centred on the quality of the *festa,* ending with the line *magħna ma'tagħmlu xejn*—'with us you won't [have to] do anything'. This was an explicit reference to the hospitality inherent in the outside festivities, to which all guests were welcome, without having to contribute anything more than their presence.

This *briju* was experientially important. Young children would be carried on shoulders and swung around in time to the music, to enable them to participate. Many adult *Pawlini* recalled the excitement and exhilaration of their earliest *festi,* which had impressed upon them the value of St Paul and his commemoration. On the first *Marċ tal-Ħadd Filgħodu,* however, the *briju* became too violent and excessive. The march had been intended to end in front of the parish church, after having processed around the streets, but the small 'ruck' in front of the band became so involved in its own swaying, drunken celebration, that the march stopped short. It was held up, and the band eventually dispersed without finishing their set. One experienced onlooker told me that this was a warning from La Valette, that if the *Pawlini* could not control themselves, the band would not honour their agreement to complete the march. Older *Pawlini,* and one or two mothers of the young revellers intervened to berate them for their excesses. Although *briju* was a welcome and even necessary part of *festa,* this time they had taken things too far. Thus, although for the most part the outside festivities provided unity among diverse *Pawlini,* it also had the potential to consolidate tensions between younger and older, male and female, 'polite' and less polite.

IL-LEJLET

Since 1992, on the third night of the *Tridu,* a 'demonstration' has taken place, which involves the newly built statue of St Paul's conversion being carried through the streets of Valletta, to the main square in front of the law courts on Republic Street, where it is winched onto a huge pedestal, to stand presiding over Valletta until the end of the *festa.* A less significant event than the main procession, the demonstration combines the *briju* of a normal band march with the novelty of a mini-procession. Like the main *vara,* the statue of St Paul's conversion is placed on an ornate pedestal, but this framing mechanism does not animate the statue in the same way as the *vara,* which becomes an embodiment of St Paul himself. Rather, it remains a representation of the saint's conversion.

Following the three days of *Tridu,* the 9th February is known as the *Lejlet tal-Festa*—Festa Eve. On this day, the Archbishop is involved for the first time, in the translation of the relic of St Paul, a small shard of bone. The relic is held in the side Oratory of Our Lady of Charities throughout the year, and on the morning of *Il-Lejlet* is taken from there by the Archbishop to its place on the main altar of the church. The event takes place in the evening, and groups of people congregate outside the church to watch as the Diocesan limousines pull up and the Archbishop gets out. Within an hour, he is gone again, having performed the translation. The movement of the relic from the fringes of the Oratory into the centre of the church further signifies the actual presence of the saint on his *festa* day.

The church actually houses two relics of St Paul. The other is his right wrist-bone—*Id-Drieħ*—which is normally held behind the church altar in a glass dome, but is placed on the main altar during important functions such as marriages, funerals and during *festa.* The significance of *Id-Drieħ* is that it is a fragment of the saint's preaching hand. All representations of him, including the *vara* itself, show the right hand held aloft as he instructs the Maltese in the gospel stories. The representations depict the moment of national conversion, and *Id-Drieħ* is part of the actual hand that preached.

After the translation, a mass is held in the church, and yet another band march begins outside. This is the *Marċ tal-Arċipierku*—the *Arċipierku* march. *L-Arċipierku* is considered the heart of St Paul's parish, and the march is one of the most popular. As the march descends into *L-Arċipierku* the revellers encroach ever more imposingly on the band. The lively atmosphere increases, as do the levels of alcohol and enthusiastic *briju.* In 1993 the enthusiasm spilled over into violence, when an argument began between two young men over the reputation of *L-Arċipierku.* One, from Valletta 'high' town said that it was a 'low' place—*ħamallu*—where prostitutes lived. The other, himself from *L-Arċipierku* retaliated, trying to throw a punch. The two were held back by friends, and bundled out of each others' way. Reactions to the scuffle reveal the sensitivity of *Pawlini* to the public nature of such events. Even though the march was considered among the more intimate of outside festivities, it was nevertheless still a public event, that attracted visitors and tourists. Violent behaviour gave them the wrong impression about the *festa,* it was argued. As with criticisms at the excessive *briju* during the inaugural Sunday morning march, there was concern that *festa* should maintain a 'polite' public image. One of the older *Pawlini,* Joe Zarb commented to me:

What a disgrace, fighting in front of the tourists.

The *Arċipierku* march ends at the bastion road that overlooks the Grand Harbour breakwater, where a display of ground fireworks are organised. In Maltese terms, the fireworks for *San Pawl* have never been particularly spectacular. Where some rural *festi* involved elaborate moving sculptures, the St Paul's fireworks were static wooden structures fashioned from wood and covered in flares, catherine wheels and rockets. In 1993 there were six pieces in all, including the popular *tapit*—a 'carpet' of flares—and the familiar logo *VSP,* standing for *Viva San Pawl.* As the fireworks were set off Joe Zarb, who had wanted to shield the tourists from the young men's violence, now began to mock them. The first flare led to an impromptu 'wow' of surprise and pleasure from the tourist groups, and when subsequent fireworks were set off, Joe joined in with them. 'Oooooh', he said, laughing heartily each time. The implication was that although the tourists might have seen aspects of the *Pawlini* they had rather not have shown, they were still naïve of local 'tradition'. He mocked the tourists because they were displaying a wonder at fireworks that by Maltese standards were not particularly impressive, and with which any Maltese would be totally familiar. By drawing attention in this way to a division in the audience for the fireworks, Joe was demonstrating that the tourists, although welcome and encouraged to turn up to the *festa,* were nevertheless ignorant of its subtleties.

The naivete towards the fireworks was also naivete in the face of *festa* as a whole. If the tourists saw the fireworks display as simply a spectacle, then this marked their ignorance of the manifestation's significance for the *festa.* They were the climax of the lead-up to *festa* day itself, and a long-awaited event. Their design and purchase was a matter of debate and disagreement, as discussed in chapter seven. They were also an important part of the sensory experience of *festa.* When I inquired about their meaning, among *Pawlini* I was assured that they had no symbolic function—they did not mean anything. However, they were a vital part of *festa.* As Charlie Zammit put it:

> You can't have *festa* without fireworks. They make *festa* what it is. When you hear them you feel ... excited. I love the smell of them.

For him, as for others, *festa* was built up of such visceral elements. Over and above the doctrinal content of the *Tridu* and other inside festivities, the imagistic, experiential elements of the outside festivities contributed to its significance, and its ability to engender a profound sense of unity. As with the Melanesian rituals discussed by Whitehouse and others, the focus of people's recollections and descriptions of *festa* is its collective nature—who was with them and who did what.

FESTA DAY

If the *festa* is characterised by a distinction between inside and outside festivities, that are aimed at 'insiders' and 'outsiders' respectively, and involve different modes of religiosity, then the events of *festa* day bring these two together. Inside festivities are turned outside, by bringing 'outsiders' into the church during a solemn *Pontifikal* mass, and by taking the inside festivities outside during the *Purċissjoni* of the saint's *vara. Festa* day is marked by three events—the *Pontifikal* mass, the most lively of band marches, and the *Purċissjoni.* All are well-attended by locals and outsiders, and for the whole day Valletta is busy.

Most *Pawlini* like to fulfil their obligation to take mass during the *Pontifikal,* and the church is packed. Unlike the *Tridu,* however, the *Pontifikal* is not considered a primarily local event. It attracts public figures from high up in the Nationalist Party, and is presided over by the Archbishop of Malta. It is common for the Prime Minister and President of Malta to attend, consolidating the *festa's* status as a national event. Everybody wears their best possible clothes, and many buy new dresses or suits which are worn for the first time at the *Pontifikal,* then later in the day, for the *Purcissjoni.* Many of the adult *Pawlini,* both men and women, said they had looked forward to *festa* when they were young because they were bought new clothes—a new dress or new shoes. These were worn with pride, and contributed to the sense of *festa* as a special occasion. People's personal memories of these new clothes, or other treats associated with *festa*—some children were given gifts, and most bought sweets—complemented the collective memories of *festa* as a whole, just as people's personal experience of the emotional and imagistic side of *festa* produced a sense of unity.

Festa day combines intense personal, emotional experience with the invocation of collective unity, through the juxtaposition of doctrinal and imagistic modes of religiosity.

The *Pontifikal* is the climax of the doctrinal, inside festivities. The most important part of the *Pontifikal* is the *Panegyrku*—panegyric—said by an invited priest, as homage to St Paul. It lasts for between sixty and ninety minutes, during which total silence reigns over the crowded church. As with the *Tridu,* the *Panegyrku* is characterised by familiar aspects of the saint's life, but each priest attempts to draw out original conclusions or implications from his speech. Also like the *Tridu,* the *Panegyrku* is assessed by those present, on the basis of its ability to draw new insights from the teachings and life of St Paul.

In 1993, the *Panegyrku* focused on the providentiality of St Paul's shipwreck in Malta. Before Paul arrived, the priest argued, the Maltese were pagans. They were uneducated, but nevertheless ready to receive the words of the Lord as delivered by St Paul. They were therefore seen as the chosen people, predestined to become Christians, thus mirroring the arguments in defence of the Pauline story that were mobilised against Warnecke—see chapter one. In 1994 the *Panegyrku* focused on the mixture of Hellenic and Jewish cultures that created Christianity, and which St Paul represented. Despite being culturally mixed, however, St Paul's Christianity arrived in Malta in its purest form. The Maltese were thus the original, and purest Christians. Both sermons linked up the life of St Paul to the spiritual life of the nation, conceived as a continuous Christian tradition that can be traced back to the miracle of Paul's shipwreck. They therefore link what is the climax of the inside festivities, with the incorporative, national focus of *San Pawl.* Although it is the *festa tal-Pawlini,* it is also the *festa tal-Maltin*—the Maltese feast.

This was confirmation, in narrative form, of the significance of St Paul in the history of Malta. Moreover, it was a moment when the presence of the national dignitaries and, after 1993, the presence of television cameras confirmed the *festa*'s status as a national feast. At this point, the inside of the church was opened up to the whole nation, and in the process, the *festa* incorporated the whole nation as its main constituency.

After the *Panegyrku,* the Archbishop leads mass, and then the crowds disperse, many returning home to eat. This is usually a large and important family meal, drawing together extended family groups to celebrate *festa* with food. Following this, comes the much-loved *Marċ tas-siegħa*—one o'clock march—that was renowned for its effervescent *briju.* Participants changed for this march, knowing that their clothes were likely to get covered in beer or whisky or worse. The march begins and ends outside the church, starting an hour after the end of the *Pontifikal* and ending in time for the beginning of the *Purċissjoni.* It is renowned for excessive drunkenness. As the march progresses, the crowd of men in front of the band increases, and their dancing and chanting escalates. They link shoulders into large scrums which sway and topple to the ground. Beer is thrown into the air, as are caps, balloons and umbrellas decorated with the *Pawlini* insignia. This is the pinnacle of *festa briju*—of the collective effervescence produced by and constituting the effectiveness of *festa.* Again, it combines collective and personal foci—the experiential and the imagistic.

As the march reaches St Paul's Street, the final downhill leg towards the church, it comes to a virtual stand-still. The street is packed to over-flowing, and by now the participants are tiring. Men are raised shoulder-high and dance aloft. The whole occasion has more the atmosphere of a rock concert or football match than a religious ritual. As with other band marches, the main participants in the excessive 'rucks' are young men, but others—women, children, older men—are also present. Joining in the loud chants and triumphalist songs, their participation may not seem as active, but is by no means passive.

By the time the march reaches the bottom of St Paul's Street, it begins to encounter smartly-dressed people, waiting for the *Purċissjoni,* which leaves the church after dusk. Crowds congregate both inside and outside the church, to watch the statue, the saint, crossing the boundary between the two. The moment is marked by a long volley of airborn fireworks, some of which light up the sky with colourful flourishes, whilst others simply explode with a large boom. There is also a string of fire-crackers set off on the roof of the church. This marks the exit of the saint. This contributes both to the ritualisation of the *festa* and to the imagistic significance of the *Purċissjoni.*

St Paul is carried by a group of twelve men—*reffiegħa*—who take turns throughout the *Purcissjoni*. Only eight are required at any one time, and the other four walk alongside with the supporting *forċina*—ornate forked poles that are used to support the statue when it rests at street corners. Care is taken to walk in time to the music, and sway from side to side as though St Paul himself were dancing. The *Purċissjoni* proceeds along St Paul's Street, stopping at each corner, before cutting across the Republic Street. Before the turn, the *vara* sits for a while at the edge of *L-Arċipierku,* just before the land slopes down into 'low' town. Here, the *reffiegħa* turn the statue around, to 'look' down the streets towards *L-Arċipierku,* to demonstrate that the saint is still maintaining his patronage over the area—over the whole parish. Every effort is made to animate the statue—to make sure he becomes more than mere representation—that he becomes St Paul himself. In 1993, on his way up Republic Street, the *vara* was halted alongside a plaque that had recently been put up, commemorating the visit of the Pope in 1991. Here the saint, taken from his year-long place in the sacred world of the church, into the everyday or mundane world of Valletta's main street, was acknowledging that he passed over the same ground as God's own emissary on earth.

At the top of the Republic Street hill, the *Purċissjoni* turns left into St John's Square, where there is a longer wait. The statue is placed on large trestles, while a liturgical function is performed by the Archpriest and the *reffiegħa* go into the Cathedral sacristy for a drink. A large crowd packs into the square, and the service is broadcast on a public address system. Prayers are said, and the hymn of St Paul sung, before the *reffiegħa* once more emerge and the statue is taken back down St Paul's Street towards the church. On this last leg, the official *reffiegħa* leave the *vara,* and there is an opportunity for all men to try carrying the statue. It is a chance for those who have not, or will not, be official *reffiegħa* to show their commitment to the saint through a physical engagement with his statue. Men crowd round the *vara,* and jostle to get a position on one of the long poles, or *bsaten* (sing. *bastun*) on which it was carried. Each *bastun* ends up with two or three temporary *reffiegħa,* who 'take a piece'—*jieħu biċċa*—before returning to their families or groups of friends with stories of how heavy it had been. It is an opportunity for them to share in the experience of the *reffiegħa,* lifting the statue in front of their friends, neighbours, families.

For the *reffiegħa* proper, lifting the statue confers a certain status. They achieve public recognition as trustworthy, reliable and strong through this performance in front of the *festa* crowd (see Mitchell 1998c). The public is extended, moreover, by the coverage of the procession on the national news, and the circulation, after *festa*, of private video-tapes depicting the *reffiegħa* during the *Purċissjoni.* These are played back and scrutinised in the months that follow, at home or in bars such as *Għand Lawrenz*, where mistakes are remarked upon and reputations set. This relatively extraordinary performance on behalf of the *reffiegħa,* therefore, is judged in the context of the everyday masculine performances discussed in chapter three. For these temporary *reffiegħa*, taking an *ad hoc* 'piece', however, the rewards are experiential, rather than status-enhancing.

Many people describe carrying the statue as a kind of penance, or *werda*. The physical and symbolic subjection of the body to the trauma of being underneath the heavy statue is a literal and figureative subjection of the person to the power of the saint (see Scarry 1985). The somatic response, or physiological symptoms of this trauma produce a kind of euphoria, that many people find difficult to describe. It is described as *tal-ostja*—'of the host', a rather blasphemous but common phrase for 'amazing'. One man, a regular *reffiegħ*, described it as follows:

> It's incredible, the feeling that you get. I remember the first time I did it. It was like the biggest 'high' you could possibly get. You get taken over by it—it's amazing. Like [St] Paul is with you.

The feeling of physical proximity to not only the statue but the very saint, confirms the process of projection inherent in *festa,* and the importance of the statue as a literal embodiment, rather than mere representation, of St Paul. It is this engagement that the young men seek at the end of the *Purċissjoni.* Afterwards, they described to me the feelings associated with the engagement—of awe and pride at having taken a 'piece'. This they would then report to their friends and family, who although not themselves joining in would nevertheless participate by taking photographs and applauding.

When the *vara* arrives at the doors of the church, the official *reffiegħa* once more take over, and the young men who crowded round to take a 'piece' rejoined their family groups. The re-entry into the church is marked by another set of loud, colourful fireworks, which the statue is turned around to 'watch'. Then with a final burst of fireworks, the five steps into the church are taken at running pace, to the shouts of the crowd. Once inside, the *antifon* is played for a final time, and the Archbishop blesses all those present. It is a moment of intense emotion. Members of the crowd turn to each other and hug, with tears in their eyes. Many are tired from the previous days' festivities, and drunk from the many *festa* drinks they have bought. It is the climax of proceedings—the point at which the saint, and the *festa,* goes once more inside, to wait for next year's commemoration. It is also a moment of unity, that brings together all *Pawlini.* At this moment in 1993, I overheard two of the *Pawlini* who had been at loggerheads over the fireworks incident of the previous years, refer to the matter once again. They hugged each other, both in tears. 'Listen', said one, 'it's all over. All that business with the fireworks. What's gone is gone. Let's get on with the rest. This is what's important. *San Pawl.*'

CONCLUSIONS

The emotion of this moment produces salient memories heightened by the bodily experience of participation—of *being there* and joining in the *festa*. Such experiential or body memories contribute to the effectiveness of *festa* in providing a palliative against the ambivalences and ambiguities of early nineties Malta. Personal experiences, they are nevertheless achieved in the public context of the *festa,* and it is through the invocation of these salient experiences, that a form of unity is suggested which rails against the tensions and antagonisms between different *festa* constituencies, and between young and old Maltese, providing a reassurance of 'tradition' to counterpose the apparently imminent threat of 'modern' life. Participating in a ritual activity that simultaneously commemorates the national patron saint, celebrates national unity, local community and the family draws attention away from the ambivalences surrounding these areas of life.

Boissevain (1992a) suggests that in late twentieth century Europe, in a context that sees the threat of globalisation uppermost on people's minds, such 'tradition', and particularly ritual tradition, is increasingly sought as an answer to these anxieties. This book has traced this operation in the feast of St Paul, examining how ambivalences emerge in respect to 'modernisation' in various areas of life, and how these ambivalences both contribute to and are in some senses mitigated by *festa*.

Chapter seven investigated the substantial dilemmas inherent in organising this *festa*, over how best to ritualise the occasion—how to maintain the *festa* as 'traditional' whilst at the same time serving its unique needs as both local and national feast, and improving its scale and substance. It traced the emergence of a range of ritual constituencies—young and old, clergy and laity, 'high' and 'low', local and national—which needed to be catered for in the organisation of *festa*. The disagreements between such ritual constituencies revolved around the debates over how best to ritualise the commemoration—what forms should the image and publicity for the *festa* take, and what forms should the *festa* itself take. The emergence of these debates revealed fault-lines that lay behind the apparent unity of *festa*, and confirmed a profound concern with maintaining *festa* in 'traditional' form.

One of the main issues at stake in organising such a feast is to maintain its national focus, the dilemma being that *San Pawl* is simultaneously a National*ist* feast, and also a feast of local significance. It commemorates St Paul, the *Pawlini* and *L-Arċipierku*. Chapter six explored the origins of this political association of St Paul with the Nationalists, linking it to a mode of political practice that combines public with personal relationships—the distant and the intimate. The Nationalist orientation derives from a long-term personalisation of politics, and its entrenchment in St Paul's parish, though this in turn presents another area of debate and ambivalence. Debates centred on the extent to which Malta may be termed 'southern' in character, and therefore essentially predisposed to a non-bureaucratic political culture. This in turn had implications for the nation's European ambitions. If Nationalism—and indeed the story of St Paul's ship-wreck—located Malta in a European cultural sphere, then the representation and essentialisation of Maltese political culture as non- or even anti-European, threatened the claims to European identity.

The ambivalence of early nineties Maltese to political modernisation was matched by a similar ambivalence towards the modernisation of Valletta itself. Memories of *L-Arċipierku* and the circumstances under which it was demolished were discussed in chapter five, and demonstrated a nostalgia that was offset by both an acknowledgement that the past had not been as idyllic as the memories might suggest, and an unwillingness to allow Valletta to become a mere heritage site. As a consequence, the nostalgia became central to both claims that the state, and politicians more widely, should take more interest in the plight of 'the people', and the vilification of Mintoff's 1970s Labour Party. Its elaboration was a strategy that implicated politics in general and party politics in particular.

The sense of injustice at *L-Arċipierku's* demolition derived from an overall sense of the inadequacy of political representation and public opinion. Experienced as a 'sense of limits', or exclusion from the central 'clique' or cliques of Maltese 'polite' society, this can be seen as the structural effect of a range of everyday practices of distinction between 'high' and 'low' society, 'polite' and 'uncouth'. These practices were discussed in chapter four, and centred around modes of bodily comportment but particularly consumption, which has increased in Malta over the last twenty years. The increase comes partly from the unprecedented availability of imported consumer goods, and an overall rise in the standard of living, but is also related to the increased desire of Maltese to be seen as 'modern' and European. This desire is not unequivocal. At the same time as being attractive, consumption is seen as problematic, particularly in its association with materialism—*materialiżmu*—one of the threats that increased modernisation and Europeanisation poses to 'traditional' Maltese life. At the centre of that life is the family, which is oriented around notions of household and indeed the house itself. As concern for the family expanded, so too consumption about the house, which symbolically strengthened and indeed embellished what was seen as an ailing institution.

The sense of crisis in family life was discussed in chapter three. It emerged from the cross-generational antagonisms over 'correct' gender roles and the transgression of 'traditional' family values. Such transgressions become possible to theorise only if we recognise that gender roles and gender identities derive not from a rigid blueprint of ineradicable 'values', but from everyday performances which although they may support a 'hegemonic' version of gender may just as often resist or subvert it. Such resistances and subversions were an everyday feature of early nineties Malta, and were perceived to come from the exposure of young Maltese to the erosive effects of northern European morality.

Such exposure comes in particular from tourists, but also from Italian and other European television that was increasingly available in the early nineties. The presence of these 'outside' influences was, again, treated with a certain ambivalence. Although tourists were a welcome and necessary part of early nineties Maltese economy, their presence caused concern, and they were often, unwittingly, the objects of Maltese humour. Particularly through language, they were kept at arms' length—welcome on the fringes, but not as part of everyday life. This tension between the pragmatic acceptance of the large numbers of tourists and the wish to avoid them taking over was mirrored by attitudes towards Valletta as a whole. These were discussed in chapter two. Here, the pragmatism of a working city that attracted thousands of visitors everyday contrasted with the nostalgia of a monumental city to represent the nation and attract tourists.

Caught on the margins of Europe, between 'tradition' and 'modernity', Maltese turned increasingly towards commemorations such as *San Pawl* for solace and stability at a time of anxiety. Maintaining the centrality of St Paul in national history, as discussed in chapter one, means simultaneously maintaining claims to European identity whilst at the same time demonstrating separateness. As aboriginal Europeans, the *Pawlini* were also ambivalent Europeans—looking to the past and commemoration to allay the anxieties of present and future.

NOTES

[29] The phrase *bla qaddisin ma titlax il-ġenna*—'without saints you can't get to heaven'—refers to the need for political patrons in everyday life (Aquilina 1972: 146, Boissevain 1993: 121).

[30] This scheme, initially developed for rites of passage alone, has been used to explain the structure of all ritual, most notably by Bloch (1992) who examines the formal similarities of a range of diverse rituals. The unifying feature, according to him, is the movement from the mundane to the transcendent and back again, that achieves a conquest of the mundane by the transcendent.

Epilogue

I opened and closed this book with a description and discussion of St Paul's *festa—San Pawl*. The ground covered in between was intended to explain the significance of *San Pawl* for those who participate in it and organise it. This explanation was rooted in an understanding of the lives of the *Pawlini* not merely in their explicit contact with the *festa,* but 'in the round'. I therefore presented an holistic ethnography, dealing with different areas of social life—community, gender, family, politics, religion, ritual.

Central to this ethnography were local understandings of 'tradition' and 'modernity'. In a recently-translated collection of essays (1998), Niklas Luhmann demonstrates that rather than being a homogenising process geared towards producing a unified social whole, modernity is above all characterised by a continuous self-denial and constant creation of otherness. Rather than being a fixed, stable essence modernity is a process that has differentiation at its core. This suggests that attempts to pin down a definition or 'check-list' of modernity's characteristics are at best problematic, at worst naïve. Rather than attempt such a check-list, therefore, I have located my understanding of modernity in differentiation, and particularly the temporalising and hierarchising axis of 'tradition' and 'modernity'. This axis, I have argued, must take centre stage in any exploration of modernity—and modern lives.

Contrary to the pluralising tendencies of much recent writing on 'modernities', I assume with Van der Veer (1998) that modernity is a singular process, but one which has had different historical trajectories in different times and different places. Moreover, these different trajectories reveal different articulations of the central polarity 'tradition'–'modernity'. It is the job of socio-cultural anthropology, which has always concerned itself with 'local' understandings of social process, to explore the particularities of such different articulations—to examine the ways in which modernity is manifest in different socio-cultural settings.

Common to all manifestations of modernity is ambivalence, and throughout the book I have tried to show ambivalence and anxiety at play in early 1990s, particularly as they were reflected in the idea of Europe, which was seen as both a promise and threat—a promise of increased security, affluence, democracy, modernity, but a threat to family, morality, community, tradition. This suggests that the temporal hierarchy of tradition–modernity can be switched either way, to valorise tradition or modernity at different moments. Modernity does not straightforwardly uphold the value of the 'modern' over the 'traditional'.

This ambivalence—and consequent anxiety about present and future—are particularly acute at the edges of Europe, in marginal places such as Malta. Here, as the power and influence of the European Union expands, so the consequences of inclusion and exclusion become more significant.[31] As the stakes are raised, so people's anxiety and ambivalence are heightened. This much has been observed in a number of countries on the fringes of Europe such as Denmark, Greece and Poland, where a similar ambivalence towards Europeanisation can be observed (see Ayres 1996, Blazyca and Kolkiewicz 1999, Carabott 1995, Lavdas 1997, Lippert and Becker 1998, Petersen 1998). Although it is tempting to regard the dilemmas of European integration, and the ambivalence of countries towards accession, as deriving from the practicalities of political or economic policy, I have shown that they are also morally charged dilemmas which go to the heart of what people regard as their identities, their cultures, their traditions.

In such circumstances, one might see *festa* as a stable element of fixed tradition amongst the flux of geo-political change. As such, one might emphasise its role in resisting modernity—in shoring up traditional life against the regional or global flows of capital and information characteristic of the late twentieth- and early twenty-first-centuries. To do so, however, is to take indigenous explanation at face value. As shown in chapter seven, one of the features of *festa* that is emphasised by *Pawlini* themselves is its ability to unite an otherwise disparate population through tradition. However, I would argue that this *appeal* to the traditional is itself a modern act. As Comaroff and Comaroff have argued (1993), such appeals to the tradition of ritual serve as a means of mediating the ambiguities inherent in modernity—of globalising the local and localising the global.

Assuming the traditionality of *festa* also denies its role in *promoting* the global. In particular, it ignores its significance in the promotion of cultural tourism—one of the major areas of economic expansion in post-Independence Malta (see Mitchell 1996b, Sant Cassia 1999). *Festa* was, and is, marketed to tourists from abroad, to attract them to the traditions of Malta. Travel features seldom omit to mention *festa,* and during the summer months a *festa* schedule is produced for tourists, to help them attend. In marketing their *festa,* then, Maltese incorporate global modernity through apparent appeals to local tradition.

Although this book is located in the ethnography of St Paul's parish and the *Pawlini* more broadly, it has wider comparative significance. There are specific elements of nostalgia which link the *Pawlini* back to *L-Arċipierku*—the area of lower Valletta that had much of its core demolished in the early 1970s. However, this nostalgia also can be seen as a more general phenomenon for Malta, and indeed globally. Shaw and Chase argue that nostalgia is a central feature of modernity—which assumes that the modern 'now' is characterised by a fragmentation when compared to the unity of the traditional 'then' (1989: 6). This nostalgia increased throughout the twentieth century, as history appeared to accelerate and displace the traditional 'then' more rapidly and more efficiently. If we accept modernity to be a singular, global phenomenon, then nostalgia too is global, feeding the ever-growing politics of tradition and culture throughout the globe (see for example Handler 1988, Macdonald 1997, Schwartz 1993, Turner 1991, Wright 1998, Yoshino 1992). This book presents simply one example of this global phenomenon, in which tradition and nostalgia combine in ritual to help accommodate modernity's ambivalence. As modern subjects, Maltese are caught in this ambivalence. Located in the margins of Europe, they are also, therefore, ambivalent Europeans.

NOTES

[31] I am indebted to my colleague Jeff Pratt for this observation.

Bibliography

Abela, A.M. (1991). *Transmitting Values in European Malta.* Malta: Jesuit Publications.

Abu-Lughod, L. (1990). The Romance of Resistance: tracing transformations of power through Bedouin women. In *Beyond the Second Sex: New Directions in the Anthropology of Gender,* edited by P.R. Sanday and R.G. Goodenough. Philadelphia: University of Pennsylvania Press.

Abu-Lughod, L. (1991). Writing Against Culture. In *Recapturing Anthropology: working in the present,* edited by R.G. Fox. Santa Fe: School of American Research.

Al-Ali, N. (forthcoming). *Standing on Shifting Ground: women's activism in contemporary Egypt.* Cambridge: Cambridge University Press.

Anderson, B. (1983). *Imagined Communities: reflections on the origin and spread of nationalism.* London: Verso.

Ang, L. (1992). Dallas and the Ideology of Mass Culture. In *The Cultural Studies Reader,* edited by S. During. London: Routledge.

Appadurai, A. and Breckenridge, C.A. (1988). Why Public Culture? *Public Culture Bulletin,* **1,1:** 5–9.

Appleby, J.O., Hunt, L.A. and Jacob, M.C. (1994). *Telling the Truth About History.* New York: Norton.

Aquilina, J. (1972) *A Comparative Dictionary of Maltese Proverbs.* Malta: University of Malta.

Aquilina, J. (1987, 1990). *Maltese-English Dictionary.* Malta: Midsea Books.

Aquilina, J. (1989). L-Ilsien Malti: Dokument ta'L-Istorja. In *L-Identità Kulturali ta'Malta,* edited by T. Cortis. Malta: Department of Information.

Argyrou, V. (1996). *Tradition and Modernity in the Mediterranean. The Wedding as Symbolic Struggle.* Cambridge: Cambridge University Press.

Arnheim, R. (1986). A Plea for Visual Thinking. In *New Essays on the Psychology of Art,* by R. Arnheim. Berkeley: University of California Press.

Attard, J. (1988). *Britain and Malta: the story of an era.* Malta: P.E.G.

Attard, L. (1983). *Early Maltese Emigration, 1800–1914.* Malta: Gulf.

Attard, L. (1989). *The Great Exodus (1918–1939).* Malta: P.E.G.

Attard, L. (1997). *The Safety Valve : a history of Maltese emigration from 1946.* Valletta: P.E.G.

Aull Davies, C. (1998). 'A oes heddwch?' Contesting Meanings and Identities in the Welsh National Eisteddfod. In *Ritual, Performance, Media,* edited by F. Hughes-Freeland. London: Routledge.

Austin, D. (1971). *Malta and the End of Empire.* London: Frank Cass.

Ayres, R. (1996). European Integration: the case of Cyprus. *Cyprus Review,* **8,1:** 39–62.

Barnard, A. and Spencer, J. (1996). Culture. In *Encyclopedia of Social and Cultural Anthropology,* edited by A. Barnard and J. Spencer. London: Routledge.

Barth, F. (1987). *Cosmologies in the Making: a generative approach to cultural variation in inner New Guinea.* Cambridge: Cambridge University Press.

Bartlett, F. (1932). *Remembering.* Cambridge: Cambridge University Press.

Bauman, Z. (1991). *Modernity and Ambivalence.* Cambridge: Polity Press.

Baumann, G. (1992). Ritual Implicates 'Others': rereading Durkheim in a plural society. In *Understanding Rituals,* edited by D de Coppet. London: Routledge.

Beeley, B. (1959). *The Farmer and Rural society in Malta.* Durham: Department of Geography.

Behar, R. (1990). The Struggle for the Church: popular anticlericalism and religiosity in post-Franco Spain. In *Religious Orthodoxy and Popular Faith in European Society,* edited by E. Badone. Princeton: Princeton University Press.

Bell, C. (1992). *Ritual Theory, Ritual Practice.* Oxford: Oxford University Press.

Bennet, T. (1991). The Shape of Things to Come: Expo '88. *Cultural Studies,* **5,1:** 30–51.

Blazyca, C. and Kolkiewicz, M. (1999). Poland and the EU: internal disputes, domestic politics and accession. *Journal of Communist Studies and Transition Politics,* **15,4:** 131–143.

Bloch, M. (1974). Symbol, Song, Dance and Features of Articulation: is religion an extreme form of traditional authority? *Archives Europeenes de Sociologie,* **15:** 55–81.

Bloch, M. (1975). *Political Language and Oratory in Traditional Society.* New York: Academic Press.

Bloch, M. (1977). The Past and the Present in the Present. *Man,* **12:** 278–292.

Bloch, M. (1992). *Prey Into Hunter: the politics of religious experience.* Cambridge: Cambridge University Press.

Blok, A. (1974). *The Mafia of A Sicilian Village 1860–1960: a study of violent peasant entrepreneurs.* Cambridge: Polity Press.

Blouet, B. (1993). *The Story of Malta.* Malta: Progress Press.

Boissevain, J. (1974). *Friends of Friends: networks, manipulators and coalitions.* Oxford: Blackwell.

Boissevain, J. (1980). *A Village in Malta.* New York: Holt, Rinehart and Winston.

Boissevain, J. (1984). Ritual Escalation in Malta. In *Religion, Power and Protest in Local Communities: the northern shores of the Mediterranean,* edited by E. Wolf. New York: Mouton.

Boissevain, J. (1991). Ritual, Play and Identity: changing patterns of celebration in Maltese villages. *Journal of Mediterranean Studies,* **1:** 87–100.

Boissevain, J. (1992a). Introduction. In *Revitalising European Rituals,* edited by J. Boissevain. London: Routledge.

Boissevain, J. (1992b). Play and Identity: ritual change in a Maltese village. In *Revitalising European Rituals,* edited by J. Boissevain. London: Routledge.

Boissevain, J. (1993). *Saints and Fireworks: religion and politics in rural Malta.* Malta: Progress Press.

Boissevain, J. (1994). A Politician and his Audience: Malta's Dom Mintoff. In *Maltese Society: a sociological inquiry,* edited by R.G. Sultana and G. Baldacchino. Malta: Mireva.

Boissevain, J. and Theuma, N. (1998). Contested Space: planners, tourists, developers and environmentalists in Malta. In *Anthro-*

pological Perspectives on Local Development, edited by S. Abram and J. Waldren. London: Routledge.

Bonavia, K. (1993). *Mikiel Anton Vassalli (1764–1829): missier l-ilsien Malti*. Malta: National Library of Malta.

Bondin, R. (1981). *Ir-Rikostruzzjoni tal-Belt Valletta*. Malta: Rama Publications.

Bonnici, A. (1967). *History of the Church in Malta Volume I*. Malta: Empire Press.

Bonnici, J. (1989). *Valletta and the Three Cities*. Narni-Terni: Edizioni Plurigraf.

Boswell, D.M. (1994). The Social Prestige of Residential Areas. In *Maltese Society: a sociological inquiry*, edited by R.G. Sultana and G. Baldacchino. Malta: Mireva.

Bourdieu, P. (1977). *Outline of a Theory of Practice*. Cambridge: Cambridge University Press.

Bourdieu, P. (1984). *Distinction: a social critique of the judgement of taste*. London: Routledge.

Bourdieu, P. (1990). *The Logic of Practice*. Cambridge: Polity Press.

Boyarin, J. (1994). *Remapping Memory: The Politics of Time-Space*. London: University of Minnesota Press.

Bradford, E. (1964). *The Great Siege: Malta 1565*. Harmondsworth: Penguin.

Brandes, S.H. (1981). Like Wounded Stags: male sexual ideology in an Andalusian town. In *Sexual Meanings: the cultural construction of gender and sexuality*, edited by S.B. Ortner and H. Whitehead. Cambridge: Cambridge University Press.

Brandes, S.H. (1992). Sex Roles and Anthropological Research in Rural Andalusia. In *Europe Observed*, edited by J. Pina-Cabral and J.K. Campbell. Oxford: MacMillan.

Brown, R. and Kulick, J. (1982). Flashbulb Memory. In *Memory Observed: remembering in natural contexts*, edited by U. Neisser. San Francisco: W.H. Freeman.

Burke, P. (1991). *New Perspectives on Historical Writing*. Cambridge: Polity.

Burke, P. (1997). *Varieties of Cultural History*. Cambridge: Polity.

Butler, J. (1990). *Gender Trouble: feminism and the subversion of identity*. London: Routledge.

Cachia, M. (1998). Within the House: behaviour and house decoration in the domestic space. BA Dissertation, University of Malta.

Calhoun, C. (1992). Introduction: Habermas and the Public Sphere. In *Habermas and the Public Sphere,* edited by C. Calhoun. Cambridge, Mass: MIT Press.

Campbell, J.K. (1964). *Honour, Family and Patronage: a study of institutions and moral values in a Greek mountain community.* Oxford: Clarendon.

Carrier, J. (1996). Consumption. In *Encyclopedia of Social and Cultural Anthropology,* edited by A. Barnard and J. Spencer. London: Routledge.

Carrithers, M., Collins, S., and Lukes, S. (1985). *The Category of the Person: Anthropology, Philosophy, History.* Cambridge: Cambridge University Press.

Cassar Pullicino, J. (1992). *Studies in Maltese Folklore.* Malta: Malta University Press.

Cassar, C. (1988). Everyday Life in Malta in the Nineteenth and Twentieth Centuries. In *The British Colonial Experience 1800–1964: the impact on Maltese society,* edited by V. Mallia-Milanes. Malta: Mireva.

Cassar, C. (1994). Economy, Society and Identity in Early Modern Malta. PhD thesis, University of Cambridge.

Central Office of Statistics. (1998). Labour. *http://www.magnet.mt/home/cos/cosnews/news98/news2298.htm.*

Centre for Social Studies. (1970). *The Housing Problem.* Malta: Social Action Movement.

Chapman, M., McDonald, M. and Tonkin, E. (1989). *History and Ethnicity.* London: Routledge.

Chatterjee, P. (1993). *The Nation and its Fragments: Colonial and Postcolonial Histories.* Princeton: Princeton University Press.

Christian, W. (1972). *Person and God in a Spanish Valley.* Princeton: Princeton University Press.

Ciaparra, F. (1988). *Marriage in Malta in the Late Eighteenth Century.* Malta: Associated News (M) Ltd.

Ciarlò, J. (1995). *The Hidden Gem: St Paul's Shipwreck Collegiate Church, Valletta, Malta.* Malta: Progress Press.

Clifford, J. (1988). On Ethnographic Authority. In *The Predicament of Culture,* by J. Clifford. Cambridge, Mass: Harvard University Press.

Clifford, J. and Marcus, G.E. (1986). *Writing Culture: the poetics and politics of ethnography*. Berkeley: University of California Press.

Cohen, A. (1993). *Masquerade Politics: explorations in the structure of urban cultural movements*. Oxford: Berg.

Cohen, A.P. (1982). *Belonging: Identity and Social Organisation in British Rural Cultures*. Manchester: Manchester University Press.

Cohen, A.P. (1985). *The Symbolic Construction of Community*. London: Routledge.

Cohen, A.P. (1987). *Whalsay: Symbol, Segment and Boundary in a Shetland Island Community*. Manchester: Manchester University Press.

Cohen, A.P. (1994). *Self-Consciousness: an alternative anthropology of identity*. London: Routledge.

Collier, J. (1997). *From Duty to Desire: remaking families in a Spanish village*. Princeton: Princeton University Press.

Comaroff, J. (1985). *Body of Power, Spirit of Resistance : the culture and history of a South African people*. Chicago: Chicago University Press.

Comaroff, J. (1989). *Sui Genderis:* feminism, kinship theory, and structural 'domains'. In *Gender and Kinship,* edited by J. Collier and S. Yanagisako. Stanford: University of California Press.

Comaroff, J. and Comaroff, J. (1992). *Ethnography and the Historical Imagination*. Chicago: Chicago University Press.

Comaroff, J. and Comaroff, J. (1993). *Modernity and its Malcontents: ritual and power in post-colonial Africa*. Chicago: Chicago University Press.

Connell, R.W. (1983). *Which Way is Up? essays on sex, class and culture*. Sydney: Allen & Unwin.

Connell, R.W. (1995). *Masculinities*. Cambridge: Polity.

Connerton, P. (1989). *How Societies Remember*. Cambridge: Cambridge University Press.

Cowan, J.K. (1991). *Dance and the Body Politic in Northern Greece*. Princeton: Princeton University Press.

Cowan, J.K. (1991). Going out for Coffee? contesting the grounds of gendered pleasures in everyday sociability. In *Contested Identities: gender and kinship in modern Greece,* edited by P. Loizos and E. Papataxiarchis. Princeton: Princeton University Press.

Crompton, R. (1993). *Class and Stratification: an introduction to current debates*. Cambridge: Polity.

Csordas, T. (1994). *Embodiment and Experience: the existential grounds of culture and self*. Cambridge: Cambridge University Press.

Dahlgren, P. (1991). Introduction. In *Communication and Citizenship: journalism and the public sphere in the new media age*, edited by P. Dahlgren and C. Sparks. London: Routledge.

Dahlgren, P. and Sparks, C. (1991). *Communication and Citizenship: journalism and the public sphere in the new media age*. London: Routledge.

Dahrendorf, R. (1959). *Class and Class Conflict in an Industrial Society*. London: Routledge.

Davis, J. (1977). *People of the Mediterranean*. London: Routledge and Kegan Paul.

Davis, J. (1984). The Sexual Division of Religious Labour in the Mediterranean. In *Religion, Power and Protest in Local Communities: the northern shores of the Mediterranean*, edited by E. Wolf. New York: Mouton.

Denich, B. (1994). Dismembering Yugoslavia: nationalist ideologies and the symbolic revival of genocide. *American Ethnologist*, **21,2:** 367–390.

Department of Information. (1992). *Malta Information*. Malta: Department of Information.

DiLeonardo, M. (1987). The Female World of Cards and Holidays: women, family and the work of kinship. *Signs*, **12:3**, 440–453.

Dirks, N., Eley, G. and Ortner, S.B. (1994) *Culture/Power/History*. Princeton: Princeton University Press.

Douglas, M. (1966). *Purity and Danger: an analysis of the concepts of pollution and taboo*. London: Routledge and Kegan Paul.

Dubisch, J. (1991). Gender, Kinship and Religion: 'Reconstructing' the anthropology of Greece. In *Contested Identities: gender and kinship in modern Greece*, edited by P. Loizos and E. Papataxiarchis. Princeton: Princeton University Press.

Dubisch, J. (1993). 'Foreign Chickens ' and Other Outsiders: gender and community in Greece. *American Ethnologist*, **20,2:** 272–287.

Dubisch, J. (1996). *In a Different Place: pilgrimage, gender and politics at a Greek island shrine*. Princeton: Princeton University Press.

Durkheim, E. (1966). *The Elementary Forms of the Religious Life*. New York: Free Press.

Durkheim, E. (1982). *The Rules of Sociological Method*, edited by S. Lukes. London:

Eisenstadt, S.N. and Lemarchand, R. (1981). *Political Clientelism, Patronage and Development.* Beverly Hills: Sage

Eley, G. (1992). Nations, Publics and Political Cultures. In *Habermas and the Public Sphere,* edited by C. Calhoun. Cambridge, Mass: MIT Press.

Englund, H. and Leach, J. (2000). Ethnography and the Meta-Narratives of Modernity. *Current Anthropology,* **41,2:** 225–248.

European Commission. (1993). *Commission Opinion on Malta's Application for Membership.* Brussels: European Commission.

Fabian, J. (1983). *Time and the Other: How Anthropology Makes its Object.* New York: Columbia University Press.

Featherstone, M. (1990). *Global Culture.* London: Sage.

Featherstone, M., Lash, S. and Robertson, R. (1995). *Global Modernities.* London: Sage.

Feld, S. and Basso, K.H. (1997). *Senses of Place.* Santa Fe: School of American Research Press.

Fentress, J. and Wickham, C. (1992). *Social Memory.* Oxford: Blackwells.

Foster, G.M. (1967). *Tzintzuntzan: Mexican Peasants in a Changing World.* Boston: Little, Brown and Company.

Frank, A.G. and Gills, B. (1996). *The World System: Five Hundred Years or Five Thousand?* London: Routledge.

Fraser, N. (1987). What's Critical about Critical Theory? The case of Habermas and gender. In *Feminism as Critique,* edited by S. Benhabib and D. Cornell. Cambridge: Polity Press.

Frendo, H. (1979). *Party Politics in a Fortress Colony: the Maltese experience.* Malta: Midsea.

Frendo, H. (1988). Maltese Colonial Identity: Latin Mediterranean or British Empire? In *The British Colonial Experience 1800–1964: the impact on Maltese society,* edited by V. Mallia-Milanes. Malta: Mireva.

Frendo, H. (1992). Italy and Britain in Maltese Colonial Nationalism. *History of European Ideas,* **15,4:** 733–739.

Friedman, J. (1992). Narcissism, Roots and Postmodernity: The Constitution of Selfhood in the Global Crisis. In *Modernity and Identity,* edited by S. Lash and J. Friedman. Oxford: Blackwell.

Fsadni, R. (1993). The Wounding Song: honour, politics and rhetoric in Maltese *ghana. Journal of Mediterranean Studies,* **3:2**, 335–353.

Fustel de Coulanges. (1955). *The Ancient City: a study on the religion, laws and institutions of Greece and Rome*. New York: Doubleday.

Galea, M. and Ciarlò, J. (1992). *St Paul in Malta: a compendium of Pauline studies*. Malta: The Editors.

Galt, J. (1812). *Voyages and Travels, in the Years 1809, 1810 and 1811, containing statistical, commercial and miscellaneous observations on Gibraltar, Sardinia, Sicily, Malta, Serigo and Turkey*. London: T. Cadell and W. Davies.

Gambetta, D. (1996). *The Sicilian Mafia: the business of private protection*. Cambridge, Mass: Harvard University Press.

Gellner, E. (1977). Patrons and Clients. In *Patrons and Clients in Mediterranean Societies*, edited by E. Gellner and J. Waterbury. London: Duckworth.

Giddens, A. (1979). *Central Problems in Social Theory: action, structure and contradiction in social analysis*. Oxford: MacMillan.

Giddens, A. (1987). *Social Theory and Modern Sociology*. Cambridge: Polity.

Giddens, A. (1990). *The Consequences of Modernity*. Cambridge: Polity Press.

Giddens, A (1991). *Modernity and Self-identity : self and society in the late modern age*. Cambridge: Polity Press.

Gilmore, D. (1987). *Honor and Shame and the Unity of the Mediterranean*. Washington: American Anthropological Association.

Gilsenan, M. (1977). Against Patron-Client Relations. In *Patrons and Clients in Mediterranean Societies*, edited by E. Gellner and J. Waterbury. London: Duckworth.

Gluckman, M. (1962). *Essays on the Ritual of Social Relations*. Manchester: Manchester University Press.

Goddard, V. (1987). Honour and Shame: the control of women's sexuality and group identity in Naples. In *The Cultural Construction of Sexuality*, edited by P. Caplan. London: Tavistock.

Goddard, V. (1996). *Gender, Family and Work in Naples*. Oxford: Berg.

Good, A. (1981). Prescription, Preference and Practice: marriage patterns among the Kondaiyankottai Maravar of South India. *Man* **16:1**, 108–129.

Goody, J. and Tambiah, S.J. (1973). *Bridewealth and Dowry*. Cambridge: Cambridge University Press.

Government of Malta. (1972). *Malta Government Gazette.* Malta: Department of Information.

Government of Malta. (1990). *Malta Structure Plan.* Malta: Department of Information.

Grima, R. and Zammit, D. (1996). Selling Spaces and Times: an investigation of *sejjieħ dekorattiv. Economic and Social Studies,* **8:** 41–52.

Gudeman, S. and Rivera, A. (1990). *Conversations in Columbia: The Domestic Economy in Life and Text.* Cambridge: Cambridge University Press.

Gullestad, M. (1993). Home Decoration as Popular Culture: constructing homes, genders and classes in Norway. In *Gendered Anthropology,* edited by T. del Valle. London: Routledge.

Gullick, C.M.J.R. (1975). Issues in the Relationship between Minority and National Language: Maltese reactions to non-Maltese speakers of Maltese. Paper presented at the 34th annual meeting of the Society for Applied Anthropology, Amsterdam.

Gupta, A. and Ferguson, J. (1997). *Anthropological Locations: boundaries and grounds of a field science.* Berkeley: University of California Press.

Habermas, J. (1974). The Public Sphere: an encyclopedia article (1964). *New German Critique,* **3:** 49–55.

Habermas, J (1984). *Reason and the Rationalisation of Society.* Boston: Beacon Press.

Habermas, J. (1987). *The Philosophical Discourse of Modernity.* Cambridge, Mass: MIT Press.

Habermas, J. (1989). *The Structural Transformation of the Public Sphere.* Cambridge, Mass: MIT Press.

Halbwachs, M. (1992). *On Collective Memory,* edited by L. Coser. Chicago: Chicago University Press.

Handler, R. (1988). *Nationalism and the Politics of Culture in Quebec.* Madison: Wisconsin University Press.

Hannerz, U. (1980). *Exploring the City: inquiries toward an urban anthropology.* New York: Columbia University Press.

Hannerz, U. (1996). *Transnational Connections.* London: Routledge.

Harrison, H. and Hubbard, D. (1945). *Valletta: a report to accompany the outline plan for the region of Valletta and the Three Cities.* Malta: Government of Malta.

Herdt, G. (1989). *Guardians of the Flutes: idioms of masculinity*. New York: Colombia University Press.

Herzfeld, M. (1980). *Ours Once More: folklore, ideology, and the making of modern Greece*. New York: Pella.

Herzfeld, M. (1984). The Horns of the Mediterraneanist Dilemma. *American Ethnologist*, **11:** 439–454.

Herzfeld, M. (1985). *The Poetics of Manhood: contest and identity in a Cretan mountain village*. Princeton: Princeton University Press.

Herzfeld, M. (1987). *Anthropology Through the Looking-Glass: critical ethnography in the margins of Europe*. Cambridge: Cambridge University Press.

Herzfeld, M. (1991). *A Place in History: social and monumental time in a Cretan town*. Princeton: Princeton University Press.

Herzfeld, M. (1992). *The Social Production of Indifference : exploring the symbolic roots of Western bureaucracy*. New York: Berg.

Herzfeld, M. (1997). *Cultural Intimacy: Social Poetics in the Nation-State*. London: Routledge.

Hill, S.A. (1986). The Politics of Development in Malta with Special Reference to Post-War Change in the Village of Mellieha. PhD thesis, University of London.

Hirschon, R. (1981). Essential Objects and the Sacred: interior and exterior space in an urban Greek locality. In *Women and Space: ground rules and social maps,* edited by S. Ardener. London: Croom Helm.

Hobsbawm, E.J. and Ranger, T. (1983). *The Invention of Tradition.* Cambridge: Cambridge University Press.

Howell, S. (1997). Cultural Studires and Social Anthropology: Contesting or Complementary Discourses? In *Anthropology and Cultural Studies,* edited by S. Nugent and C. Shore. London: Pluto.

Hughes, Q. (1969). *Fortress: Architecture and Military History of Malta*. London: Lund Humphries.

Hull, G. (1993). *The Malta Language Question: a case study in cultural imperialism.* Malta: Said.

Humphrey, C. and Laidlaw, J. (1994). *The Archetypal Actions of Ritual.* Oxford: Oxford University Press.

In-Nazzjon Tagħna

Joyce, P. (1995). *Class.* Oxford: Oxford University Press.

Kahn, J.S. (1989). Culture: Demise or Resurrection? *Critique of Anthropology*, **9,2:** 5–25.

Kahn, J.S. (1997). Demons, Commodities and the History of Anthropology. In *Meanings of the Market*, edited by J. Carrier. Oxford: Berg.

KANA (1980). *Studju Dwar Il-Familja Maltija*. Malta: KANA.

Kapferer, B. (1988). *Legends of People, Myths of State*. Washington: Smithsonian Institute.

Kelly, J.D. and Kaplan, M. (1990). History, Stucture and Ritual. *Annual Review of Anthropology*, **19:** 119–150.

Kertzer, D. (1980). *Comrades and Christians: religion and political struggle in communist Italy*. Cambridge: Cambridge University Press.

Kertzer, D. (1988). *Ritual, Politics and Power*. London: Yale University Press.

Koster, A. (1984). *Prelates and Politicians in Malta*. Assen: Van Gorcum.

Kugelmass, D. (1995). Bloody Memories: encountering the past in contemporary Poland. *Cultural Anthropology*, **10,3:** 279–301.

Lacqueur, T.W. (1990). *Making Sex: body and gender from the Greeks to Freud*. Cambridge, Mass: Harvard University Press.

Laferla, A.V. (1939). *The Story of Man in Malta*. Malta: Government Printing Office.

Latour, B. (1993). *We Have Never Been Modern*. New York: Harvester Wheatsheaf.

Lave, J., Duguid, P., Fernandez, N. and Axel, E. (1992). Coming of Age in Birmingham: cultural studies and conceptions of subjectivity. *Annual Review of Anthropology*, **21:** 257–282.

Leach, E. (1968). Ritual. In *International Encyclopedia of the Social Sciences*, edited by D.L. Sills. London: MacMillan.

Lever, A. (1986). Honour as a Red Herring. *Critique of Anthropology*, **6,3:** 830106.

Lewis, G. (1980). *Day of shining Red : an essay on understanding ritual*. Cambridge: Cambridge University Press.

LiCausi, L. (1975). Anthropology and Ideology: the case of 'patronage' in Mediterranean societies. *Critique of Anthropology*, **4,5:** 90–107.

Lippert, B. and Becker, P. (1998). *Towards EU-Membership: transformation and integration in Poland and the Czech Republic*. Bonn: Europa Union Verlag.

Loizos, P. (1994). A Broken Mirror: masculine sexuality in Greek ethnography. In *Dislocating Masculinity: comparative ethnographies,* edited by A. Cornwall and N. Lindisfarne. London: Routledge.

Loizos, P. and Papataxiarchis, E. (1991). *Contested Identities: gender and kinship in modern Greece.* Princeton: Princeton University Press.

L-Orizzjont

Lowenthal, D. (1985). *The Past is a Foreign Country.* Cambridge: Cambridge University Press.

Luhmann, N. (1998). *Observations on Modernity,* translated by W. Whobrey. Stanford: Stanford University Press.

Luke, H. (1960). *Malta: an account and an appreciation.* London: Corgi.

Lukes, S. (1975). Political Ritual and Social Integration. *Sociology,* **9:** 289–308.

Luttrell, A. (1977). Girolamo Manduca and Gian Francesco Abela: tradition and invention in Maltese historiography. *Melita Historica,* **7,2:** 105–132.

Macdonald, S. (1997). *Reimagining Culture: histories, identities and the gaelic renaissance.* Oxford: Berg.

Madigan, R. and Munro, M. (1996) 'House Beautiful': style and consumption in the home. *Sociology,* **30,1:** 41–57.

Malta Year Book. (Annual). Malta: De La Salle Brothers.

Marcus, G.E. (1989). Imagining the Whole: ethnography's contemporary efforts to situate itself. *Critique of Anthropology,* **9,3:** 7–30.

Marcus, G.E. and Fischer, M.M.J. (1986). *Anthropology as Cultural Critique: an experimental moment in the human sciences.* Chicago: Chicago University Press.

Marx, K. (1959). The Eighteenth Brumaire of Louis Bonaparte. In *Marx and Engels: basic writings on politics and philosophy.* New York: Doubleday Anchor.

Marx, K. and Engels, F. (1967). *The Communist Manifesto.* Harmondsworth: Penguin.

Mauss, M. (1979).*Body Techniques. In* Sociology and Psychology: essays by Marcel Mauss. *London: Routledge.*

Miceli, P. (1994). The Visibility and Invisibility of Women. In *Maltese Society: a sociological inquiry,* edited by R.G. Sultana and G. Baldacchino. Malta: Mireva.

Miller, D. (1987). *Material Culture and Mass Consumption.* Oxford: Basil Blackwell.

Miller, D. (1988). Appropriating the State on the Council Estate. *Man* **23:** 353–372.

Miller, D. (1994). *Modernity: an ethnographic approach.* Oxford: Berg.

Mills, M.B. (1999). *Thai Women in the Global Labor Force: Consuming Desires, Contested Selves.* New Brunswick: Rutgers University Press.

Ministry of Finance. (1992) *Economic Survey.* Malta, Government Press.

Mitchell, J.P. (1996a). Patrons and Clients. In *Encyclopedia of Social and Cultural Anthropology,* edited by A. Barnard and J. Spencer. London: Routledge.

Mitchell, J.P. (1996b). Presenting the Past: cultural tour-guides and the sustaining of European identity in Malta. In *Sustainable Tourism in Islands and Small States: Case Studies,* edited by L. Briguglio, R. Butler, D Harrison and W. Leal Filho. London: Cassell.

Mitchell, J.P. (1997). A Moment with Christ: the importance of feelings in the analysis of belief. *Journal of the Royal Anthropological Institute,* **3:** 79–94.

Mitchell, J.P. (1998a) The Nostalgic Construction of Community: memory and social identity in urban Malta. *Ethnos,* **63: 1**, 81–101.

Mitchell, J.P. (1998b). A Providential Storm: Myth, History and the Story of St Paul's Shipwreck in Malta. In *Memory, History and Critique: European identity at the Millennium,* edited by F. Brinkhuis and S. Talmor. Utrecht: University for Humanist Studies.

Mitchell, J.P. (1998c). Performances of Masculinity in a Maltese *Festa.* In *Recasting Ritual: performance, media, identity,* edited by F. Hughes-Freeland and M. Crain. London: Routledge.

Mitchell, J.P. (2000). The Devil, Satanism and the Evil Eye in Contemporary Malta. In *Powers of Good and Evil: social transformation and popular belief,* edited by P. Clough and J.P. Mitchell. Oxford: Berghahn.

Mizzi, S.O. (1981). Women of Senglea: the changing role of urban, working-class women in Malta. PhD thesis, SUNY Stony Brook.

Montalto, J. (1979). *The Nobles of Malta 1530–1800.* Malta: Midsea.

Moore, H. (1988). *Feminism and Anthropology : feminist perspectives.* Cambridge: Polity.

Morris, R.C. (1995). All Made Up: performance theory and the new anthropology of sex and gender. *Annual Review of Anthropology,* **24:** 567–592.

Mumford, L. (1961). *The City in History: its origins, its transformations and its prospects.* New York: Secker.

Mumford, L. (1970). *The Culture of Cities.* New York: Greenwood.

Nugent, S. and Shore, C. (1997). *Anthropology and Cultural Studies.* London: Pluto.

Organisation of World Heritage Cities. (1996). *The Management Guide: a case study guide to managing conservation programmes within historic towns.* http://www.ovpm.org/ovpm/english/guide/cas/gec-vale.html.

Ortner, S.B. (1974). Is Female to Male as Nature is to Culture? In *Woman, Culture and Society,* edited by M.Z. Rosaldo and L. Lamphere. Stanford: Stanford University Press.

Ortner, S.B. (1984). Theory in Anthropology Since the Sixties. *Comparative Studies in Society and History,* **28:** 126–166.

Ortner, S.B. and Whitehead, H. (1981). *Sexual Meanings: the cultural construction of gender and sexuality.* Cambridge: Cambridge University Press.

Papataxiarchis, E. (1991). Friends of the Heart: male commensal solidarity, gender and kinship in Aegean Greece. In *Contested Identities: gender and kinship in modern Greece,* edited by P. Loizos and E. Papataxiarchis. Princeton: Princeton University Press.

Pardo, I. (1996). *Managing Existence in Naples: morality, action and structure.* Cambridge: Cambridge University Press.

Parkin, D. (1985). Introduction. In *The Anthropology of Evil,* edited by D. Parkin. Oxford: Basil Blackwell.

Passerini, L. (1988). *Fascism in Popular Memory: the cultural experience of the Turin working class.* Cambridge. Cambridge University Press.

Pavlides, E. and Hesser, J. (1986). Women's Roles and House Form and Decoration in Eressos, Greece. In *Gender and Power in Rural Greece,* edited by J. Dubisch. Princeton: Princeton University Press.

Peristiany, J.G. (1965). *Honour and Shame: the values of Mediterranean society.* London: Weidenfeld and Nicolson.

Petersen, N. (1998). National Strategies in the Integration Dilemma: an adaptation approach. *Journal of Common Market Studies,* **36,1: 33–54.**

Piaget, J. (1977). The Construction of Reality in the Child. In *The Essential Piaget,* edited by H.E. Gruber and J.J. Voneche. London: Routledge and Kegan Paul.

Piano, R. (1989). *Rehabilitation of the Historic Centre: La Valetta.* Paris: Renzo Piano.

Pina-Cabral, J. (1989). The Mediterranean as a Category of Regional Comparison: a critical view. *Current Anthropology,* **30,3:** 399–406.

Piot, C. (1999). *Remotely Global: Village Modernity in West Africa.* Chicago: University of Chicago Press.

Pitt-Rivers, J. (1961). *People of the Sierra.* Chicago: Phoenix Books.

Pitt-Rivers, J. (1977). *The Fate of Schechem or the Politics of Sex.* Cambridge: Cambridge University Press.

Poole, F.J.P. (1982). The Ritual Forging of Identity: aspects of person and self in Bimin-Kuskusmin male initiation. In *Rituals of Manhood: male initiation in Papua New Guinea,* edited by G. Herdt. Berkeley: University of California Press.

Pynchon, T. (1956). *V.* London: Picador.

Reiter, R.R. (1975). Men and Women in the South of France: public and private domains. In *Toward an Anthropology of Women,* edited by R.R. Reiter. London: Monthly Review Press.

Ritter, H. (1996). Memory, Certified History, and Consciousness of the Past. Paper presented at the fifth conference of the International Society for the Study of European Ideas, Utrecht.

Robertson, R. (1995). Glocalization: Time-Space and Homogeneity-Heterogeneity. In *Global Modernities,* edited by M. Featherstone, S. Lash and R. Robertson. London: Sage.

Rofel, L. (1999). *Other Modernities: Gendered Yearnings in China After Socialism.* Berkeley: University of California Press.

Roniger, L. The Comparative Study of Clientelism and the Changing Nature of Civil Society in the Contemporary World. In *Democracy, Clientelism and Civil Society,* edited by L. Roniger and A. Günes-Ayata. London: Lynne Rienner Publishers.

Rosaldo, M.Z. (1974). Woman, Culture and Society: a theoretical overview. In *Woman, Culture and Society,* edited by M.Z. Rosaldo and L. Lamphere. Stanford: Stanford University Press.

Rosaldo, R. (1980). *Ilongot Headhunting 1883–1974: a study in society and history*. Stanford: Stanford University Press.

Said, E. (1978). *Orientalism*. New York: Basic Books.

Salole, G.M. (1982). Politics in a Sardinian Town. PhD thesis, University of Manchester.

Sant Cassia, P. (1989). L-Għana: bejn il-folklor u l-ħabi. In *L-Identità Kulturali ta'Malta,* edited by T. Cortis. Malta: Department of Information.

Sant Cassia, P. (1992). The Nostalgia of Nostalgia: reflections on the semiotics of city gate and the opera house. Paper presented at Mediterranean Institute, University of Malta.

Sant Cassia, P. (1993). History, Anthropology and Folklore in Malta. *Journal of Mediterranean Studies,* 3,2: 291–315.

Sant Cassia, P. (1999). Tradition, Tourism and Memory in Malta. *Journal of the Royal Anthropological Institute,* 5,2: 247–263.

Sant, C. (1992). *Bible Translation and Language: essays in the history of Bible translation in Maltese*. Malta: University of Malta.

Schachter, D.L. (1996). *Searching for Memory*. New York: Basic Books.

Schama, S. (1995). *Landscape and Memory*. London: Harper Collins.

Schiavone, M.J. (1992). *L-Elezzjonijiet f'Malta 1849–1992: Storja, Fatti, Cifri*. Malta: Pubblikazjonijiet Indipendenza.

Schneider, J. and Schneider, P. (1976). *Culture and Political Economy in Western Sicily: studies in social discontinuity*. New York: Academic Press.

Schwartz, T. (1993). 'Kastom', 'Custom', and Culture: conspicuous culture and culture-constructs. *Anthropological Forum,* **6,4:** 515–540.

Scott, J. (1996). *Stratification and Power: structures of class, status and command*. Cambridge: Polity Press.

Serracino-Inglott, P. (1988). Was Malta a Nation in 1964? In *The British Colonial Experience 1800–1964: the impact on Maltese society,* edited by V. Mallia-Milanes. Malta: Mireva.

Shaw, C. and Chase, M. (1989). *The Imagined Past: History and Nostalgia*. Manchester: Manchester University Press.

Shore, C. (1993). Inventing the 'People's Europe': critical approaches to European Community 'cultural policy'. *Man,* **28:** 779–800.

Silverman, S. (1977). Patronage as Myth. In *Patrons and Clients in Mediterranean Societies,* edited by E. Gellner and J. Waterbury. London: Duckworth.

Spencer, J. (1996). Modernism, Modernity and Modernisation. In *Encyclopedia of Social and Cultural Anthropology,* edited by A. Barnard and J. Spencer. London: Routledge.

Spencer, J. (1997). Post-colonialism and the Political Imagination. *Journal of the Royal Anthropological Institute,* **3,1:** 1–19.

Spivak, G. (1987). *In Other Worlds : essays in cultural politics.* New York: Methuen.

Strathern, A. (1996). *Body Thoughts.* Ann Arbor: University of Michigan Press.

Sultana, R.G. (1994). Towards a Sociology of Consumption in Malta. In *Maltese Society: a sociological inquiry,* edited by R.G. Sultana and G. Baldacchino. Malta: Mireva.

Suttles, G. (1971). *The Social Construction of Communities.* Chicago: Chicago University Press.

Tabone, C. (1987). *The Secularisation of the Family in Changing Malta.* Malta: Dominican Publications.

Taussig, M. (1980). *The Devil and Commodity Fetishism in South America.* Chapel Hill: University of North Carolina Press.

Taylor, C. (1995). *Liberal Politics and the Public Sphere.* London: LSE.

The Malta Independent

The Sunday Times (Malta)

The Times of Malta

The Times of Malta.

Thompson, J.B. (1984). *Studies in the Theory of Ideology.* Cambridge: Cambridge University Press.

Thompson, P. (1978). *The Voice of the Past: oral history.* Oxford: Oxford University Press.

Thompson, P. and Samuel, R. (1990). *The Myths We Live By.* London: Routledge.

Thornton, R. (1988). The Rhetoric of Ethnographic Holism. *Cultural Anthropology,* **3,3:** 285–303.

Tonkin, E. (1992). *Narrating Our Pasts: the social construction of oral history.* Cambridge: Cambridge University Press.

Tonna, B. (1994). *Malta Trends 1994.* Malta: Centre for Research into Signs of the Times.

QM LIBRARY
(MILE END)